SWEET CRAVINGS

SWEET CRAVINGS

13-Digit ISBN: 978-1-60433-899-7

10-Digit ISBN: 1-60433-899-7

This book may be ordered by mail from the publisher. Please include $5.99 for postage and handling. Please support your local bookseller first!

Books published by Cider Mill Press Book Publishers are available at special discounts for bulk purchases in the United States by corporations, institutions, and other organizations. For more information, please contact the publisher.

Cider Mill Press Book Publishers
"Where good books are ready for press"
PO Box 454
12 Spring Street
Kennebunkport, Maine 04046
Visit us online!
www.cidermillpress.com

Typography: Adobe Garamond Pro, Gotham, Blackjack, Type Embellishments One

Printed in China

1 2 3 4 5 6 7 8 9 0

First Edition

SWEET CRAVINGS

Over 300 Desserts to Satisfy and Delight

CIDER MILL PRESS

BOOK PUBLISHERS
KENNEBUNKPORT, MAINE

TABLE *of* CONTENTS

❖ ❖ ❖

INTRODUCTION:
SWEET SALVATION

❋ ❋ ❋

Everyone knows that something sweet can salvage the otherwise forgettable and erase the thoroughly awful. Even the simplest desserts have the miraculous ability to put any unpleasantness firmly in the past and fix our attention on the encouraging aspects of the world before us.

While being saved by sweets and turning to the sugary in a time of need are both universal experiences, an antidote cannot be prescribed so generally.

More often than not, the desire to wipe away the gray of the day through indulgence trains itself upon a specific flavor. Frequently, it is a confection that features the unique abilities of chocolate. Other times it is the sweetness Mother Nature has freighted berries and stone fruits with. And there are moments when only a decadent cheesecake or luscious caramel can provide the required bit of solace.

As these cravings are not confined to just one treat or one flavor, the individual is also never locked in to just one. Instead, a craving for each element along the spectrum of sweetness resides in each and every one of us. What satisfied us last week may be the last thing we want today, and, fortunately, we live in a world plentiful enough to accommodate our continually shifting desires.

It is generally better to take matters into your own hands when your palate makes a specific demand. Not only is a homemade dessert more likely to satiate, as you can tailor it exactly to your tastes, but taking a step back to turn out something special means your satisfaction won't be limited to your consumption of it. By committing to making your own sweets, you gain the power to provide a solution to whatever plea your body makes, and continually get to enjoy the sensation of watching a series of seemingly disparate elements come together to form an appealing whole. This alchemy, which can be managed with little more than a few mixing bowls, a couple of simple implements, and a standard-issue stove and oven, is a process that never ceases to amaze.

Whatever confectionary concerns arise for you or your loved ones, *Sweet Cravings* is here to help. A mix of classic treats that are certain to satisfy and innovative offerings that will set the heart and mind aflame and generate a series of new inclinations, you can suddenly find an answer to soothe even the most insistent sweet tooth.

So the next time life has you up against the wall or you are simply looking to make a good day better, turn to this book, and remember this: all that really matters is how you finish.

CHAPTER 1

IN THE KITCHEN

If you're intent on taking responsibility for soothing your sweet tooth, it's a must that you get, and keep, your kitchen in line. From outfitting your kitchen properly to helpful techniques that will provide the confidence needed to tackle any recipe, this chapter is filled with information that ensures that when a craving strikes you are always equipped to satisfy it.

KITCHEN ESSENTIALS

※ ※ ※

This checklist of kitchen essentials is by no means exhaustive, but a cook working in a kitchen provisioned with these items should have no problem preparing the recipes included in this book.

COOKWARE

Cast-iron skillet
Dutch oven
4-quart saucepan with lid
Large nonstick frying pan
Steamer basket
10" to 14" sauté pan with lid
2- to 3-quart saucepan with lid

BAKEWARE

8 oz. ramekins
8" square baking pan
Madeleine pan
Muffin tin
9 x 13-inch baking dish
9 x 5-inch loaf pan
9" pie plate
9" round cake pan
9" tart pan
Sheet pans
Souffle dish
Springform pan
12-cup Bundt pan
Wire cooling racks

UTENSILS

Bench scraper
Box grater
Bread knife
Can opener
Chef's knife
Corkscrew
Ladle
Large wooden cutting board
Locking metal tongs
Mandoline
Microplane
Oven mitts
Paring knife
Pastry blender
Pasta maker
Popsicle molds
Pot holders
Potato masher
Rolling pin
Rubber spatulas
Serrated carving knife
Slotted spoon
Small plastic cutting board
Vegetable peeler
Whisks
Wooden spoons

MEASURING

Dry ingredient measuring cups
4-cup liquid measuring cup
Instant-read thermometer
Kitchen scale
Measuring spoons
Oven thermometer

BOWLS & CONTAINERS

Large colander
Nest of mixing bowls
Strainers

SMALL KITCHEN APPLIANCES

Blender
Coffee maker
Food processor
Handheld mixer
Ice cream maker*
Kitchen torch
Stand mixer
Toaster

---

*It may seem a bit extravagant to include on a list of essentials, but quality ice cream makers are available online for around $40. Considering the cost of purchasing high-quality ice cream at the store, we're elevating the ice cream maker to must-have status for dessert aficionados.

HOW TO CARE FOR YOUR KITCHEN TOOLS

✳ ✳ ✳

We invest a great deal in our kitchens. Cookware, knives, and the like do not come cheaply, and to keep these tools working well for the long haul, it's best to clean and maintain your kitchen tools after every use.

Common sense is key when cleaning your kitchen tools. Be sure to follow the manufacturer's instructions and, when in doubt, wash by hand. Most kitchen tools can be easily cleaned with just soap and water. When cleaning small appliances like a blender or food processor, take the pieces apart and clean them separately. Always make sure that any electrical appliances are unplugged and that they have cooled before washing.

✳ ✳ ✳

POTS & PANS

When using a nonstick pan, avoid metal utensils that can damage the nonstick finish. Instead, use wood, plastic, or silicone utensils.

Once your pots and pans have cooled after use, be sure to clean them in a timely manner. Avoid leaving them soiled or soaking them overnight, which can damage the finish and/or cause rust. While many pots and pans claim to be dishwasher-safe, hand washing and drying are better options if you want to extend the life of your cookware.

For both stainless steel and nonstick pans, never use abrasive cleaners or a scouring pad, which will scratch surfaces and ruin nonstick coatings. Instead, use a nylon net pad or sponge. Copper-bottom pots and pans should be cleaned with a copper cleaner after every use.

To avoid rusting or pitting, be sure your cookware is completely dry before storing, and refrain from stacking your cookware if space allows.

KNIVES

Knives are at their best and last longer when sharpened. Before each use, hone your blade by using the steel that came with your knife set, and have your knives sharpened by a professional once or twice a year. Local sharpeners can be found online or at many farmers markets, and the cost is inexpensive, particularly compared to the cost of a new, high-quality knife.

After you've used a knife, clean and dry it by hand. Never leave knives soaking, which can warp the wooden handles. Likewise, never wash knives in the dishwasher, as they can be damaged. Any rust can be removed with scouring powder and a gentle scrubbing.

Make sure your knives are completely dry before you store them, as this will keep them free from rust. Store your knives in a wooden knife block or sheathed in a drawer. These precautions will keep your knife from coming into contact with anything that can damage the blade.

WOODEN ITEMS

Never soak wooden items like cutting boards or spoons, and never wash them in a dishwasher, as the heat will cause the wood to swell and crack. Instead, wash with mild dish detergent and hand dry them immediately.

Keep in mind that wood is prone to bacteria growth, so wash immediately after use, and rub with a lemon before using to help fight the spread of bacteria.

Wooden cutting boards and spoons need to be oiled every few months to prevent them from drying and cracking. Use a cloth to coat your wooden items with mineral or walnut oil, allow the oil to soak in, and wipe away any excess after 30 minutes.

PLASTIC & RUBBER ITEMS

Most plastic and rubber cutting boards, spatulas, and measuring cups are generally dishwasher-safe, but some cheaper plastic utensils may melt or crack if exposed to excessive heat. Be cautious when using plastic in the dishwasher; hand washing and hand drying your plastic and rubber items will ensure that they last as long as possible.

COFFEE MAKERS

Coffee makers can be cleaned using equal parts white vinegar and water. Fill the coffee maker with the mixture and run it halfway through a cycle. Turn the machine off and let sit for 1 hour. Then turn the machine on and complete the cycle. Next, rinse the filter chamber and the pot to eliminate the vinegar odor and run a final cycle with only fresh water. Repeat as necessary.

CAST-IRON COOKWARE

If you go shopping for a new cast-iron skillet, you'll come across the name Lodge—a company that has been making cast-iron skillets since the late 1800s. They brand themselves as "America's Original Cookware," but Lodge isn't resting on its laurels. Instead, the company has recently developed a method to season its cookware so that it will last as it always has but with minimal (consistent) care. Lodge coats the pan with vegetable oil and bakes it in at very high heat, which is just what you need to do to an unseasoned pan. With a new Lodge pan, you can begin cooking with it almost immediately.

But let's start at the beginning, with an unseasoned skillet. Wash it with hot, soapy water, rinse, and dry thoroughly.

If there's any rust on the pan, sand it lightly with fine-grained sandpaper. Apply Coca-Cola to the rust spots and let it sit for 10 to 15 minutes. Wash again with soapy water, rinse, dry, and put the skillet over low heat to dry any excess moisture.

Once there's no rust, use a paper towel to apply a light layer of cooking oil (vegetable oil, not olive oil) all over the pan, even the handle. The pan should have a slight sheen to it.

Place the skillet upside down on the middle rack of the oven and heat the oven to 400°F with the pan inside. Put a piece of foil or a baking sheet on the lower rack to catch any oil. Let the pan bake in the oven for about 2 hours.

Turn the oven off and let the pan cool (upside down) in the oven.

Take it out, wipe it down with a clean paper towel, and it's good to go.

If the skillet has taken on a slightly brown color, you can repeat the process, which will further season the pan and darken its color, improving its appearance. This will also happen naturally over time.

Now that you've got a seasoned pan, you're going to want to stick by a few guidelines: never wash your seasoned pan with soapy water, and never put a cast-iron pan in the dishwasher.

Why? Soap breaks down the seasoning you spent so much time building, meaning you'll have to season the pan all over again. Leaving any kind of moisture on the pan will lead to rusting, which will also require you to re-season. It may seem counterintuitive, since you're used to thinking "it's not clean unless it's been washed in (really) hot, soapy water," but this is one of the great advantages of cast iron.

After you've cooked in your skillet, clean it with hot water (no soap) and a plastic, rough-surfaced scrub brush. Dry the cookware completely after washing. Put a teaspoon of vegetable oil in the pan and use a paper towel to rub it in until the entire pan has a nice sheen.

Got it? On to the next cast-iron commandment: never use steel wool.

Cast iron is softer than steel, meaning that using an abrasive sponge on your cast iron has the potential to strip the pan's seasoning.

If there's a mess that water and a scrub brush cannot handle, you can create a scrubbing paste by adding coarse kosher salt to your hot water before using the brush to loosen the stubborn residue. They can also be loosened from your cookware by soaking very briefly in water, but do not leave it submerged in water for long. You can also add water to the messy cookware and simmer over medium-low heat to aid the loosening process in instances of extreme grime.

Again, once the pan has been scrubbed clean, dry your cast iron extremely well and rejuvenate the lovely sheen by rubbing in vegetable oil.

With cast iron, cleaning is only half the battle. If you don't store it in a dry place, all your careful tending will be for naught.

To ensure that your pan stays rust-free and ready to go, you need a moisture-free storage space with good air circulation. If you need to stack it with other pans in your pantry or cupboard, put paper towels between the pieces of cookware to prevent scratches or other damage.

Storing cast-iron cookware in an oven is also a popular option, so that it is nearby and ready for use whenever you're cooking. Just be sure to remain mindful and remove any pans before preheating your oven.

Other than these simple tips, the best thing to do with your cast-iron cookware is use it. When you start using it for all the different things it can do, you'll probably find that the cookware lives on your stovetop, waiting for its next assignment. The more you use it, the better it gets. Nothing will stick to its surface. You can go from the frying pan to the fire, as it were, starting a dish on the stove and finishing it in the oven.

In short, with regular use, cast iron is like a fine wine, getting better and better with age and use.

AT WORK IN THE KITCHEN

❈ ❈ ❈

*While most of us like tinkering in the kitchen, not all of us have the skill set
of a professional chef. If you find yourself looking through these recipes
and wondering what something refers to, here are some basic kitchen tips
and techniques that will help you navigate this book.*

❈ ❈ ❈

BEATING EGGS: Using a fork or whisk, break the yolks and then mix in a rapid, circular motion to combine the yolks and the egg whites.

BEATING EGG WHITES: Use fresh eggs at room temperature, and make sure that your bowl is totally clean. When using a handheld mixer, it's best to start on a slower setting and gradually increase the speed, taking care not to overbeat, as overbeaten eggs will liquefy. When removing the beaters and holding them upside down, "soft peaks" will curl down, and "stiff peaks" will stand straight up. Use beaten egg whites right away.

CLARIFYING BUTTER: Butter is clarified by removing the water and milk fat, leaving only the butterfat that stands up to high temperatures. To make clarified butter, melt and then simmer unsalted butter in a saucepan. The milk fat will gather on top. Remove the butter from the heat and skim off the milk fat. Pour through a piece of cheesecloth to remove any remaining or browned milk fat.

CREAMING BUTTER AND SUGAR: Use butter that's at room temperature; butter that's too firm won't incorporate the sugar as well and the resulting mixture will be lumpy. Beat the butter and sugar together until the mixture is fluffy with peaks.

CRIMPING A PIECRUST: Crimping creates a defined and decorative edge on your piecrust. Place your left thumb and left index finger 1" from each other. Working your way around the pie plate, use your right index finger to press the inside edge of the piecrust into that 1" space.

CUTTING A MANGO: Mangos are difficult to work with because they have a long, thin seed in the middle. To keep from getting foiled by this obstacle, hold the mango and envision a centerline. Cut about a ¼" on either side of this centerline to avoid the seed.

DOUBLE BOILER: To melt something in a double boiler, fill a saucepan approximately one-quarter of the way with water and bring it to a boil. Reduce to a simmer and place a heatproof bowl on top of the pot, making sure that the bottom of the bowl does not touch the water. Add the ingredient and gently stir as it melts.

FOLDING: Combines ingredients without removing air from the mixture. Using a rubber spatula, add the lighter mixture (i.e. whipped cream) to the heavier mixture (i.e. chocolate) by running the spatula along the side of the bowl and "folding" the latter on top of itself.

PROOFING YEAST: Proofing helps ensure that you get the rise you want out of your baked goods. Proof your yeast by adding it to the water called for in the recipe, plus a pinch of sugar. Stir gently and let stand for 10 minutes. The yeast will react with the sugar and the resulting foam is "proof" that the yeast is working.

PUMPKIN PUREE: While you can buy pumpkin puree at your grocery store, it's easy to make at home. Just cut a sugar pumpkin in half and remove the seeds and pulp. Place the pumpkin halves face down on a baking sheet and roast for an hour at 325°F. Scoop the pumpkin flesh from the shell and puree in a food processor.

SAUTÉING: Frying your ingredient with a small amount of butter or fat in a shallow pan over high heat. Sauté is French for "jump," and the trick is to keep the food moving so it doesn't stick to the pan and burn.

SCRAPING A VANILLA BEAN: Using a sharp paring knife, slice the vanilla bean in half lengthwise. Separate the two halves, lay the cut sides face up, and run the tip of the knife along the inside of each half to remove the seeds.

SEPARATING AN EGG: Get a clean bowl and crack an egg in half over it. Separate the two halves of shell and pass the yolk back and forth between the two halves, allowing the egg white to drip into the bowl below. Eventually all the white will be in the bowl, and the yolk will be in one of the pieces of shell. If you find this method too difficult to master, you can also pour the yolk into the palm of one hand. With your fingers spread, pass the yolk between your hands while letting the white fall into the bowl.

TEMPERING EGGS: This is adding a hot mixture to room-temperature eggs. While whisking, slowly pour the hot mixture into the eggs, gradually bringing the eggs up to temperature without creating scrambled eggs.

WHISKING: Used to combine ingredients. For best results, put your mixing bowl at an angle and utilize a side-to-side motion with your wrist, as opposed to stirring or beating (see page 18).

ZESTING CITRUS: Using a microplane, gently grate the exterior of the fruit, rotating the fruit as you go so that you do not remove the bitter white pith.

❋ ❋ ❋

THE BUILDING BLOCKS:
FLOUR, SALT, EGGS & SUGAR

❊ ❊ ❊

FLOUR

For most people, flour is just a powdery substance that is sold in a paper bag and stored in a cabinet.

But once you start getting serious about baking, you will quickly realize that the type of flour you choose is a big part of both your successes and your failures. In no time, hunting for flours will become just as natural as hunting for the freshest and plumpest fruits at the grocery store.

Technically, flour derives from the grinding of seeds, nuts, or roots. The most commonly used flour comes from wheat, but flours from other grains, or cereals, are also very common.

Hearty and able to be processed into an affordable staple that can then be made into a dizzying variety of foodstuffs, wheat is the world's most widely grown cereal, accounting for nearly one-third of the global cereal harvest as of 2017.

Wheat seeds consist of a large, starchy endosperm and an oily germ, which are enclosed in an outer layer of bran. The fibers are primarily in the bran, while the endosperm is where the starches and most of the proteins are stored. Fats are stocked in the germ of the wheat kernel.

Wheat and other cereals can be ground into flours featuring varying degrees of fineness. Coarse flours, like semolina, are best suited for pasta making. Fine flours, like the widely used all-purpose flour, are ideal for baking. And if you want to make a pastry with a feathery texture, you need to look for superfine flour, which is silky to the touch and confers that elegant feel to the baked goods it produces.

Research shows that wheat flour's ability to absorb water increases with a reduction in particle size. Dough development time and stability also grow as the flour increases in fineness. This is due to the tendency of flour proteins to be more readily available in the finest fractions of milled flour. A dough made with finer flour is also more extensible, allowing for easier shaping. In all, this results in baked goods with higher volumes, lighter textures, and better colors compared to those made with coarser flours.

In order to obtain an even lighter and airier consistency in baked goods made from wheat flour, the bran is either partially or totally eliminated, or sifted out. Bran removal, which has been done since antiquity, now relies on increasingly sophisticated milling and sifting techniques.

Based on the amount of bran present in wheat flour, different labels are applied, such as: whole wheat, sifted, unbleached white, and white (i.e. bleached).

Whole wheat flour is obtained when all the bran contained in the wheat kernel is included in the milled flour. However, not all whole wheat flours are the same. Most whole wheat flours available at the store are not made by grinding the whole seed at once. Instead, the bran, which was previously removed, is added back to the refined flour. The resulting flour, which is called whole wheat, will not truly include the whole ground wheat kernel, but only the endosperm and bran fractions. In fact, the vitamin-rich wheat germ is not included in most industrially produced whole wheat flours.

Sifting flour aims to remove the bran and leave the endosperm and wheat germ. Different methods and degrees of sifting are used to create flours with different percentages of bran content, also known as "ashes."

Unbleached white flour is obtained via roller mill technology. This sophisticated method involves mechanically isolating the endosperm from the bran and the wheat germ and milling only the endosperm. This results in a flour that is lighter and whiter than that which can be produced by sifting. Unbleached white flour is extremely versatile and has a long shelf life, but the term does not mean that the flour is necessarily free from chemical additives. A very common additive in unbleached white flour is potassium bromate, which improves performance in the oven by strengthening the dough and allowing it to rise higher. However, this additive has been cited as a possible carcinogen, and is banned in the United Kingdom, Canada, and the European Union. Because of this, you may want to seek out unbleached white flour that is also unbromated.

If you see flour that is identified as "white flour," and does not specify being unbleached, this might mean that the flour has been bleached. Bleaching is done to increase whiteness and improve performance in the oven. Through bleaching, the flour is oxidized, which can mimic the natural aging of flour.

FLOURS USED IN BAKING

ALL-PURPOSE FLOUR: A versatile white flour that can be relied upon to produce outstanding results in nearly every baking preparation. It is generally a combination of flour from hard (bronze-colored wheat that has a higher protein, and thus higher gluten, content) and soft wheat (wheat with a light golden color; also referred to as "white wheat"). It is overwhelmingly the most frequently recommended flour in this book.

PASTRY FLOUR: Superfine white wheat flour with relatively low protein content (around 9 percent) that is ideal for light, flaky baked goods. It is not a must, and the results it achieves can be duplicated with an all-purpose flour with a protein content on the lower end of the spectrum, but some baking enthusiasts swear by it for piecrusts and croissants.

CAKE FLOUR: Another smooth, superfine white wheat flour, and its protein content is even lower (ranging from 6 to 8 percent) than pastry flour. It lends baked goods the tender texture and high rise that is particularly desirable for cakes and biscuits.

BREAD FLOUR: White flour with a high protein content, which is ideal for bread baking, since the extra-elastic dough it produces can capture and hold more carbon dioxide than recipes using cake or pastry flour. Generally obtained from hard wheat, it is to be avoided when making desserts, as its high-protein content will result in cakes and cookies that are far tougher and denser than anyone is in the market for.

LOCAL OR STORE-BOUGHT FLOUR?

Not so long ago, there were thousands of mills in the United States. But, with the advent of modern milling techniques in the 19th century, large mills reduced the need for smaller, less technologically advanced gristmills. By the turn of the last century, mass-produced flour was the norm across the globe.

But the locavore movement has ushered in a revival of local, artisan milling, and the availability of flour that has been milled without the use of industrial technology is on the rise. However, local mills are still too few and too scattered to provide a significant proportion of our flour. And, as distribution channels are limited for artisan mills, the best way for most people to buy small-batch flour is online.

Most contemporary artisan mills use the ancient technique of stone milling. This technology is as old as farming, although important developments have since occurred, with stone mills powered by electricity now in operation.

Most flours produced by an authentic stone mill will not be the superfine, powdery, white substance that is fundamental to turning out quality desserts. Artisan mills can utilize more advanced technology to produce flours that are better suited to baking than what is traditionally produced by a stone mill, but the main point of artisan mills is to provide a more wholesome flour, not mimic the products of industrial giants.

SALT

Contrary to what most non-bakers think, the primary reason to add salt to a dough is not for taste. Although salt does improve the taste, the other functions it serves are far more important.

Baking without salt will result in flat baked goods that are miles away from the airy delight you were envisioning when you set out. The presence of salt in dough also slows down the activity of yeasts, bacteria, and enzymes, reducing acidity and allowing more time for the sweet, flavorful sugars to develop.

Salt also helps the dough create a better structure by making gluten (the protein that holds together baked goods) more resistant and more effective at keeping the gasses in, producing results that are higher in volume and feature a more open crumb.

Salt absorbs water, thus, a dough containing salt will be more dry and elastic, and will be less sticky and difficult to work with during handling and shaping.

Keep in mind that salt stiffens the dough, which is why you should generally try to add it during the last phases of mixing/kneading rather than at the beginning, so as not to make the dough too tough too early.

EGGS

For the purposes of making glorious desserts, it is best to secure the highest-quality eggs available.

Eggs provide more protein, which, when combined with the gluten, enhances the structure of a dough, making it elastic, soft, and easier to roll out without tearing.

It is important to use eggs that have a vibrantly orange yolk, as it is a sign of a healthy, happy, and well-fed chicken. Egg yolks get their color from carotenoids, which are also responsible for strengthening the chicken's immune system. Because chickens only hatch eggs if they have sufficient levels of carotenoids, the yolks possess hues of dark gold and orange. Paler yolks are often a result of chickens feeding on barley or white cornmeal, which don't nourish them as completely as a diet based on yellow corn and marigold petals.

Using brown or white eggs is up to personal preference, since they have the same nutritional profiles and taste. However, there are good arguments for buying brown eggs. First, brown eggs come from larger breeds that eat more, take longer to produce their eggs, and produce eggs with thicker protective shells, which prevents internal moisture loss over time and helps them maintain their freshness.

Eggs in the United States are graded according to the thickness of their shell and the firmness of their egg whites. Agricultural advances have made it possible for large egg producers to assess the quality of each individual egg and to efficiently sort them by size, weight, and quality. With almost scientific precision, eggs are graded AA (top quality), A (good quality found in most supermarkets), and B (substandard eggs with thin shells and watery egg whites that don't reach consumers but are used commercially and industrially). They are also further categorized by size: medium, large (the most common size), and extra large.

The past decade or so has seen a rise in the popularity of free-range and organic eggs. The chickens that produce these eggs are fed organic feed and are caged with slightly more space at their disposal than those raised at standard chicken farms. The jury is still out on whether free-range eggs taste better, but they constitute an additional, and perhaps politically oriented, option for aspiring bakers.

SUGAR

The standards—granulated sugar, confectioners' sugar (which is the same as powdered sugar), and brown sugar—will be what are required in almost all of the recipes in this book. But in your endeavors you may come across a recipe that calls for one of these sugars, which are less common:

CASTER SUGAR: A superfine sugar with a consistency that sits somewhere between granulated sugar and confectioners' sugar. Since it can dissolve without heat, unlike granulated sugar, it is most commonly called for in recipes where the sugar needs to melt or dissolve quickly, as in meringues. This ease can come with a hefty price tag that scares some people off, but you can easily make caster sugar at home with nothing more than a food processor or a blender and some granulated sugar. Place the granulated sugar in the food processor or blender and pulse until the consistency is superfine, but short of powdery. Let the sugar settle in the food processor, transfer it to a container, and label to avoid future confusion.

DEMERARA SUGAR: A large-grained raw sugar that originated in Guyana and is now produced in a number of countries around the globe. It is commonly referred to as a "brown sugar" due to its color, but brown sugar is refined white sugar that has been bathed in molasses. Demerara has a natural caramel flavor that comes through in any dish it is added to. Famous for the depth and complexity it can lend to recipes, it is worth experimenting with if a certain recipe is falling short of your ideal flavor. Demerara's large grains also pack a pleasant crunchy quality, making it perfect for sprinkling on muffins, cakes, and cookies.

TURBINADO SUGAR: Very similar to demerara sugar, possessing the large, crunchy grains and rich flavor that has made demerara fashionable of late. If you're going to give either of these sugars a try, keep in mind that they contain more moisture than granulated sugar. This probably won't be a problem in preparations featuring a moist batter, such as brownies. But in recipes that are on the arid side, like pastry and cookie doughs, substituting demerara or turbinado might take you wide of the mark.

MUSCOVADO SUGAR: A cane sugar with a very moist texture and a molasses-forward flavor. It is best suited to savory dishes, but may be worth incorporating into preparations where you're after something other than standard sweetness. As with demerara and turbinado, you want to keep moisture in mind whenever you're thinking of utilizing it in a recipe.

As far as sugar alternatives go, substituting an equivalent amount of a combination of maple syrup and honey is probably the easiest route when baking. Agave nectar is another option, but it will affect the tenderness and flavor of baked goods. If you want to use agave nectar, swap it in for the suggested amount of sugar and add ¼ cup of flour to your preparation.

For those who have blood sugar concerns, stevia is the best bet to approximate the effect sugar would provide. Avoid saccharin (which will leave a strong aftertaste) and aspartame.

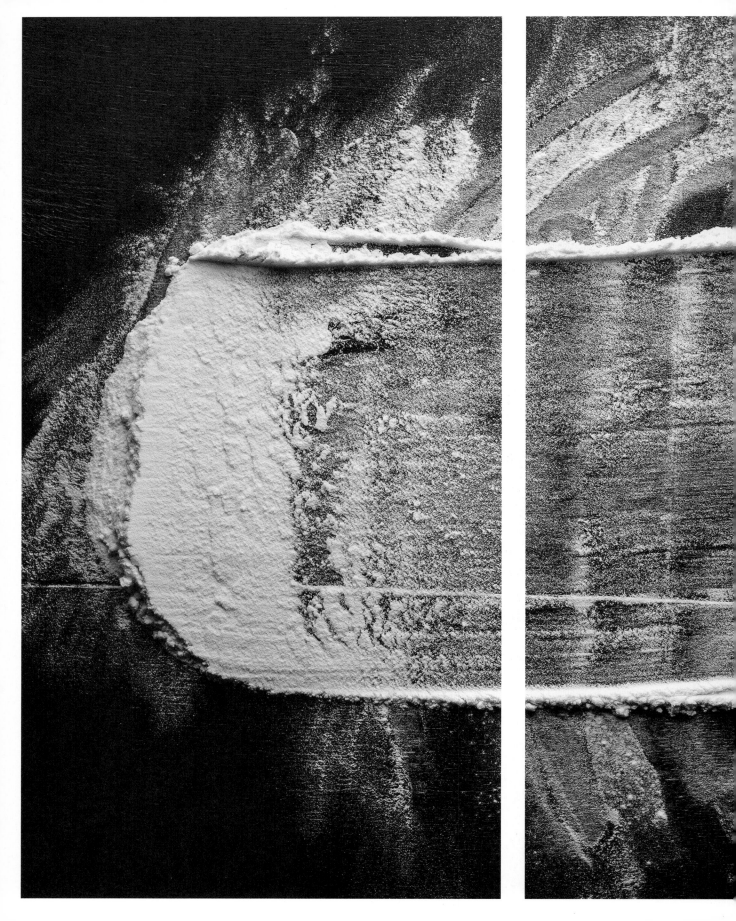

CHAPTER 2

ESSENTIAL

RECIPES

Getting serious about your sweet tooth means getting ready to make the foundational pieces from scratch. Yes, you can easily purchase each of the following cornerstones at your local grocery store, but we're certain you'll feel better tackling tough preparations and serving them to your loved ones if you get in the habit of whipping them up yourself.

While these recipes are meant to be added to, a number of them—such as the Pound Cake, Caramel, and Hot Fudge—are treats in their own right, able to delight with nothing further required of you.

Leaf Lard Piecrusts

YIELD: **9" PIECRUSTS**

ACTIVE TIME: **12 MINUTES**

TOTAL TIME: **2 HOURS**

INGREDIENTS

2½ CUPS ALL-PURPOSE FLOUR

1½ TABLESPOONS GRANULATED SUGAR

1 TEASPOON SALT

6 OZ. COLD LEAF LARD, CUBED

2 TABLESPOONS UNSALTED BUTTER, CHILLED AND DIVIDED INTO TABLESPOONS

5 TABLESPOONS ICE-COLD WATER, PLUS MORE AS NEEDED

DIRECTIONS

1. Place the flour, sugar, and salt in a bowl and stir until combined.

2. Add the lard and butter and use a pastry blender to work them into the flour mixture. Work the mixture until it is a coarse meal, making sure to smooth out any large chunks.

3. Add the water and continue to work the mixture until it is a smooth dough. If it feels too dry, add more water in 1-teaspoon increments. Form the dough into a large ball and then cut it in half. Wrap each piece in plastic wrap and place in the refrigerator for 2 hours before using. The dough will keep in the refrigerator for up to 3 days. It also freezes very well, and can be stored in a freezer for 3 to 6 months.

NOTE: Leaf lard is the highest grade of lard, coming from the visceral fat around a pig's kidneys and loin. It is spreadable at room temperature, making it the perfect base for a flaky, flavorful piecrust. If you cannot locate it, substitute an equivalent amount of shortening.

Graham Cracker Crust

YIELD: **9" PIECRUST**

ACTIVE TIME: **20 MINUTES**

TOTAL TIME: **50 MINUTES**

INGREDIENTS

1½ CUPS GRAHAM CRACKER CRUMBS

2 TABLESPOONS GRANULATED SUGAR

1 TABLESPOON MAPLE SYRUP

6 TABLESPOONS UNSALTED BUTTER, MELTED

DIRECTIONS

1. Preheat the oven to 375°F. In a large bowl, add the graham cracker crumbs and sugar and stir to combine. Add the maple syrup and 5 tablespoons of the melted butter and stir until thoroughly combined.

2. Liberally grease a 9" pie plate with the remaining butter. Pour the dough into the pie plate and lightly press into shape. Line with tin foil and fill with uncooked rice. Bake for 10 to 12 minutes until the crust is golden.

3. Remove from the oven, discard the rice, and allow the crust to cool before filling.

A LOOK AHEAD

The technique of baking a piecrust before filling it is also known as "blind baking." When working with a custard filling, as in a lemon meringue or pumpkin pie, baking the crust ahead of time has several advantages. It prevents pockets of steam from forming in the crust once it is filled, which can cause the crust to become puffy and uneven. Blind baking also keeps the bottom of the crust from becoming soggy, and allows the edge of the pie to be sturdy, as opposed to saggy. Uncooked rice is the most typical weight when blind baking a pie, though dried beans and weights designed specifically for the task can also be utilized.

Gluten-Free Crust

YIELD: **9" PIECRUST**

ACTIVE TIME: **20 MINUTES**

TOTAL TIME: **1 HOUR**

INGREDIENTS

1¼ CUPS GLUTEN-FREE MULTI-PURPOSE FLOUR BLEND, PLUS MORE FOR DUSTING

1 TABLESPOON GRANULATED SUGAR

½ TEASPOON XANTHAN GUM

½ TEASPOON SALT

6 TABLESPOONS UNSALTED BUTTER, CHILLED AND CUT INTO SMALL PIECES

1 LARGE EGG

2 TEASPOONS FRESH LEMON JUICE

1 TO 2 TABLESPOONS ICE-COLD WATER

DIRECTIONS

1. In a large bowl, combine the flour blend, sugar, xanthan gum, and salt. Add the butter and work it into the flour mixture with a pastry blender or your fingers to form a coarse meal that includes large chunks of butter.

2. In a small bowl, whisk the egg and lemon juice together briskly until the mixture is very foamy. Add to the dry mixture and stir until the dough holds together. If the dough isn't quite holding, add the cold water in 1-tablespoon increments until it does. Shape into a disk, wrap tightly in plastic wrap, and refrigerate for 30 minutes or overnight.

3. When ready to make the pie, take the dough out of the refrigerator and allow to rest at room temperature for about 10 minutes before rolling out on a lightly floured work surface.

Tart Pastry Shell

YIELD: **9" PASTRY SHELL**

ACTIVE TIME: **30 MINUTES**

TOTAL TIME: **3 HOURS AND 15 MINUTES**

INGREDIENTS

YOLK FROM 1 LARGE EGG

1 TABLESPOON HEAVY CREAM

½ TEASPOON PURE VANILLA EXTRACT

1¼ CUPS ALL-PURPOSE FLOUR, PLUS MORE FOR DUSTING

⅔ CUP CONFECTIONERS' SUGAR

¼ TEASPOON SALT

1 STICK UNSALTED BUTTER, CUT INTO 4 PIECES

DIRECTIONS

1. Place the egg yolk, cream, and vanilla in a small bowl, whisk to combine, and set aside. Place the flour, sugar, and salt in a food processor and pulse to combine. Add the pieces of butter and pulse until the mixture resembles a coarse meal. Set the food processor to puree and add the egg mixture as it is running. Puree until the dough just comes together, about 20 seconds. Transfer the dough onto sheet of plastic wrap, press into 6" disk, wrap, and refrigerate for at least 2 hours.

2. Approximately 1 hour before you are planning to start constructing your tart, remove the dough from the refrigerator. Lightly dust a large sheet of parchment paper or plastic wrap with flour and place the dough in the center. Roll out to 9" and line the tart pan with it. Place the pan containing the rolled-out dough in the freezer.

3. Preheat the oven to 375°F. Place the chilled tart shell on cookie sheet, line the inside of the tart shell with foil, and fill with uncooked rice. Bake for 30 minutes, rotating the shell halfway through.

4. After 30 minutes, remove the shell from the oven and discard the rice and foil. Leave the tart shell on the cookie sheet and place it on the upper rack of the oven. Bake until the shell is golden brown, about 5 minutes. Remove and fill as desired.

Pound Cake

YIELD: **1 LOAF**

ACTIVE TIME: **20 MINUTES**

TOTAL TIME: **2 HOURS AND 15 MINUTES**

INGREDIENTS

2 STICKS UNSALTED BUTTER, CHILLED AND DIVIDED INTO TABLESPOONS, PLUS MORE FOR GREASING THE PAN

3 LARGE EGGS

YOLKS OF 3 LARGE EGGS

2 TEASPOONS PURE VANILLA EXTRACT

1¾ CUPS CAKE FLOUR, PLUS MORE FOR DUSTING

½ TEASPOON SALT

1¼ CUPS GRANULATED SUGAR

DIRECTIONS

1. Place the butter in the bowl of a stand mixer and let stand until room temperature, about 25 minutes.

2. Place the eggs, egg yolks, and vanilla in a bowl and beat until combined. Set the mixture aside.

3. Preheat the oven to 325°F and generously butter a 9 x 5-inch loaf pan, dust it with flour, and knock out any excess.

4. Attach the paddle attachment to the stand mixer. Add the salt and beat until the mixture is smooth and creamy, 2 to 3 minutes. Gradually add the sugar and beat until the mixture is fluffy and almost white, 5 to 8 minutes. Scrape down the bowl as needed while mixing the batter.

5. Gradually add the egg mixture in a steady stream and beat mixture until light and fluffy, 3 to 4 minutes. Remove bowl from the mixer and scrape it down.

6. Working in 3 or 4 portions, sift the cake flour over the mixture and use a rubber spatula to fold the flour in before adding the next portion. Stir until all of the flour has been incorporated.

7. Transfer the batter to the prepared loaf pan and smooth the top with a rubber spatula. Place the cake in the oven and bake until golden brown and a toothpick inserted in the center of the cake comes out clean, approximately 1 hour and 15 minutes. Remove the pan from the oven and let the cake cool in the pan on a wire rack for 15 minutes. Invert the cake onto wire rack and let it cool completely before serving.

Sugar Glaze

YIELD: **1½ CUPS**

ACTIVE TIME: **5 MINUTES**

TOTAL TIME: **5 MINUTES**

INGREDIENTS

4 CUPS CONFECTIONERS' SUGAR

¼ CUP WATER, PLUS MORE AS NEEDED

½ TEASPOON PURE VANILLA EXTRACT

FOOD COLORING (OPTIONAL)

DIRECTIONS

1. Combine the confectioners' sugar, water, and vanilla in a mixing bowl. Stir until the mixture is smooth, adding additional water if it is too thick.

2. If you want to color the glaze, transfer it to small cups and add the food coloring a few drops at a time until the desired color is achieved.

Chocolate Frosting

YIELD: **1½ CUPS**

ACTIVE TIME: **15 MINUTES**

TOTAL TIME: **1 HOUR AND 30 MINUTES**

INGREDIENTS

1 LB. MILK CHOCOLATE, CHOPPED

⅔ CUP HEAVY CREAM

2 STICKS UNSALTED BUTTER, DIVIDED INTO TABLESPOONS AND AT ROOM TEMPERATURE

DIRECTIONS

1. Place 1" of water in a saucepan and bring it to a simmer over medium heat.

2. Place the chocolate and cream in a large heatproof bowl and place it over the saucepan, making sure that the water does not touch bottom of bowl. Stir occasionally until the mixture is smooth and glossy, 10 to 15 minutes.

3. Remove the bowl from heat, add the butter, and stir briefly. Let mixture stand until the butter is melted, about 5 minutes, and then stir until the mixture is smooth.

4. Place in the refrigerator until the frosting has cooled and thickened, 30 minutes to 1 hour.

Cream Cheese Frosting

YIELD: **3 CUPS**

ACTIVE TIME: **5 MINUTES**

TOTAL TIME: **5 MINUTES**

INGREDIENTS

1 (8 OZ.) PACKAGE OF CREAM CHEESE, AT ROOM TEMPERATURE

5 TABLESPOONS UNSALTED BUTTER, AT ROOM TEMPERATURE

1 TABLESPOON SOUR CREAM

½ TEASPOON PURE VANILLA EXTRACT

1¼ CUPS CONFECTIONERS' SUGAR

DIRECTIONS

1. Place the cream cheese, butter, sour cream, and vanilla in a food processor and blitz until combined. Scrape down the bowl as needed.

2. Add the confectioners' sugar, blitz until smooth, and refrigerate until ready to use.

Vanilla Buttercream Frosting

YIELD: **1½ CUPS**

ACTIVE TIME: **10 MINUTES**

TOTAL TIME: **10 MINUTES**

INGREDIENTS

10 TABLESPOONS UNSALTED BUTTER, AT ROOM TEMPERATURE

SEEDS OF ½ VANILLA BEAN

1¼ CUPS CONFECTIONERS' SUGAR

PINCH OF SALT

½ TEASPOON PURE VANILLA EXTRACT

1 TABLESPOON HEAVY CREAM

DIRECTIONS

1. Using a stand or handheld mixer fitted with the whisk attachment, beat the butter until smooth.

2. Add the vanilla seeds, confectioners' sugar, and salt and beat until the mixture is fully combined. Scrape down the bowl as needed while mixing.

3. Add the vanilla extract and heavy cream and beat until the mixture is light and fluffy, about 4 minutes, stopping to scrape down the bowl as needed.

FOR CHOCOLATE BUTTERCREAM FROSTING:
Remove the heavy cream from the ingredients. After adding the vanilla extract, add 4 oz. of room-temperature melted chocolate, and beat until the mixture is light and fluffy, about 4 minutes.

Pastry Cream

YIELD: **2½ CUPS**

ACTIVE TIME: **15 MINUTES**

TOTAL TIME: **1 HOUR**

INGREDIENTS

2 CUPS WHOLE MILK

1 TABLESPOON UNSALTED BUTTER

½ CUP GRANULATED SUGAR

3 TABLESPOONS CORNSTARCH

2 LARGE EGGS

PINCH OF SALT

½ TEASPOON PURE VANILLA EXTRACT

DIRECTIONS

1. Place the milk and butter in a saucepan and bring to a simmer over medium heat.

2. As the milk mixture is coming to a simmer, place the sugar and cornstarch in a small bowl and whisk to combine. Add the eggs and whisk until the mixture is smooth and creamy.

3. Pour half of the hot milk mixture into the egg mixture and stir until incorporated. Add the salt and vanilla extract, stir to incorporate, and pour the tempered egg mixture into the saucepan. Cook, while stirring constantly, until the mixture is very thick and boiling.

4. Remove from heat and pour the pastry cream into a bowl. Place plastic wrap directly on the surface to prevent a skin from forming. Place in the refrigerator until cool.

Whipped Cream

YIELD: **2 CUPS**

ACTIVE TIME: **5 MINUTES**

TOTAL TIME: **5 MINUTES**

INGREDIENTS

2 CUPS HEAVY CREAM

1 TEASPOON PURE VANILLA EXTRACT

DIRECTIONS

1. Place the cream and vanilla in a bowl and whisk until soft peaks begin to form. Be sure not to over-mix, as this will result in butter.

2. Place in refrigerator until ready to serve.

Hot Fudge

YIELD: **2 CUPS**

ACTIVE TIME: **15 MINUTES**

TOTAL TIME: **15 MINUTES**

INGREDIENTS

⅔ CUP HEAVY CREAM

½ CUP LIGHT CORN SYRUP

⅓ CUP DARK BROWN SUGAR

¼ CUP UNSWEETENED COCOA POWDER

½ TEASPOON SALT

½ LB. BITTERSWEET CHOCOLATE, CHOPPED

½ TEASPOON INSTANT ESPRESSO POWDER

2 TABLESPOONS UNSALTED BUTTER

1 TEASPOON PURE VANILLA EXTRACT

DIRECTIONS

1. Place the cream, corn syrup, brown sugar, cocoa powder, salt, half of the chocolate, and the espresso grounds in a saucepan and cook over medium heat until the chocolate is melted.

2. Reduce heat and simmer for 5 minutes. Remove from heat and whisk in the remaining chocolate, the butter, and the vanilla. Serve immediately.

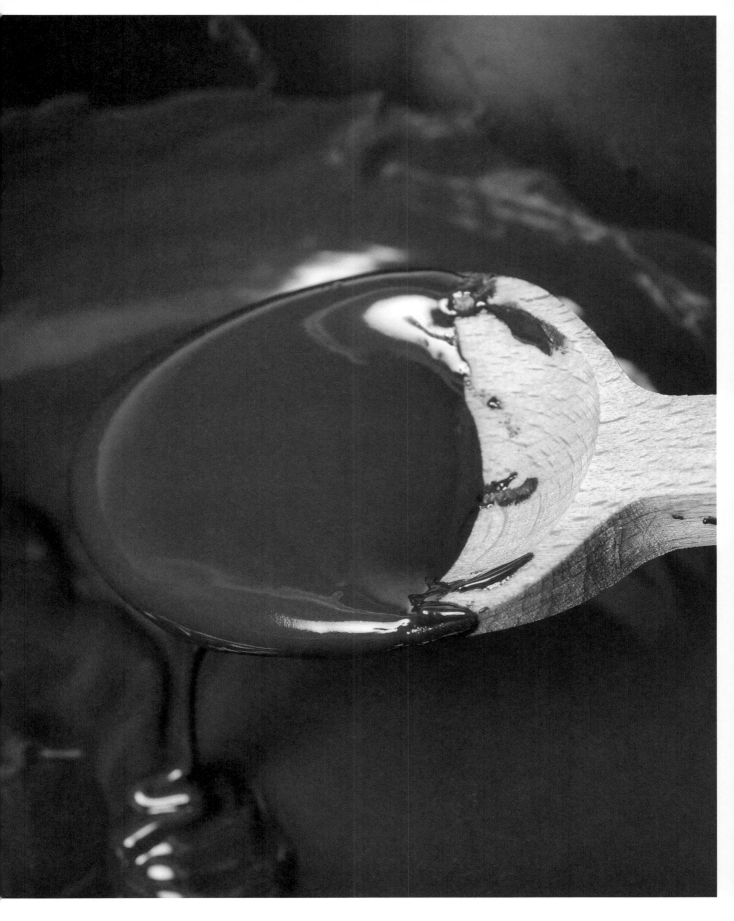

Caramel

YIELD: **1 CUP**

ACTIVE TIME: **5 MINUTES**

TOTAL TIME: **10 MINUTES**

INGREDIENTS

1 CUP GRANULATED SUGAR

¼ CUP WATER

3 TABLESPOONS UNSALTED BUTTER

½ TEASPOON SALT

DIRECTIONS

1. Place the sugar, water, butter, and salt in a small saucepan and cook over medium-high heat until it is light brown. Be sure not to stir the mixture; instead, gently swirl the pan a few times as it cooks.

2. Reduce heat to medium and cook for about 3 to 5 minutes, or until the mixture caramelizes. Stir the mixture once or twice to make sure it does not burn.

CHAPTER 3

CHOCOLATE

We start with the most beloved of all sweets-related flavors, the only one that gets the addiction signifier of "-holic" appended to it. Whether it be milk or dark, sweet, bitter, or white, the array of flavors that chocolate provides, and the number of desserts this versatility can carry, causes people all across the globe to be powerless against its sweet song.

The rare ingredient that is as comfortable playing with others as it is standing on its own, it's quite possible that chocolate is responsible for putting more smiles on people's faces than any other food.

Chocolate Chip Cookies

YIELD: **16 COOKIES**

ACTIVE TIME: **15 MINUTES**

TOTAL TIME: **45 MINUTES**

INGREDIENTS

14 TABLESPOONS UNSALTED BUTTER

1¾ CUPS ALL-PURPOSE FLOUR

½ TEASPOON BAKING SODA

½ CUP GRANULATED SUGAR

¾ CUP PACKED DARK BROWN SUGAR

1 TEASPOON SALT

2 TEASPOONS PURE VANILLA EXTRACT

1 LARGE EGG

YOLK OF 1 LARGE EGG

1¼ CUPS SEMISWEET CHOCOLATE CHIPS

DIRECTIONS

1. Preheat the oven to 350°F.

2. Place the butter in a saucepan and cook over medium-high heat until it is dark brown and has a nutty aroma. Transfer to a heatproof mixing bowl.

3. Place the flour and baking soda in a bowl and whisk until combined.

4. Add the sugars, salt, and vanilla to the bowl containing the melted butter and whisk until combined. Add the egg and egg yolk and whisk until mixture is smooth and thick. Add the flour-and-baking soda mixture and stir until incorporated. Add the chocolate chips and stir until evenly distributed. Form the mixture into 16 balls and place on parchment-lined baking sheets, leaving about 2″ between each ball.

5. Working with 1 baking sheet at a time, place it in the oven and bake until golden brown, 12 to 16 minutes while rotating the sheet halfway through the bake time. Remove from the oven and let cool to room temperature before serving.

Chocolate & Almond Crinkle Cookies

YIELD: **24 COOKIES**

ACTIVE TIME: **10 MINUTES**

TOTAL TIME: **2 HOURS AND 30 MINUTES**

INGREDIENTS

⅔ CUP SLIVERED ALMONDS

2 TABLESPOONS GRANULATED SUGAR

6 OZ. BITTERSWEET CHOCOLATE, FINELY CHOPPED

¼ CUP WHOLE MILK

1 STICK UNSALTED BUTTER

1½ CUPS PACKED LIGHT BROWN SUGAR

2 LARGE EGGS, AT ROOM TEMPERATURE

½ TEASPOON PURE ALMOND EXTRACT

2 TABLESPOONS UNSWEETENED COCOA POWDER

2 TEASPOONS BAKING POWDER

½ TEASPOON SALT

2¾ CUPS ALL-PURPOSE FLOUR

¾ CUP CONFECTIONERS' SUGAR

DIRECTIONS

1. Preheat the oven to 350°F. Place the almonds on a baking sheet and toast for 5 to 7 minutes, until lightly browned. Remove from the oven and transfer to a food processor. Add the granulated sugar and pulse until the mixture is very fine.

2. Combine the chocolate and milk in a microwave-safe bowl and microwave on medium for 15-second intervals until melted and smooth, removing to stir in between each interval.

3. Combine the butter and brown sugar in a mixing bowl and beat at low speed with a handheld mixer to combine. Increase the speed to high and beat for 3 to 4 minutes, until light and fluffy. Add the eggs one at a time and beat until incorporated. Add the chocolate-and-milk mixture, almond extract, cocoa powder, baking powder, and salt and beat for 1 minute. Slowly add the flour and beat until a stiff dough forms. Stir in the almonds and place the dough in the refrigerator for at least 2 hours, until it is firm.

4. Preheat the oven to 350°F and line two baking sheets with parchment paper. Sift the confectioners' sugar onto a sheet of waxed paper. Remove tablespoon-sized portions of the dough, form them into balls, and roll each ball in the confectioners' sugar until well coated. Place the balls 2″ apart on the baking sheets, place in oven, and bake for 14 to 16 minutes, until the cookies are cracking and the edges feel dry. Remove, let cool for 2 minutes, and then transfer to wire racks to cool completely.

Chocolate Cake

YIELD: **4 SERVINGS**

ACTIVE TIME: **10 MINUTES**

TOTAL TIME: **1 HOUR**

INGREDIENTS

6 TABLESPOONS UNSALTED
BUTTER, CUT INTO SMALL PIECES

1 CUP GRANULATED SUGAR

2 EGGS

½ TEASPOON PURE VANILLA
EXTRACT

1 CUP ALL-PURPOSE FLOUR

1 TEASPOON BAKING POWDER

2 TABLESPOONS UNSWEETENED
COCOA POWDER

½ CUP WHOLE MILK

CHOCOLATE BUTTERCREAM
FROSTING (SEE PAGE 49)

DIRECTIONS

1. Preheat the oven to 350°F.

2. In a large bowl, beat the butter and sugar together until the mixture is light and fluffy. Add the eggs one at a time, stirring to combine thoroughly after each addition. Stir in the vanilla extract.

3. In a small bowl, combine the flour, baking powder, and cocoa powder and mix together. Alternate adding the flour mixture and the milk to the butter-and-sugar mixture, stirring after each addition until it has been incorporated.

4. Pour the batter into a greased round 9" cake pan.

5. Put the pan in the oven and bake for about 20 to 25 minutes, until a toothpick inserted in the middle comes out clean. Remove the pan from the oven and let the cake cool completely before applying the frosting.

German Chocolate Cake

YIELD: **8 SERVINGS**

ACTIVE TIME: **10 MINUTES**

TOTAL TIME: **1 HOUR AND 30 MINUTES**

INGREDIENTS

6 EGGS

1⅓ CUPS GRANULATED SUGAR

1 STICK UNSALTED BUTTER, MELTED

½ CUP SOUR CREAM

1 TEASPOON ORANGE ZEST

1⅓ CUPS CAKE FLOUR

⅔ CUP ALL-PURPOSE FLOUR

½ CUP COCOA POWDER

½ CUP OVALTINE

2 TEASPOONS BAKING POWDER

½ TEASPOON BAKING SODA

1 TABLESPOON SALT

COCONUT-PECAN FROSTING (SEE RECIPE)

DIRECTIONS

1. Preheat the oven to 350°F.

2. Place the eggs and sugar in the bowl of a stand mixer fitted with the whisk attachment and beat on medium until pale and fluffy. Add the butter, sour cream, and orange zest and beat until combined.

3. Sift the flours, cocoa powder, Ovaltine, baking powder, baking soda, and salt into a bowl. Add the dry mixture to the wet mixture and beat until just combined. Scrape the bowl as needed while mixing the batter.

4. Divide the batter between two greased round 9" cake pans. Place them in the oven and bake for 20 to 25 minutes, until a toothpick inserted into the center comes out clean.

5. Remove from the oven and let cool in the pan for 10 minutes before transferring to a wire rack to cool completely. When the cakes have cooled, spread some of the frosting on the top of one cake. Place the other cake on top and cover the entire cake with the remaining frosting.

COCONUT-PECAN FROSTING

½ CUP EVAPORATED MILK

½ CUP GRANULATED SUGAR

YOLK OF 1 EGG

4 TABLESPOONS UNSALTED BUTTER,
CUT INTO SMALL PIECES

SEEDS OF ½ VANILLA BEAN

½ CUP SWEETENED SHREDDED
COCONUT

½ CUP CHOPPED PECANS

1. In a large saucepan, combine the evaporated milk, sugar, egg yolk, butter, and vanilla. Cook over medium heat, while stirring frequently, until it is thickened, about 10 to 12 minutes.

2. Add the coconut and pecans, stir to combine, and remove the saucepan from heat. Let cool, while stirring occasionally, and then spread over the cooled cake.

Double Chocolate Decadence Cake

YIELD: **8 TO 10 SERVINGS**

ACTIVE TIME: **10 MINUTES**

TOTAL TIME: **1 HOUR**

INGREDIENTS

6 EGGS

1⅓ CUPS GRANULATED SUGAR

1 STICK UNSALTED BUTTER, MELTED

½ CUP SOUR CREAM

1 TEASPOON ORANGE ZEST

½ LB. CHOCOLATE, MELTED

1⅓ CUPS CAKE FLOUR

⅔ CUP ALL-PURPOSE FLOUR

1 CUP COCOA POWDER

2 TEASPOONS BAKING POWDER

½ TEASPOON BAKING SODA

1 TABLESPOON SALT

CHOCOLATE BUTTERCREAM FROSTING (SEE PAGE 49)

CHOCOLATE SHAVINGS, FOR TOPPING

DIRECTIONS

1. Preheat the oven to 350°F.

2. Place the eggs and sugar in the bowl of a stand mixer fitted with the whisk attachment and beat on medium until pale and fluffy. Add the butter, sour cream, orange zest, and melted chocolate and beat until combined.

3. Sift the flours, cocoa powder, baking powder, baking soda, and salt into a bowl. Add the dry mixture to the wet mixture and beat until just combined. Scrape the bowl as needed while mixing the batter.

4. Divide the batter between two greased round 9″ cake pans. Place them in the oven and bake for 20 to 25 minutes, until a toothpick inserted into the center comes out clean.

5. Remove from the oven and let cool in the pan for 10 minutes before transferring to a wire rack to cool completely. When the cakes have cooled, spread some of the frosting on the top of one cake. Place the other cake on top and cover the entire cake with the remaining frosting. Sprinkle the chocolate shavings on top and serve.

Dark Chocolate & Stout Brownies

YIELD: **16 BROWNIES**

ACTIVE TIME: **15 MINUTES**

TOTAL TIME: **1 HOUR AND 15 MINUTES**

INGREDIENTS

12 OZ. GUINNESS OR OTHER STOUT

¾ LB. DARK CHOCOLATE CHIPS

2 STICKS UNSALTED BUTTER

1½ CUPS GRANULATED SUGAR

3 LARGE EGGS

1 TEASPOON PURE VANILLA EXTRACT

¾ CUP ALL-PURPOSE FLOUR

1¼ TEASPOONS SALT

COCOA POWDER, FOR DUSTING

DIRECTIONS

1. Preheat your oven to 350°F and grease a square 8″ cake pan. Place the stout in a medium saucepan and bring to a boil. Cook until it has reduced by half. Remove pan from the heat and let cool.

2. Place the chocolate chips and the butter in a microwave-safe bowl and microwave until melted, removing to stir every 20 seconds.

3. Place the sugar, eggs, and vanilla in a large bowl and stir until combined. Slowly whisk in the chocolate-and-butter mixture and then whisk in the stout.

4. Fold in the flour and salt. Pour batter into greased pan, place in oven, and bake for 35 to 40 minutes, until the surface begins to crack and a toothpick inserted in the center comes out with a few moist crumbs attached. Remove the pan from the oven, place on a wire rack, and let cool for at least 20 minutes. When cool, sprinkle the cocoa powder over the top and cut the brownies into squares.

Marble Brownies

YIELD: **16 BROWNIES**

ACTIVE TIME: **15 MINUTES**

TOTAL TIME: **1 HOUR AND 15 MINUTES**

INGREDIENTS

½ CUP ALL-PURPOSE FLOUR, PLUS MORE FOR DUSTING

1 STICK UNSALTED BUTTER

4 OZ. MILK CHOCOLATE CHIPS

3 LARGE EGGS, AT ROOM TEMPERATURE

1 CUP GRANULATED SUGAR

PINCH OF SALT

1 (8 OZ.) PACKAGE OF CREAM CHEESE, AT ROOM TEMPERATURE

½ TEASPOON PURE VANILLA EXTRACT

DIRECTIONS

1. Preheat the oven to 350°F. Grease and flour a square 8" cake pan.

2. Place the butter and chocolate chips in a microwave-safe bowl and microwave on medium until melted and smooth, removing to stir every 20 seconds. Let cool for 5 minutes.

3. Place 2 of the eggs and ¾ cup of the sugar in a mixing bowl and beat with a handheld mixer on medium speed for 1 minute. Add the chocolate-and-butter mixture, beat for 1 minute, and then add the flour and salt. Beat until just blended and then pour into the prepared pan.

4. In a separate bowl, combine the cream cheese, remaining sugar, remaining egg, and vanilla. Beat with a handheld mixer on medium speed until light and fluffy. Spread on top of the batter and use a fork to stir the layers together. Place in the oven and bake for 35 minutes, until the top is springy to the touch. Remove, allow the brownies to cool in the pan, and then cut into bars.

Whoopie Pies

YIELD: **6 SERVINGS**

ACTIVE TIME: **15 MINUTES**

TOTAL TIME: **1 HOUR**

INGREDIENTS

2½ STICKS UNSALTED BUTTER, AT ROOM TEMPERATURE

1¼ CUPS CONFECTIONERS' SUGAR

2 PINCHES OF SALT

2½ TEASPOONS PURE VANILLA EXTRACT

2½ CUPS MARSHMALLOW CRÈME

2 CUPS ALL-PURPOSE FLOUR

½ CUP UNSWEETENED COCOA POWDER

1 TEASPOON BAKING SODA

1 CUP PACKED LIGHT BROWN SUGAR

1 LARGE EGG, AT ROOM TEMPERATURE

1 CUP BUTTERMILK

DIRECTIONS

1. Place 12 tablespoons of the butter and the confectioners' sugar in a mixing bowl and beat until the mixture is fluffy. Add a pinch of salt and 1½ teaspoons of the vanilla and beat until combined. Add the marshmallow crème and beat until incorporated. Place the filling in the refrigerator and chill for at least 30 minutes.

2. Preheat the oven to 350°F.

3. Place the flour, cocoa powder, baking soda, and the remaining salt in a bowl and whisk to combine. Place the remaining butter and the brown sugar in another mixing bowl and beat until the mixture is fluffy. Add the egg, beat until incorporated, and then add the remaining vanilla. Gradually add the dry mixture and the buttermilk, alternating between them. Beat until incorporated and then scoop the batter onto parchment-lined baking sheets, making sure to leave plenty of room between the scoops.

4. Place the sheets in the oven and bake, while rotating and switching their positions halfway through, for 15 minutes. The cakes should feel springy when done. Remove from the oven and let cool on the baking sheets.

5. Place filling in the center of one cake, top with another cake, and press down to spread the filling to the edges. Repeat with the remaining filling and cakes and then serve.

CRÈME OF THE CROP

Marshmallow crème is a marshmallow confectionary spread, the best-known version of which is Marshmallow Fluff. Fluff was invented by Archibald Query in Somerville, Mass., near the turn of the 20th century. After selling his creation door-to-door for a time, Query sold it to two candy makers in nearby Lynn, H. Allen Durkee and Fred Mower, for $500 in 1920. Durkee and Mower's version (originally called Toot Sweet Marshmallow Fluff) hit the market in 1917, and it remains a pantry staple throughout the Northeast, where the whoopie pie and the Fluffernutter sandwich remain regional favorites.

Marshmallow crème is also a traditional part of Middle Eastern cuisine. While this iteration, which is known as *natef*, was mentioned in a 10th-century cookbook, modern commercial varieties are practically identical to those produced in the U.S.

WHITE CHOCOLATE

While some apocryphal tales assert that white chocolate is the result of cocoa beans that have not been roasted, that is far from the case. White chocolate is instead made with cocoa butter (a product resulting from roasted cocoa beans), sugar, and milk powder. As it does not contain the cocoa mass that is produced by grinding the roasted nibs of the cacao bean finely, some do not consider white chocolate to be a true chocolate.

White Chocolate Almond Bars

YIELD: **16 SQUARES**

ACTIVE TIME: **10 MINUTES**

TOTAL TIME: **1 HOUR**

INGREDIENTS

1 CUP BLANCHED AND CHOPPED ALMONDS

2 STICKS UNSALTED BUTTER

1 CUP PACKED DARK BROWN SUGAR

YOLK OF 1 LARGE EGG, AT ROOM TEMPERATURE

1 TEASPOON PURE VANILLA EXTRACT

2 CUPS ALL-PURPOSE FLOUR

¼ TEASPOON SALT

½ LB. QUALITY WHITE CHOCOLATE, CHOPPED

DIRECTIONS

1. Preheat the oven to 350°F and line a 9 x 13-inch baking dish with parchment paper. Place the almonds on a baking sheet and toast for 5 to 7 minutes, until lightly browned.

2. Combine the butter and sugar in a mixing bowl and beat at low speed with a handheld mixer to blend. Increase the speed to high and beat for 3 to 4 minutes, until light and fluffy.

3. Add the egg yolk and vanilla and beat for 1 minute. Slowly add the flour and salt and beat until a stiff dough forms. Pat the dough evenly into the baking dish and prick it with a fork. Place the pan on the middle rack in the oven and bake for 20 minutes, or until light brown.

4. Remove the pan from the oven and scatter the white chocolate evenly over the crust. Return the pan to the oven for 1 minute, remove, and spread the chocolate into an even layer. Sprinkle the almonds on top, allow to cool in the pan, and then cut into bars.

Chocolate & Coconut Bars

YIELD: **16 BARS**

ACTIVE TIME: **15 MINUTES**

TOTAL TIME: **1 HOUR**

INGREDIENTS

2 STICKS UNSALTED BUTTER

¾ CUP GRANULATED SUGAR

¾ CUP PACKED LIGHT BROWN SUGAR

2 LARGE EGGS, AT ROOM TEMPERATURE

1 TEASPOON PURE ALMOND EXTRACT

¼ CUP UNSWEETENED COCOA POWDER

1 TEASPOON BAKING SODA

½ TEASPOON SALT

2 CUPS ALL-PURPOSE FLOUR

1 CUP MINIATURE CHOCOLATE CHIPS

1 (14 OZ.) CAN OF SWEETENED CONDENSED MILK

1 CUP PACKED UNSWEETENED SHREDDED COCONUT

DIRECTIONS

1. Preheat the oven to 375°F and grease a 9 x 13-inch baking dish. Combine the butter and sugars in a mixing bowl and beat at low speed with a handheld mixer to blend. Increase the speed to high and beat for 3 to 4 minutes, until light and fluffy.

2. Add the eggs and almond extract and beat until well combined. Add the cocoa powder, baking soda, and salt and beat at medium speed. Reduce the speed to low, add the flour, beat until incorporated, and then fold in the chocolate chips.

3. Spread the batter in the pan. Combine the condensed milk and coconut in a small bowl and stir well. Spread this in an even layer on top of the batter. Place the pan in the oven and bake for 25 to 30 minutes, until a toothpick comes out clean after being inserted into the middle. Remove from the oven, allow to cool in the pan, and then cut into bars.

YIELD: **6 TO 8 SERVINGS**

ACTIVE TIME: **25 MINUTES**

TOTAL TIME: **3 HOURS**

INGREDIENTS

¼ TEASPOON ACTIVE DRY YEAST

¼ TEASPOON GRANULATED SUGAR

1½ CUPS LUKEWARM WATER (90 TO 100°F)

2 STICKS UNSALTED BUTTER, CUT INTO SMALL PIECES

1 CUP SEMISWEET CHOCOLATE CHIPS

1 TEASPOON GROUND CINNAMON

YOLKS OF 6 LARGE EGGS

1 TEASPOON SALT

3 CUPS ALL-PURPOSE FLOUR, PLUS MORE FOR DUSTING

Chocolate & Cinnamon Brioche

DIRECTIONS

1. Put the yeast and sugar in a measuring cup and add about ½ cup of the water in a drizzle. Cover the measuring cup with plastic wrap and set it aside for about 15 minutes. If the yeast doesn't foam, it is not alive and you'll need to start over.

2. Place the butter and the chocolate chips in a microwave-safe bowl. Melt the chocolate and butter in the microwave on medium, removing to stir every 20 seconds. Remove, stir in the cinnamon, and let cool to room temperature.

3. When the yeast is proofed, pour it into a large bowl and add the egg yolks and remaining water. Stir gently to combine. Combine the salt and the flour in a separate bowl, and then add to the yeast mixture. Stir with a wooden spoon until combined. The dough should be wet and sticky.

4. Put a dusting of flour on a flat surface and lift out the dough. With flour on your hands and more at the ready, begin kneading the dough so that it loses its stickiness. Don't overdo it, and don't use too much flour—just enough that the dough becomes more cohesive. While kneading, add the chocolate-and-cinnamon mixture in small increments. Place the dough in a large bowl, cover the bowl with plastic wrap, and allow to rise for at least 1 hour. Gently punch it down, re-cover with the plastic, and allow to rise for another 30 minutes or so.

5. While the dough is on its final rise, preheat the oven to 450°F. Put a piece of parchment paper on the bottom of a Dutch oven, cover it, and place it in the oven. When the oven is ready, use pot holders to remove the lid of the Dutch oven, scoop the dough from the bowl to the pot, put the lid back on, and bake with the lid on for 15 minutes. Remove the lid and bake for another 15 to 20 minutes, until the top is golden and the bread sounds hollow when tapped. Remove the pot from the oven and use tea towels to carefully remove the bread. Allow to cool before slicing.

Black Forest Trifle with Preserved Cherries & Cocoa Crumble

YIELD: **10 TO 12 SERVINGS**

ACTIVE TIME: **45 MINUTES**

TOTAL TIME: **2 HOURS**

DIRECTIONS

1. Preheat the oven to 350°F and grease a round 9″ cake pan.

2. Place the eggs and sugar in the bowl of a stand mixer fitted with the whisk attachment and beat on medium until pale and fluffy. Add the butter, sour cream, orange zest, and half of the cherry liqueur and beat until combined.

3. Sift the flours, cocoa powder, baking powder, baking soda, and salt into a bowl. Add the dry mixture to the wet mixture and beat until just combined. Scrape the bowl as needed while mixing the batter.

4. Pour the batter into the prepared pan, place it in the oven, and bake for 20 to 25 minutes, until a toothpick inserted into the center comes out clean. Remove from the oven and let cool in the pan for 10 minutes before transferring to a wire rack to cool completely. Keep the oven at 350°F.

5. Place the Cherries in Syrup and the remaining liqueur in a bowl and let sit for at least 30 minutes. Strain, set the cherries aside, and combine the strained liquid with the water. Set aside.

6. Prepare the crumble. Sift the sugar, flour, and cocoa powder into a bowl. Add the melted butter and work the mixture with a fork until it is crumbly. Place the mixture on a parchment-lined baking sheet in an even layer, place it in the oven, and bake until crunchy, about 25 minutes. Remove from the oven and let cool completely.

7. Prepare the whipped cream. Place the heavy cream, confectioners' sugar, salt, and liqueur in a mixing bowl and whip until stiff peaks form.

8. When you are ready to assemble the trifle, cut the cake into 1½″ pieces. Cover the bottom of a 3-quart trifle bowl with pieces of cake, breaking pieces as needed to fill up any empty space. Brush the pieces of cake with the reserved liqueur-and-water mixture. Top with layers of whipped cream, cherries, and cocoa crumble. Repeat this layering process two more times. Top the trifle with a layer of whipped cream and sprinkle any remaining cherries and crumble on top.

INGREDIENTS

FOR THE CAKE & TRIFLE

3 EGGS

⅔ CUP GRANULATED SUGAR

4 TABLESPOONS UNSALTED BUTTER, MELTED

¼ CUP SOUR CREAM

½ TEASPOON ORANGE ZEST

¼ CUP CHERRY LIQUEUR

⅔ CUP CAKE FLOUR

⅓ CUP ALL-PURPOSE FLOUR

½ CUP COCOA POWDER

1 TEASPOON BAKING POWDER

¼ TEASPOON BAKING SODA

1½ TEASPOONS SALT

2 CUPS CHERRIES IN SYRUP (SEE RECIPE), QUARTERED

¼ CUP WATER, AT ROOM TEMPERATURE

FOR THE COCOA CRUMBLE

1 CUP CONFECTIONERS' SUGAR

⅔ CUP ALL-PURPOSE FLOUR

½ CUP UNSWEETENED COCOA POWDER

1 STICK UNSALTED BUTTER, MELTED

FOR THE WHIPPED CREAM

1 CUP HEAVY CREAM

2 TABLESPOONS CONFECTIONERS' SUGAR

½ TEASPOON SALT

1 TABLESPOON CHERRY LIQUEUR

CHERRIES IN SYRUP

2 CUPS CHERRIES (OR ANY STONE FRUIT)

2 CUPS GRANULATED SUGAR

1 CUP WATER

¼ CUP FRESH LEMON JUICE

1. Wash the cherries thoroughly and then remove the pits and stems.

2. Place the sugar, water, and lemon juice in a saucepan and bring to a boil over medium-high heat. Cook, while stirring, until the sugar is dissolved. Remove from heat and let cool for 5 minutes.

3. Place the cherries in sterilized mason jars and cover with the syrup. These will keep in the refrigerator for 1 week.

Chocolate Mousse Pie

YIELD: **6 TO 8 SERVINGS**

ACTIVE TIME: **10 MINUTES**

TOTAL TIME: **2 HOURS AND 15 MINUTES**

INGREDIENTS

2 CUPS SEMISWEET CHOCOLATE CHIPS

2½ CUPS HEAVY CREAM

1 TABLESPOON BOURBON

1 TEASPOON PURE VANILLA EXTRACT

1 GRAHAM CRACKER CRUST (SEE PAGE 34)

DIRECTIONS

1. Preheat the oven to 350°F.

2. Put the chocolate chips in a microwave-safe bowl. Add ½ cup of the cream and stir. Microwave on medium, removing to stir every 20 seconds. When just melted, stir in the bourbon and vanilla and let the mixture stand for about 5 minutes.

3. In a large bowl, beat the remaining 2 cups of cream at medium-high speed with a handheld mixer until medium peaks form. Fold the chocolate mixture into the whipped cream. Pour the filling into the piecrust and smooth the top with a rubber spatula.

4. Place in the refrigerator and chill for at least 2 hours before serving.

Chocolate Meringue Pie

YIELD: **8 SERVINGS**

ACTIVE TIME: **25 MINUTES**

TOTAL TIME: **1 HOUR AND 30 MINUTES**

DIRECTIONS

1. Preheat the oven to 375°F. To prepare the crust, place the flour, salt, butter, and lard in a mixing bowl and work the mixture with a pastry blender until coarse clumps start to form.

2. Add the water 2 tablespoons at a time and work it into the mixture with the pastry blender. When the dough just sticks together, place the ball between two sheets of plastic wrap and roll it out to 9". Place the crust in a greased 9" pie plate and crimp. Place the crust in the freezer for 10 minutes.

3. Remove the crust from the freezer and combine the cream and egg yolk. Brush the mixture over the crust and then use a fork to prick the bottom and sides of the crust. Place the crust in the oven and bake for 10 minutes. Check to see if it's puffing up; if it is, remove from the oven and poke more holes in the dough. Return to the oven and bake until it is a light golden brown, about 20 minutes.

4. To prepare the filling, place the flour, cocoa powder, salt, and sugar in a bowl and whisk to combine. Place the water and egg yolks in a separate bowl, whisk to combine, and then strain this mixture into the evaporated milk. Add the dry mixture and whisk to combine.

5. Place the mixture in a saucepan and bring to a boil over medium heat while stirring constantly. Remove from heat, add the vanilla seeds and butter, and beat with a handheld mixture until smooth. Cover the saucepan and set it aside.

6. Preheat the oven to 325°F. To prepare the meringue, place the egg whites and cream of tartar in the mixing bowl of a stand mixer and beat at high speed until frothy. Add the sugar very slowly with the mixer running and beat until stiff peaks form.

7. Pour the filling into the crust and top with the meringue. Place in the oven and bake until a few cracks form in the meringue, about 45 minutes.

INGREDIENTS

FOR THE CRUST

2½ CUPS CAKE FLOUR

½ TEASPOON SALT

4 TABLESPOONS UNSALTED
BUTTER, FROZEN AND GRATED

4 TABLESPOONS LARD

¼ CUP ICE-COLD WATER

1 TABLESPOON HEAVY CREAM

YOLK OF 1 EGG

FOR THE FILLING

5 TABLESPOONS CAKE FLOUR

½ CUP SIFTED UNSWEETENED
COCOA POWDER

⅛ TEASPOON SALT

2¼ CUPS GRANULATED SUGAR

¾ CUP WATER

YOLKS OF 5 LARGE EGGS

1¾ CUPS EVAPORATED MILK

SEEDS OF 2½ VANILLA BEANS

2½ TABLESPOONS UNSALTED
BUTTER, CUT INTO SMALL
PIECES

FOR THE MERINGUE

WHITES OF 1½ EGGS, AT
ROOM TEMPERATURE

½ TEASPOON CREAM OF
TARTAR

1¼ CUPS GRANULATED SUGAR

Chocolate Cream Pie

INGREDIENTS

6 CUPS CHOCOLATE PUDDING
(SEE PAGE 112)

1 GRAHAM CRACKER CRUST
(SEE PAGE 34)

2 CUPS WHIPPED CREAM
(SEE PAGE 53)

CHOCOLATE SHAVINGS,
RASPBERRIES, OR SLICED
STRAWBERRIES, FOR GARNISH

DIRECTIONS

1. Put the pudding in the Graham Cracker Crust, smooth the top with a rubber spatula, and cover with plastic wrap. Refrigerate for 1 hour.

2. When ready to serve, place the Whipped Cream on top in a thick layer. Garnish with the chocolate shavings, raspberries, or strawberries, if desired.

THAT'S USING THE OLD BEAN

In order to produce chocolate, the seeds of the cacao tree are harvested, heaped into piles to ferment, dried in the sun, and roasted at low temperatures to develop the beguiling flavors. The shells of the beans are then removed and the resulting nibs are ground into cocoa mass (which is also called cocoa liquor) and placed under extremely high pressure to produce cocoa powder and cocoa butter. From there, the cocoa mass and cocoa butter are partnered with sugar to produce dark chocolate, and sugar and milk powder to produce milk chocolate.

Chocolate Truffle Tart

YIELD: **6 SERVINGS**

ACTIVE TIME: **20 MINUTES**

TOTAL TIME: **3 HOURS AND 30 MINUTES**

INGREDIENTS

FOR THE CRUST

6 TABLESPOONS UNSALTED
BUTTER, AT ROOM TEMPERATURE

3 TABLESPOONS SIFTED
CONFECTIONERS' SUGAR

1 EGG

¼ TEASPOON PURE VANILLA
EXTRACT

5 TABLESPOONS ALL-PURPOSE
FLOUR

2 TEASPOONS UNSWEETENED
COCOA POWDER

½ TEASPOON BAKING POWDER

½ TEASPOON SALT

FOR THE FILLING

1½ CUPS HEAVY CREAM

2 CUPS BITTERSWEET CHOCOLATE
CHIPS

4 TABLESPOONS UNSALTED
BUTTER, DIVIDED INTO
TABLESPOONS

2 TABLESPOONS PREFERRED
LIQUEUR (OPTIONAL)

DIRECTIONS

1. To prepare the crust, place the butter into the mixing bowl of a stand mixer. Use the paddle attachment and beat on low until smooth. Add the sugar and beat at medium speed until smooth. Take care not to whip air into the mixture or the dough will be very hard to handle.

2. Add the egg and beat to incorporate. Add the vanilla and beat to incorporate. Scrape the mixing bowl as needed. Add the flour, cocoa powder, baking powder, and salt. Beat on low speed until incorporated, cover the dough in plastic wrap, and refrigerate for 1 hour.

3. Preheat the oven to 350°F. Roll out the dough fit a 9″ tart pan and then place it in the greased pan. Line the dough with parchment and fill with uncooked rice. Bake until it is baked through, about 15 minutes. Discard the parchment and uncooked rice and let cool.

4. To prepare the filling, place the cream in a small saucepan and bring to a boil over medium heat. Place the chocolate chips in a mixing bowl and then pour the boiling cream over the chocolate. Stir until the mixture is smooth, add the butter and liqueur, if using, and stir to incorporate.

5. Place the filling in the tart shell, making sure to distribute it evenly. You do not want to touch the surface, as it will ruin the appealing glossy finish. Place in the refrigerator and chill for at least 2 hours before serving.

Chocolate Fudge Tart

YIELD: **6 TO 8 SERVINGS**

ACTIVE TIME: **15 MINUTES**

TOTAL TIME: **1 HOUR AND 30 MINUTES**

INGREDIENTS

1 BALL OF TART PASTRY SHELL DOUGH (SEE PAGE 38)

1⅔ CUPS BITTERSWEET CHOCOLATE CHIPS

1 STICK UNSALTED BUTTER, CUT INTO SMALL PIECES

2 EGGS

1 CUP HEAVY CREAM

½ CUP GRANULATED SUGAR

1 TEASPOON PURE VANILLA EXTRACT

PINCH OF SALT

DIRECTIONS

1. Preheat the oven to 350°F.

2. Roll out the ball of dough to fit a 9″ tart pan. Place it in a greased tart pan, cover with foil or parchment paper, fill with uncooked rice, and bake until it starts to turn golden brown, about 20 to 25 minutes. Remove from the oven, discard the rice, and set the baked tart shell aside. Leave the oven at 350°F.

3. Place the chocolate and butter in a small saucepan and cook over low heat, while stirring frequently, until melted and combined. Remove from heat and aside.

4. In a bowl, whisk together the eggs, cream, sugar, vanilla, and salt. Whisk the chocolate mixture in and then whisk until well combined. Transfer the mixture into the baked tart shell and shake the pan to evenly distribute.

5. Put the pan in the oven and bake for 15 to 20 minutes until the filling is set around the edges but still soft in the center. Remove from the oven and let cool completely before serving.

White Chocolate Tart

YIELD: **6 TO 8 SERVINGS**

ACTIVE TIME: **45 MINUTES**

TOTAL TIME: **1 HOUR AND 30 MINUTES**

INGREDIENTS

1 BALL OF TART PASTRY SHELL DOUGH (SEE PAGE 38)

¾ LB. WHITE CHOCOLATE CHIPS

1 STICK UNSALTED BUTTER, CUT INTO SMALL PIECES

2 EGGS

1 CUP HEAVY CREAM

½ CUP GRANULATED SUGAR

1 TEASPOON PURE VANILLA EXTRACT

PINCH OF SALT

WHITE CHOCOLATE SHAVINGS, FOR GARNISH

¼ CUP HULLED AND SLICED STRAWBERRIES, FOR GARNISH

DIRECTIONS

1. Preheat the oven to 350°F.

2. Roll out the ball of dough to fit a 9″ tart pan. Place it in a greased tart pan, cover with foil or parchment paper, fill with uncooked rice, and bake until it starts to turn golden brown, 20 to 25 minutes. Remove from the oven, discard the rice, and set the baked tart shell aside.

3. Place the white chocolate chips and butter in a small saucepan and cook over low heat, while stirring frequently until melted and combined. Remove from heat and aside.

4. In a bowl, whisk together the eggs, cream, sugar, vanilla, and salt. Whisk the white chocolate mixture in and then whisk until well combined. Transfer the mixture into the tart shell and shake the pan to evenly distribute.

5. Put the pan in the oven and bake for 15 to 20 minutes until the filling is set around the edges but still soft in the center. Remove from the oven and let cool completely before topping with the white chocolate shavings and strawberries.

THE UPPER CRUST

A bit of crunch and a trace of mint will provide this smooth tart with some depth. If you're looking for a twist along these lines, place 8 to 10 Mint Milano cookies in a food processor and pulse until they are crumbs. Place the cookie crumbs in a bowl with 6 tablespoons of melted unsalted butter, stir to combine, and then press the mixture into a greased tart or springform pan to form the crust.

Chocolate & Coconut Soup with Brûléed Bananas

YIELD: **4 SERVINGS**

ACTIVE TIME: **25 MINUTES**

TOTAL TIME: **1 HOUR**

INGREDIENTS

2 CUPS WHOLE MILK

1 (14 OZ.) CAN OF UNSWEETENED COCONUT MILK

1 CUP HEAVY CREAM

SEEDS AND POD OF 1 VANILLA BEAN

2 BANANAS

¾ CUP GRANULATED SUGAR, PLUS MORE TO TASTE

½ FRESH COCONUT

½ CUP WATER

¾ LB. 60% DARK CHOCOLATE, CHOPPED

DIRECTIONS

1. Place the milk, coconut milk, cream, and the vanilla seeds and pod in a saucepan and bring to a simmer. Turn off the heat and let stand for 20 minutes.

2. Cut your bananas along the bias. Dip the angled piece into a dish of sugar and then use a kitchen torch to caramelize the sugar. Set aside.

3. Preheat the oven to 350°F. Remove the outer shell of the coconut and use a spoon to remove the meat. Slice the coconut meat very thin and set aside. In a small saucepan, add the ¾ cup sugar and the water and bring to a boil. Remove from heat and let stand until cool. Once the syrup is cool, dip the coconut slices into the syrup and place on a parchment-lined baking sheet. Place the sheet in the oven and bake for 8 minutes, or until the coconut is golden brown. Remove and set aside.

4. After 20 minutes, remove the vanilla pod from the soup and return to a simmer. Turn off heat, add the chocolate, and stir until the chocolate is melted. Strain the soup through a fine sieve and serve with the bruléed bananas and candied coconut.

Chocolate Fettuccine

YIELD: **1¼ POUNDS**

ACTIVE TIME: **25 MINUTES**

TOTAL TIME: **1 HOUR AND 45 MINUTES**

INGREDIENTS

1½ CUPS ALL-PURPOSE FLOUR, PLUS MORE AS NEEDED

½ CUP UNSWEETENED COCOA POWDER, PLUS MORE FOR DUSTING

3 LARGE EGGS

1 TABLESPOON WATER, PLUS MORE AS NEEDED

1 TABLESPOON EXTRA VIRGIN OLIVE OIL

DIRECTIONS

1. Combine the flour and cocoa in a mixing bowl and make a well in the center. Add the eggs, water, and olive oil. Using a fork or your fingers, gradually start pulling the flour-and-cocoa mixture into the pool. Continue to work the mixture until the dough starts holding together in a single mass, adding more water— 1 tablespoon at a time—if the mixture is too dry to stick together. Once the dough feels firm and dry and can form a craggy looking ball, it's time to start kneading.

2. Place the ball of dough on a floured work surface and knead until it has a smooth, elastic texture, about 8 minutes. If the dough still feels wet, tacky, or sticky, dust it with flour and continue kneading. If it feels too dry and is not completely sticking together, wet your hands with water and continue kneading. The dough has been sufficiently kneaded when it is very smooth and gently pulls back into place when stretched.

3. Wrap the ball of dough tightly in plastic wrap and let rest for 1 hour.

4. Unwrap the dough, cut it into thirds, and roll each one out to a thickness that can go through the widest setting on a pasta maker. Run the rolled pieces of dough through the pasta maker, adjusting the setting to reduce the thickness with each pass. When the dough is the desired thickness, roll the sheets up and cut into ¼" strips.

5. Dust the cut pasta with cocoa powder and place on a surface lightly dusted with cocoa powder. Let stand for 15 minutes before cooking.

Chocolate Fettuccine with Pecan & Caramel Sauce

YIELD: **6 TO 8 SERVINGS**

ACTIVE TIME: **15 MINUTES**

TOTAL TIME: **20 MINUTES**

INGREDIENTS

4½ TABLESPOONS UNSALTED BUTTER

⅔ CUP CRUSHED PECANS

SALT, TO TASTE

¾ CUP PACKED LIGHT BROWN SUGAR

½ CUP HEAVY CREAM

1 TEASPOON PURE VANILLA EXTRACT

¾ LB. CHOCOLATE PASTA DOUGH (SEE PAGE 100)

CHOCOLATE SHAVINGS, FOR GARNISH

RASPBERRIES, FOR GARNISH

DIRECTIONS

1. Place a small skillet over low heat for 2 minutes. Add 1 tablespoon of the butter and raise the heat to medium. Once the butter has melted, add the pecans and cook, while stirring continuously, until they give off toasty fragrance, about 2 minutes. Add 2 pinches of salt and stir. Transfer to a plate and let cool. Wipe out the skillet with a paper towel.

2. Bring a large pot of water to a boil. While the water is heating up, put the skillet you toasted the pecans in over low heat. After 1 minute, add 3 tablespoons of the butter, the brown sugar, cream, and a pinch of salt and raise the heat to medium-low. Cook, while whisking gently, until the sauce thickens, 5 to 7 minutes. Stir in the vanilla and cook for another minute. Stir in the toasted pecans, remove the pan from heat, and cover.

3. When the water is boiling, add the pasta and cook until the pasta is soft but still very firm. Right before draining the pasta, reserve ¼ cup of the pasta water. Return the empty pot to the stove. Immediately turn the heat to high and add the remaining butter and the reserved pasta water. Add the drained pasta and toss until the water is absorbed. Add the sauce and cook, while stirring, for 1 to 2 minutes. Ladle the pasta into warmed bowls and garnish with chocolate shavings and raspberries.

YIELD: **16 CROISSANTS**

ACTIVE TIME: **45 MINUTES**

TOTAL TIME: **17 HOURS**

Pain au Chocolat

INGREDIENTS

FOR THE POOLISH

1¾ CUPS ALL-PURPOSE FLOUR

1 TEASPOON INSTANT YEAST

1⅓ CUPS LUKEWARM WATER (90°F)

¾ CUP WHOLE WHEAT FLOUR

FOR THE CROISSANTS

5⅔ CUPS ALL-PURPOSE FLOUR, PLUS MORE FOR DUSTING

½ CUP GRANULATED SUGAR

1 TABLESPOON SALT

1¼ TEASPOONS INSTANT YEAST

1 CUP WHOLE MILK

3 TABLESPOONS UNSALTED BUTTER

16 PIECES OF PREFERRED CHOCOLATE

YOLK OF 1 EGG

1 TEASPOON HEAVY CREAM

FOR THE LAMINATION LAYER

4½ STICKS UNSALTED BUTTER

DIRECTIONS

1. To make the poolish, place the all-purpose flour, ½ teaspoon of the yeast, and 1 cup of the water in a mixing bowl, stir to combine, and transfer the mixture to the refrigerator for 8 hours. Place the whole wheat flour, remaining yeast, and remaining water in a separate bowl and stir to combine. Let stand at room temperature for 1 hour and then place in the refrigerator for 8 hours.

2. To make the croissant dough, add the flour, sugar, salt, yeast, milk, and butter to the mixing bowl of a stand mixer. Add both poolish mixtures and beat on low speed until the mixture is just combined, about 2 minutes. Let rest for 20 minutes and then mix for 2 minutes on low speed. Transfer the dough to a separate bowl, cover with plastic wrap, and let stand at room temperature for 1 hour.

3. Place the butter for the lamination layer in a mixing bowl and beat until it is smooth and free of lumps. Transfer the butter onto a piece of parchment paper and smash until it is a 6½ x 9-inch rectangle of even thickness. Place the butter in the refrigerator when the dough has 20 minutes left to stand.

4. Place the dough on a floured work surface and roll out into a 13 x 9-inch rectangle. Remove the butter from the refrigerator and place it on the right half of the dough. Fold the left side of the dough over the butter, making sure that the dough completely covers the butter. Essentially, you want to make a "butter sandwich."

5. Roll the dough out to a 12 x 27-inch rectangle, fold it in half, and then fold it in half again. Wrap the dough in plastic, place in the refrigerator, and chill for 1 hour.

6. Place the dough on a floured work surface and gently roll it out into a 12 x 30-inch rectangle. Cut the rectangle in half and then cut each half every 3½". Place a piece of chocolate in the center of each piece. Fold the dough over the chocolate and place the croissants, seam-side down, on a parchment-lined baking sheets, making sure not to crowd the sheet. Let them stand at room temperature for 4 hours or refrigerate until the next day.

7. When you are ready to bake the croissants, preheat the oven to 420°F. Place the egg yolk and heavy cream in a mug and stir to combine. Brush the egg wash on the tops of the croissants, place them in the oven, and bake until golden brown, 20 to 25 minutes.

Chocolate Mousse

YIELD: **6 SERVINGS**

ACTIVE TIME: **10 MINUTES**

TOTAL TIME: **1 HOUR AND 10 MINUTES**

INGREDIENTS

1 CUP BITTERSWEET CHOCOLATE CHIPS

2 CUPS HEAVY CREAM, CHILLED

2 TABLESPOONS GRANULATED SUGAR

WHITES OF 3 EGGS

½ TEASPOON PURE VANILLA EXTRACT

¼ TEASPOON SALT

WHIPPED CREAM (SEE PAGE 53), FOR SERVING

DIRECTIONS

1. Place the chocolate in a microwave-safe bowl and microwave on high for 25 to 35 seconds. Remove and stir until smooth. If chocolate is not completely melted, return to microwave for a few more seconds, but be careful to not overcook.

2. Place the cream in a mixing bowl and beat until soft peaks form. Place the sugar, egg whites, vanilla, and salt in a separate bowl and beat until soft peaks form.

3. Gradually add the chocolate to the egg white mixture and stir until almost completely combined. Gently fold in the cream.

4. Transfer the mousse into the serving dishes and refrigerate for at least 1 hour. Top each serving with Whipped Cream.

Chocolate Soufflé

YIELD: **6 TO 8 SERVINGS**

ACTIVE TIME: **15 MINUTES**

TOTAL TIME: **45 MINUTES**

INGREDIENTS

5 TABLESPOONS UNSALTED BUTTER, DIVIDED INTO TABLESPOONS AND AT ROOM TEMPERATURE

6 TABLESPOONS GRANULATED SUGAR

½ LB. SEMISWEET CHOCOLATE CHIPS

⅛ TEASPOON SALT

½ TEASPOON PURE VANILLA EXTRACT

YOLKS OF 6 LARGE EGGS

WHITES OF 8 LARGE EGGS

¼ TEASPOON CREAM OF TARTAR

DIRECTIONS

1. Preheat the oven to 375°F degrees. Grease the inside of a soufflé dish with 1 tablespoon of the butter and then coat the dish with 1 tablespoon of the sugar. Place the dish in the refrigerator.

2. Place the chocolate and remaining butter in a microwave-safe bowl and microwave on medium until melted, removing to stir every 20 seconds. Remove, stir in the salt and vanilla, and set the mixture aside.

3. Place the egg yolks and the remaining sugar in a mixing bowl and beat with a handheld mixer on medium until thick, about 3 minutes. Fold into the chocolate mixture and wipe off the beaters.

4. Place the egg whites in a mixing bowl and beat until frothy. Add the cream of tartar and beat on high until you have moist, stiff peaks. Stir one-quarter of the whipped egg whites into the chocolate mixture. Gently fold the remaining egg whites into the chocolate mixture and then transfer the mixture into the soufflé dish.

5. Place in the oven and bake until the soufflé is fully risen and set, but the interior is still creamy, about 25 minutes. Remove from the oven and serve immediately.

NOTE: Rather than one large soufflé, you can make individual ones. To do so, completely fill eight 8 oz. ramekins with the chocolate mixture and reduce the baking time to about 16 minutes.

THE BOLD AND THE BEAUTIFUL

Soufflé: the mere mention of the word strikes fear into the hearts of the uninitiated, with images of saggy, deflated confections and disappointed faces surrounding the table keeping most from ever venturing onto the hallowed ground this fragile French classic has long held.

First, know that even if your soufflé does collapse and doesn't bear the delicate, cloud-like quality that is part of its appeal, you will still have a delicious, rich dessert on your hands. Second, the key to pairing that rich flavor with equally appealing aesthetics is taking care not to overbeat the egg whites after adding the cream of tartar mixture. You want shiny, lustrous peaks, as opposed to dry and drab ones. Keep this in mind, remain patient while working through the numerous steps, and you're certain to end up with an Instagram-worthy dessert.

French Silk Parfait

YIELD: **8 SERVINGS**

ACTIVE TIME: **15 MINUTES**

TOTAL TIME: **1 HOUR AND 15 MINUTES**

INGREDIENTS

10 CHOCOLATE CHIP COOKIES
(SEE PAGE 63)

1 TABLESPOON GRANULATED
SUGAR

1 (8 OZ.) PACKAGE OF CREAM
CHEESE, AT ROOM TEMPERATURE

1 TEASPOON PURE VANILLA
EXTRACT

2 CUPS CONFECTIONERS' SUGAR

2 OZ. MILK CHOCOLATE

2 OZ. UNSWEETENED BAKER'S
CHOCOLATE

4 TABLESPOONS SALTED BUTTER

5 CUPS WHIPPED CREAM
(SEE PAGE 53)

DIRECTIONS

1. Place the cookies and granulated sugar in a food processor and blitz until both are finely ground. Set the mixture aside.

2. Place the cream cheese, vanilla, and confectioners' sugar in a bowl and beat until combined.

3. Chop up the chocolates and place them in a microwave-safe bowl with the butter. Microwave on medium until melted, removing to stir every 20 seconds. Remove and briefly let cool before adding it to the cream cheese mixture. Beat until well combined and then gently fold in 3 cups of the Whipped Cream.

4. Alternate layers of the cookie crumbs, the French silk pudding, and the remaining Whipped Cream in mason jars or tall glasses, making sure to end with a layer of whipped cream and a few cookie crumbs. Place in the refrigerator for 1 hour before serving.

Chocolate Pudding

YIELD: **8 SERVINGS**

ACTIVE TIME: **15 MINUTES**

TOTAL TIME: **2 HOURS AND 15 MINUTES**

INGREDIENTS

¼ CUP GRANULATED SUGAR

½ CUP SWEETENED COCOA POWDER

¼ CUP CORNSTARCH

¾ TEASPOON SALT

2½ CUPS WHOLE MILK

6 TABLESPOONS UNSALTED BUTTER, AT ROOM TEMPERATURE

2 TEASPOONS PURE VANILLA EXTRACT

SHREDDED COCONUT, FOR GARNISH (OPTIONAL)

RASPBERRIES, FOR GARNISH (OPTIONAL)

CHOCOLATE SHAVINGS, FOR GARNISH (OPTIONAL)

DIRECTIONS

1. Place the sugar, cocoa powder, cornstarch, and salt in a saucepan and whisk to combine. Cook over medium heat and slowly add the milk while whisking constantly. Cook until the mixture thickens and comes to a boil, approximately 8 to 10 minutes.

2. Reduce the heat to low and simmer for 1 to 2 minutes. Remove the saucepan from heat and stir in the butter and vanilla.

3. Transfer the pudding into the serving dishes and place plastic wrap directly on the pudding's surface to prevent a skin from forming. Place in the refrigerator for 2 hours and garnish with shredded coconut, raspberries, and/or chocolate shavings before serving.

Chocolate Ice Cream

YIELD: **8 SERVINGS**

ACTIVE TIME: **45 MINUTES**

TOTAL TIME: **24 HOURS**

INGREDIENTS

3 CUPS HEAVY CREAM

1 CUP WHOLE MILK

¾ CUP GRANULATED SUGAR

½ CUP UNSWEETENED COCOA POWDER

1 TEASPOON INSTANT ESPRESSO POWDER

1 TEASPOON SALT

YOLKS OF 5 LARGE EGGS, BEATEN

1 TABLESPOON PURE VANILLA EXTRACT

DIRECTIONS

1. Place the cream, milk, sugar, cocoa powder, espresso powder, and salt in a saucepan and warm over medium heat whle stirring. Once the sugar has dissolved, take approximately 1 cup from the mixture in the saucepan and whisk it into the bowl containing the egg yolks. Add the tempered eggs to the saucepan and continue cooking over medium heat until the contents have thickened to where they will coat the back of a spoon.

2. Add the vanilla extract and remove from heat. To ensure that there are no lumps, strain the mixture through a fine sieve into a nonstick bowl. Stir the contents of the bowl often as it cools.

3. When the mixture has cooled, cover the bowl with plastic wrap and place it in the refrigerator overnight.

4. Remove the mixture from the refrigerator and pour it into an ice cream maker. Churn until it has the desired consistency. Freeze for at least 6 hours before serving.

Chocolate-Covered Strawberries

YIELD: **4 SERVINGS**

ACTIVE TIME: **10 MINUTES**

TOTAL TIME: **2 HOURS AND 10 MINUTES**

INGREDIENTS

2 PINTS OF FRESH STRAWBERRIES

2 CUPS SEMISWEET CHOCOLATE CHIPS

6 GRAHAM CRACKERS, CRUSHED (OPTIONAL)

½ CUP ALMONDS, FINELY GROUND (OPTIONAL)

DIRECTIONS

1. Wash the strawberries and pat them dry.

2. Place the chocolate chips in a microwave-safe bowl. Melt in the microwave on medium, removing to stir every 20 seconds. When melted, remove from the microwave and stir until smooth.

3. Dip each strawberry into the chocolate halfway, or completely, whichever you prefer. If desired, roll the coated strawberries in the graham cracker crumbs or the ground almonds.

4. Line a baking sheet with parchment paper and place the strawberries on the sheet. Place the strawberries in the refrigerator for at least 2 hours before serving.

Chocolate-Covered Graham Crackers

YIELD: **4 TO 6 SERVINGS**

ACTIVE TIME: **15 MINUTES**

TOTAL TIME: **1 HOUR AND 15 MINUTES**

INGREDIENTS

2 CUPS SEMISWEET CHOCOLATE CHIPS

1 TABLESPOON UNSALTED BUTTER

12 GRAHAM CRACKERS, BROKEN INTO QUARTERS

SEA SALT, FOR TOPPING

DIRECTIONS

1. Place the chocolate chips in a microwave-safe bowl. Melt in the microwave on medium, removing to stir every 20 seconds. When melted, remove from the microwave and stir until smooth. Add the butter and stir until combined.

2. Dip each graham cracker into the chocolate. Line a baking sheet with wax paper and place the coated graham crackers on the sheet. Once all of the graham crackers have been used, sprinkle sea salt on top and place the baking sheet in the refrigerator until the chocolate is set, about 1 hour.

Chocolate-Covered Popcorn

YIELD: **10 TO 12 SERVINGS**

ACTIVE TIME: **10 MINUTES**

TOTAL TIME: **40 MINUTES**

INGREDIENTS

1½ LBS. SEMISWEET CHOCOLATE CHIPS

26 CUPS OF FRESHLY POPPED POPCORN (ABOUT 2 BAGS)

½ TEASPOON SALT

¼ TEASPOON GRATED NUTMEG

DIRECTIONS

1. Place the chocolate chips in a microwave-safe bowl. Melt in the microwave on medium, removing to stir every 20 seconds. When melted, remove from the microwave and stir until smooth.

2. Divide the popcorn, salt, and nutmeg between two bowls and toss to combine.

3. Drizzle the melted chocolate over the popcorn and toss to coat. Line a baking sheet with parchment paper and pour the popcorn onto the baking sheet. Place it in the refrigerator and chill for 30 minutes before serving.

Chocolate Candies

YIELD: **6 SERVINGS**

ACTIVE TIME: **15 MINUTES**

TOTAL TIME: **45 MINUTES**

INGREDIENTS

½ LB. BITTERSWEET OR DARK CHOCOLATE, CHOPPED

1 TABLESPOON FLEUR DE SEL

2 TABLESPOONS CHOPPED DRIED CHERRIES (OPTIONAL)

2 TABLESPOONS CHOPPED ROASTED ALMONDS (OPTIONAL)

2 TABLESPOONS CHOPPED PISTACHIOS (OPTIONAL)

DIRECTIONS

1. Place the chocolate in a microwave-safe bowl. Melt in the microwave on medium, removing to stir every 20 seconds. When melted, remove from the microwave and stir until smooth.

2. Scoop teaspoons of the melted chocolate into your chosen mold or onto a parchment-lined baking sheet. Sprinkle the fleur de sel on top and then place the dried cherries, roasted almonds, and/or pistachios on the chocolates, if desired. Transfer to the refrigerator and chill until set, about 30 minutes.

White Chocolate Bark

INGREDIENTS

1 LB. WHITE CHOCOLATE, CHOPPED

½ CUP DRIED CHERRIES OR CRANBERRIES

½ CUP CHOPPED PISTACHIOS

DIRECTIONS

1. Place the chocolate in a microwave-safe bowl. Melt in the microwave on medium, removing to stir every 20 seconds. When melted, remove from the microwave and stir until smooth.

2. Line a baking sheet with parchment paper. Pour melted chocolate onto baking sheet and spread it into an even layer, making sure not to spread it too thin.

3. Sprinkle the cherries or cranberries and pistachios onto the chocolate and lightly press down to ensure that they stick. Place in the refrigerator until set, about 30 minutes.

4. When the chocolate is set, break the bark up into large pieces and serve.

Chocolate & Walnut Fudge

YIELD: **16 PIECES**

ACTIVE TIME: **15 MINUTES**

TOTAL TIME: **2 HOURS AND 30 MINUTES**

INGREDIENTS

1 CUP CHOPPED WALNUTS

¾ LB. QUALITY BITTERSWEET CHOCOLATE, CHOPPED

2 OZ. UNSWEETENED BAKER'S CHOCOLATE, CHOPPED

1 STICK UNSALTED BUTTER

2 CUPS GRANULATED SUGAR

1 TEASPOON PURE VANILLA EXTRACT

DIRECTIONS

1. Preheat the oven to 350°F and line a square 8″ cake pan with heavy-duty aluminum foil so that the foil extends over the sides. Spray the foil with nonstick cooking spray.

2. Place the walnuts on a baking sheet, place it in the oven, and toast the walnuts for 5 to 7 minutes, until lightly browned. Remove from the oven and set the nuts aside.

3. Place the chocolates and the butter in a heatproof mixing bowl and set aside. Place the sugar in a deep saucepan and cook over medium heat until it has dissolved and is boiling. Continue to cook, while stirring constantly, until the sugar reaches 236°F. Pour the sugar over the chocolates and butter in the mixing bowl. Whisk until smooth and then stir in the toasted walnuts and the vanilla.

4. Spread the fudge in an even layer in the cake pan. Refrigerate until the fudge is set, about 2 hours. Use the foil to lift the fudge out of the pan and then cut the fudge into squares.

Mexican Hot Chocolate

YIELD: **4 SERVINGS**

ACTIVE TIME: **15 MINUTES**

TOTAL TIME: **15 MINUTES**

INGREDIENTS

3 CUPS WHOLE MILK

1 CUP HALF-AND-HALF

3 CINNAMON STICKS

1 RED CHILI PEPPER

¼ CUP SWEETENED CONDENSED MILK

1½ LBS. SEMISWEET CHOCOLATE CHIPS

½ TEASPOON PURE VANILLA EXTRACT

1 TEASPOON GRATED NUTMEG

½ TEASPOON SALT

WHIPPED CREAM (SEE PAGE 53), FOR GARNISH

RED PEPPER FLAKES, FOR GARNISH (OPTIONAL)

DIRECTIONS

1. Place the milk, half-and-half, cinnamon sticks, and chili pepper in a saucepan and cook over medium-low heat for 5 to 6 minutes, making sure the mixture does not come to a boil. Remove the cinnamon sticks and chili pepper.

2. Add the sweetened condensed milk and whisk until combined. Add the chocolate chips and cook, while stirring occasionally, until the chocolate is melted. Add the vanilla, nutmeg, and salt and whisk until combined.

3. Ladle into warmed mugs, top with Whipped Cream, and garnish with red pepper flakes, if desired.

A BRIEF HISTORY OF CHOCOLATE

No one is certain exactly when chocolate began its long march into the hearts of millions, but it is believed that the Olmec civilization, which inhabited present-day Mexico, used cacao in a bitter, ceremonial drink, a hypothesis borne out by the traces of theobromine—a stimulant that is found in chocolate and tea—being found on ancient Olmec pots and vessels.

While the exact role of chocolate in Olmec culture is impossible to pin down because they kept no written history, it appears that they passed their reverence for it onto the Mayans, who valued chocolate to the point that cocoa beans were used as currency in certain transactions. It is interesting that access to this precious resource wasn't restricted to the wealthy among the Mayans, but was available enough that a beverage consisting of chocolate mixed with honey or chili peppers could be enjoyed with every meal in a majority of Mayan households.

The next great Mexican civilization, the Aztecs, carried things even further. They saw cocoa as more valuable than gold, and the mighty Aztec ruler Montezuma II supposedly drank gallons of chocolate each day, believing that it provided him with considerable energy and also served as a potent aphrodisiac.

No one is certain exactly which explorer brought this New World tradition back to Europe, with some crediting Christopher Columbus and others Hernan Cortes. Whoever is responsible, they created a sensation on the continent. Chocolate-based beverages that were sweetened with cane sugar or spruced up with spices such as cinnamon became all the rage, and fashionable houses where the wealthy congregated and induldged began popping up all over Europe by the early 17th century.

Chocolate remained in the hands of Europe's elite until a Dutch chemist named Coenraad Johannes van Houten discovered how to treat cacao beans with alkaline salts to produce a powdered chocolate that was more soluble. This "Dutch cocoa" made cocoa affordable for all, and opened the door for mass production.

The first chocolate bar was produced by the British chocolatier J. S. Fry and Sons, though the amalgamation of sugar, chocolate liqueur, and cocoa butter was far chewier, and less sweet, than the bars turned out for the modern palate.

Swiss chocolatier Daniel Peter is widely credited as the individual who added dried milk powder to chocolate to create milk chocolate in 1876. Peter then teamed with his friend Henri Nestle to create the company that brought milk chocolate to the masses.

Café Mocha

YIELD: **10 CUPS**

ACTIVE TIME: **10 MINUTES**

TOTAL TIME: **20 MINUTES**

INGREDIENTS

8 CUPS WHOLE MILK

1 CUP HEAVY CREAM

½ CUP GRANULATED SUGAR, PLUS MORE TO TASTE

½ CUP BREWED ESPRESSO

½ LB. BITTERSWEET CHOCOLATE, CHOPPED

1 TABLESPOON ORANGE ZEST

½ TEASPOON SALT

WHIPPED CREAM (SEE PAGE 53), FOR GARNISH

DIRECTIONS

1. Place the milk, cream, sugar, and espresso in a saucepan and warm over medium heat.

2. Place the chocolate in a bowl. When the milk mixture is hot, ladle 1 cup into the bowl containing the chocolate and whisk until the chocolate is completely melted, adding more of the warm milk mixture if the melted chocolate mixture is too thick.

3. Pour the melted chocolate mixture into the pot of warm milk and whisk to combine. Add the orange zest and salt, stir to combine, and adjust to taste before topping with the Whipped Cream.

Cookie Dough Pops

YIELD: **15 TO 20 POPS**

ACTIVE TIME: **15 MINUTES**

TOTAL TIME: **3 HOURS AND 15 MINUTES**

INGREDIENTS

1 STICK UNSALTED BUTTER, AT ROOM TEMPERATURE

⅓ CUP GRANULATED SUGAR

⅓ CUP PACKED DARK BROWN SUGAR

½ TEASPOON SALT

½ TEASPOON PURE VANILLA EXTRACT

1 CUP ALL-PURPOSE FLOUR

1 CUP MINIATURE SEMISWEET CHOCOLATE CHIPS

LOLLIPOP STICKS

½ LB. WHITE, MILK, OR DARK CHOCOLATE, MELTED

CHOPPED NUTS (OPTIONAL)

RAINBOW OR CHOCOLATE SPRINKLES (OPTIONAL)

DIRECTIONS

1. Place the butter, sugar, and brown sugar in the bowl of a stand mixer and beat until it is light and fluffy. Add the salt and vanilla and beat until combined.

2. Add the flour in two batches and beat until almost all of it has been incorporated. Before flour is completely blended in, add the chocolate chips and mix until well combined. Cover the dough with plastic wrap and place in the refrigerator for 1 hour.

3. Line a baking sheet with parchment paper. Remove mixture from refrigerator and scoop out teaspoon-sized balls of dough. Roll into spheres and place on the baking sheet. Insert lollipop sticks into each sphere.

4. Dip each pop into the melted chocolate until completely coated. Decorate them with nuts or sprinkles, if desired, and place them back on the baking sheet. Place in the refrigerator and chill until the chocolate is set, about 2 hours.

CHAPTER 4

VANILLA

For a large group of people, vanilla is anything but boring. Equal parts smooth and sweet, its ability to both soothe and dazzle the taste buds is unmatched. Any skeptics out there should talk to their favorite baker about the crucial role vanilla plays in a number of desserts, adding a luscious aroma and lightness whose absence would be glaring, rendering the finished confection unacceptable to anyone who had experienced it previously.

From the vanilla ice cream that forms the basis of the iconic hot fudge sundae to the custard that has lifted the Boston cream pie to legendary heights, those who are hankering for the unique qualities of the vanilla bean will find a number of avenues to get their fix.

Cream Puff Cake

YIELD: **8 TO 10 SERVINGS**

ACTIVE TIME: **20 MINUTES**

TOTAL TIME: **1 HOUR AND 30 MINUTES**

INGREDIENTS

1 STICK UNSALTED BUTTER

1 CUP WATER

1 CUP ALL-PURPOSE FLOUR

4 EGGS

PASTRY CREAM (SEE PAGE 50)

DIRECTIONS

1. Preheat the oven to 375°F and grease a Bundt pan with nonstick cooking spray.

2. Place the butter and water in a large saucepan and bring to a boil over medium-high heat.

3. Reduce the heat to low and add the flour. Cook, while stirring, until the mixture forms a ball and pulls away from the edges of the pan. Remove from heat.

4. Add the eggs one at a time, beating to incorporate each one before adding the next.

5. Transfer the mixture to the prepared Bundt pan, place in the oven, and bake until golden brown and a knife inserted into the center comes out clean, about 40 to 45 minutes. Remove and allow the cake to cool completely.

6. Invert the cooled cake onto a plate. Slice the cut in half along the equator. Spread the Pastry Cream over the bottom layer, replace the top layer, and serve.

Boston Cream Pie

INGREDIENTS

FOR THE FILLING

½ CUP GRANULATED SUGAR

PINCH OF SALT

YOLKS OF 6 LARGE EGGS

¼ CUP ALL-PURPOSE FLOUR

2 CUPS HALF-AND-HALF

4 TABLESPOONS UNSALTED BUTTER, CHILLED AND DIVIDED INTO TABLESPOONS

SEEDS OF 1 VANILLA BEAN

FOR THE FROSTING

½ CUP HEAVY CREAM

2 TABLESPOONS LIGHT CORN SYRUP

4 OZ. BITTERSWEET CHOCOLATE, MINCED

FOR THE CAKES

1½ CUPS ALL-PURPOSE FLOUR

1½ TEASPOONS BAKING POWDER

¾ TEASPOON SALT

¾ CUP WHOLE MILK

6 TABLESPOONS UNSALTED BUTTER

1½ TEASPOONS PURE VANILLA EXTRACT

3 LARGE EGGS

1½ CUPS GRANULATED SUGAR

DIRECTIONS

1. To prepare the filling, place the sugar, salt, and egg yolks in a mixing bowl and whisk until smooth. Add the flour and whisk to incorporate.

2. Place the half-and-half in a saucepan and bring to a simmer over medium heat. Remove the pan from heat and slowly pour ½ cup into the flour-and-egg yolk mixture while whisking constantly. Whisk the tempered mixture into the half-and-half that remains in the saucepan. Place the saucepan over medium heat and cook, whisking constantly, until the mixture thickens, about 1 minute. Reduce heat to medium-low and simmer, while whisking constantly, for 8 minutes.

3. Raise the heat to medium and cook, while whisking vigorously, until the mixture starts to bubble, 1 to 2 minutes. Remove saucepan from heat, add the butter and vanilla seeds, and whisk until the butter is melted and incorporated. Strain through a fine sieve and let cool. When cool, press plastic wrap directly onto the surface and place in the refrigerator for 2 hours.

4. To prepare the frosting, place the cream and corn syrup in a small saucepan and bring to a simmer over medium heat. When the mixture is simmering, remove from heat and add the chocolate. Gently whisk until smooth and set aside.

5. To prepare the cakes, preheat the oven to 325°F. Grease two round 9" cake pans with nonstick cooking spray and line them with parchment paper. Place the flour, baking powder, and salt in mixing bowl and whisk to combine. Place the milk and butter in a small saucepan and warm over low heat until the butter has melted. Remove from heat, stir in the vanilla, and cover.

6. Place the eggs and sugar in the bowl of a standing mixer and beat on high until the mixture is light, about 5 minutes. Whisk the warm milk mixture into the egg-and-sugar mixture until it has all been incorporated. Whisk in the flour mixture until it has been incorporated.

7. Divide the batter between prepared pans and place them in the oven. Bake until the tops are light brown and a toothpick inserted into the center of each cake comes out clean, about 20 minutes. Remove pans from the oven and let cool completely, about 2 hours.

8. After 2 hours, invert the cakes onto wire racks and remove the parchment paper. Remove the filling from the refrigerator and whisk to loosen it slightly. Spoon the filling onto the top of one of the cakes and spread it evenly over the surface. Place the second cake, flat-side up, on top of the filling.

9. Whisk the frosting to loosen and then spread it over the top of the cake. Place the cake in the refrigerator for at least 3 hours before serving.

Vanilla Lovers' Layer Cake

YIELD: **10 TO 12 SERVINGS**

ACTIVE TIME: **15 MINUTES**

TOTAL TIME: **1 HOUR AND 15 MINUTES**

INGREDIENTS

2½ CUPS CAKE FLOUR, PLUS MORE FOR DUSTING

1¼ TEASPOONS BAKING POWDER

¼ TEASPOON BAKING SODA

¾ TEASPOON SALT

1¾ CUPS GRANULATED SUGAR

10 TABLESPOONS UNSALTED BUTTER, MELTED AND COOLED SLIGHTLY

2 TEASPOONS PURE VANILLA EXTRACT

1 CUP BUTTERMILK, AT ROOM TEMPERATURE

3 TABLESPOONS VEGETABLE OIL

YOLKS OF 6 LARGE EGGS, AT ROOM TEMPERATURE

WHITES OF 3 LARGE EGGS, AT ROOM TEMPERATURE

VANILLA BUTTERCREAM FROSTING (SEE PAGE 49)

DIRECTIONS

1. Preheat the oven to 350°F. Grease two round 9" cake pans and dust them with flour, making sure to knock out any excess.

2. Place the flour, baking powder, baking soda, salt, and 1½ cups of the sugar in a large mixing bowl and whisk until combined. Place the butter, vanilla, buttermilk, vegetable oil, and egg yolks in a separate mixing bowl and whisk until combined.

3. Place the egg whites in a bowl and beat until foamy. Gradually add the remaining sugar and beat until stiff peaks begin to form. Set aside.

4. Gradually add the butter mixture to the flour mixture and whisk until the mixture is smooth.

5. Add the beaten egg whites to the mixture and fold until they have been incorporated. Divide the batter between the prepared cake pans, place them in the oven, and bake until a toothpick inserted into the center of each cake comes out clean, about 20 minutes. Remove the pans from the oven and let cool for 10 minutes before removing the cakes from the pans. Place on wire racks and let cool completely.

6. When the cakes are completely cool, spread some of the frosting in a thin layer on the top of one cake. Place the other cake on top, flat-side up, and cover the entire cake with the remaining frosting.

Gluten-Free Vanilla Cake

YIELD: **8 TO 10 SERVINGS**

ACTIVE TIME: **15 MINUTES**

TOTAL TIME: **1 HOUR AND 30 MINUTES**

INGREDIENTS

2 CUPS GLUTEN-FREE FLOUR, PLUS MORE FOR DUSTING

1½ STICKS UNSALTED BUTTER, AT ROOM TEMPERATURE

1⅓ CUPS GRANULATED SUGAR

2 EGGS, AT ROOM TEMPERATURE

1 TEASPOON PURE VANILLA EXTRACT

1 TEASPOON XANTHAN GUM

2 TEASPOONS BAKING SODA

½ TEASPOON SALT

1 CUP BUTTERMILK

CONFECTIONERS' SUGAR, FOR DUSTING

DIRECTIONS

1. Preheat the oven to 350°F. Liberally coat a Bundt pan with nonstick cooking spray and then lightly dust it with flour, making sure to knock out the excess.

2. Place the butter and granulated sugar in the mixing bowl of a stand mixer fitted with the paddle attachment and beat on medium until the mixture is light and fluffy. Add the eggs one at a time, beating until each one is incorporated before adding the next. Scrape down the bowl after incorporating each egg. Add the vanilla and beat to incorporate.

3. Place the flour, xanthan gum, baking soda, and salt in a separate mixing bowl and whisk to combine.

4. Divide the flour mixture and the buttermilk into three portions and alternate adding them to the butter-and-sugar mixture. Incorporate each portion completely before adding the next.

5. Transfer the batter to the prepared Bundt pan and ensure that it is spread evenly. Place in the oven and bake until a toothpick inserted into the center comes out with just a few crumbs, about 45 minutes.

6. Remove from the oven and let cool in the pan for 30 minutes. Invert the cake onto a wire rack and let cool completely before dusting with the confectioners' sugar.

DOES EXTRACT SUBTRACT?

Using pure vanilla extract as opposed to the seeds of a vanilla bean will not affect the taste of your preparation, so don't be wary of any recipe that recommends the former. Ultimately, vanilla extract is made by macerating vanilla beans in a combination of water and alcohol. It is the more common recommendation due to its lower price and the ease of selling larger amounts.

While using vanilla bean in place of extract won't do much to the taste, those dark little flecks do add an aesthetic element that the extract cannot, giving any dessert that utilizes the seeds an air of sophistication. If you want to take advantage of this in any recipe that recommends vanilla extract, simply substitute the seeds of 1 vanilla bean for every 1 tablespoon of extract.

Pound Cake with Crème Anglaise

YIELD: **6 SERVING**

ACTIVE TIME: **20 MINUTES**

TOTAL TIME: **20 MINUTES**

INGREDIENTS

1 CUP WHOLE MILK

1 CUP HEAVY CREAM

¼ CUP GRANULATED SUGAR

SEEDS OF 1 VANILLA BEAN

YOLKS OF 4 LARGE EGGS

2 TABLESPOONS SPICED RUM

POUND CAKE (SEE PAGE 41), SLICED

BLUEBERRIES OR STRAWBERRIES, FOR GARNISH

WHIPPED CREAM (SEE PAGE 53), FOR GARNISH

DIRECTIONS

1. Place the milk, cream, sugar, and vanilla seeds in a medium saucepan and bring to a boil over medium-high heat. Remove the saucepan from heat.

2. Place the egg yolks in a bowl and whisk until scrambled. Add the milk mixture to the egg yolk mixture in ½-cup increments while whisking constantly. When all of the milk mixture has been incorporated, return the mixture to the saucepan, and stir in the rum.

3. Cook over low heat, while whisking constantly, until the mixture thickens, about 5 minutes. Take care to not let the mixture come to a boil.

4. Remove the saucepan from heat and strain the mixture through a fine sieve. Spoon the crème over the slices of the Pound Cake and garnish with blueberries or strawberries and Whipped Cream.

Frissants

YIELD: **8 FRISSANTS**

ACTIVE TIME: **2 HOURS**

TOTAL TIME: **5 HOURS**

INGREDIENTS

3 CUPS ALL-PURPOSE FLOUR,
PLUS MORE FOR DUSTING

3¼ TABLESPOONS GRANULATED
SUGAR

¾ TEASPOON SALT

2¼ TABLESPOONS CAKE YEAST

⅔ TABLESPOON EGG YOLK

1 STICK UNSALTED BUTTER, PLUS
1⅓ TABLESPOONS

¾ CUP WATER

VEGETABLE OIL, FOR FRYING

PASTRY CREAM (SEE PAGE 50)

CONFECTIONERS' SUGAR, FOR
DUSTING

DIRECTIONS

1. Place the flour, sugar, salt, yeast, egg yolk, 1⅓ tablespoons butter, and water in a stand mixer fitted with the dough hook attachment. Beat on low for 5 minutes, until the dough is just combined. Transfer to a baking sheet, flatten the dough, cover with plastic wrap, and place in the freezer for 1 hour.

2. Place the stick of butter in a large resealable plastic bag and flatten it with a rolling pin until the butter is pliable and fills up as much of the bag as possible. The butter should not be melted.

3. Remove the dough from the freezer and place it onto a flour-dusted work surface. Roll it out so it is twice the size of the butter in the bag. Remove the butter from the bag and place it on one side of the dough. Fold the other side over the butter, making sure that the butter is fully enclosed by dough. Roll out the dough and fold it over once. Transfer to the refrigerator and let rest for 30 minutes.

4. Remove the dough from the refrigerator and roll it out. Fold it as you would a letter before placing it in an envelope, return to the refrigerator, and chill for 30 minutes.

5. Remove the dough from the refrigerator and roll it out. Repeat the envelope fold made in Step 4, return the dough to the refrigerator, and chill for 30 minutes.

6. Place the dough on a flour-dusted work surface and roll it out until it is ¼" thick. Cut the dough into 8 pieces, place the pieces on a greased piece of parchment paper in a warm area, and let sit until they have doubled in size, about 2 hours.

7. Add vegetable oil to a large Dutch oven until it is 1" deep and warm to 360°F over medium-high heat.

8. Working in batches, place the frissants in the oil and fry, while turning once, until they are golden brown all over. Transfer the cooked frissants to a paper towel-lined plate to drain.

9. Use a toothpick to poke 4 holes into the top of each frissant and, using a piping bag fitted with a #4 tip, pipe the Pastry Cream into them. Dust with confectioners' sugar and serve.

NOTE: Cake yeast is fresh yeast that adds a floral aroma to baked goods that dry yeast does not. Despite this advantage, it is not widely employed due to its shorter shelf life (a few weeks compared to a few months) and higher cost compared to dry yeast.

Mille-Feuille

YIELD: **4 TO 6 SERVINGS**

ACTIVE TIME: **20 MINUTES**

TOTAL TIME: **45 MINUTES**

INGREDIENTS

2 SHEETS FROZEN PUFF PASTRY, THAWED

CONFECTIONERS' SUGAR, FOR DUSTING

PASTRY CREAM (SEE PAGE 50)

ZEST OF 1 ORANGE

1 TABLESPOON GRAND MARNIER

1 PINT OF FRESH RASPBERRIES

DIRECTIONS

1. Preheat the oven to 400°F.

2. Roll out the sheets of puff pastry and place each one on a greased baking sheet. Dust with confectioners' sugar, place them in the oven, and bake until golden brown, about 12 to 15 minutes. Remove from the oven, transfer to a wire rack, and let cool.

3. Place the Pastry Cream in a bowl, add the orange zest and Grand Marnier, and fold to incorporate. Transfer the mixture into a piping bag and place it in the refrigerator to chill while the puff pastry continues to cool.

4. Divide each sheet of the cooled puff pastry into 3 equal portions. Remove the piping bag from the freezer and place a thick layer of cream on one of the pieces of puff pastry. Dot the edges of the cream with the raspberries and press down on them gently. Fill the space between the raspberries with more of the cream and place another piece of puff pastry on top. Repeat the process with the cream and raspberries and then place the last piece of puff pastry on top. Carefully cut into the desired number of portions and serve.

Vanilla Ice Cream

YIELD: **4 CUPS**

ACTIVE TIME: **45 MINUTES**

TOTAL TIME: **13 HOURS**

INGREDIENTS

3 CUPS HEAVY CREAM

1 CUP WHOLE MILK

¾ CUP GRANULATED SUGAR

1 TEASPOON SALT

YOLKS OF 5 LARGE EGGS, BEATEN

SEEDS OF 2 VANILLA BEANS

DIRECTIONS

1. In a medium saucepan, warm the cream, milk, sugar, and salt over medium heat. Stir until the sugar has dissolved.

2. While whisking constantly, add 1 cup of the warm milk mixture to the bowl containing the egg yolks. Add the tempered eggs to the saucepan and cook over medium heat until the mixture thickens enough to coat the back of a wooden spoon.

3. Add the vanilla seeds and remove the pan from heat. Strain into a bowl through a fine sieve and stir the mixture as it cools.

4. When the mixture has cooled completely, cover with plastic wrap and place it in refrigerator for 6 hours.

5. Remove the mixture from the refrigerator and pour it into an ice cream maker. Churn until the desired texture is achieved. Place the churned cream in the freezer for 6 hours before serving.

PARISIAN FASHION

Vanilla is typically categorized according to where the bean is grown (as in the popular Madagascar and Tahitian varieties), but that is not the case when you see "French vanilla."

Instead, this appellation refers to the traditional French method for making ice cream, which utilizes a rich egg custard base. Those eggs, some claim, give vanilla a richness and depth that the bean can't attain on its own, forming such a memorable match that the flavor, which carries caramel and floral notes, resides in a category all its own.

This classification begs the question: What of vanilla ice cream made without eggs? Ice cream prepared in this manner is referred to as "Philadelphia-style."

Hot Fudge Sundaes

INGREDIENTS

HOT FUDGE (SEE PAGE 54)

2 PINTS OF VANILLA ICE CREAM
(SEE PAGE 152 FOR HOMEMADE)

WHIPPED CREAM (SEE PAGE 53)

½ CUP CHOPPED PECANS OR
WALNUTS

4 LUXARDO MARASCHINO
CHERRIES, FOR GARNISH

DIRECTIONS

1. Place the Hot Fudge in the bottom of four tulip sundae dishes or bowls.

2. Scoop the ice cream into the bowls.

3. Top each with Whipped Cream, pecans or walnuts, and a maraschino cherry and serve.

LUXURIATE IN LUXARDO

Luxardo maraschino cherries are a far cry from the glowing, sweet red cherries that the supermarket has accustomed you to. Luxardo cherries are made with the sour Marasca cherries that grow in the sandy soil of the Croatian coast. These sour cherries are then candied in a syrup consisting of Marasca cherry juice and sugar, producing a nutty and fruity maraschino that features far more depth than its American imposter—and none of the cloying sweetness.

Vegan Vanilla Ice Cream

YIELD: **4 CUPS**

ACTIVE TIME: **30 MINUTES**

TOTAL TIME: **24 HOURS**

INGREDIENTS

2 (14 OZ.) CANS OF COCONUT MILK

¾ CUP MAPLE SYRUP

SEEDS OF 2 VANILLA BEANS

1 TEASPOON SEA SALT

DIRECTIONS

1. Place the coconut milk, maple syrup, vanilla seeds, and salt in a blender or food processor and blitz until combined. Transfer the mixture in the refrigerator and chill overnight.

2. Pour the chilled mixture into an ice cream maker and churn until the desired consistency is achieved. Transfer the churned cream to the freezer and freeze for 1 hour before serving.

Classic Vanilla Milkshakes

YIELD: **4 SERVINGS**

ACTIVE TIME: **2 MINUTES**

TOTAL TIME: **2 MINUTES**

INGREDIENTS

2 PINTS OF VANILLA ICE CREAM
(SEE PAGE 152 FOR HOMEMADE)

½ CUP WHOLE MILK

½ TEASPOON SALT

2 TEASPOONS PURE VANILLA
EXTRACT

MINT, FOR GARNISH (OPTIONAL)

DIRECTIONS

1. Place all of the ingredients, other than the mint, in a blender and puree until combined.

2. Pour the milkshakes into tall glasses and, if desired, garnish with mint.

Root Beer Floats

YIELD: **4 SERVINGS**

ACTIVE TIME: **5 MINUTES**

TOTAL TIME: **5 MINUTES**

INGREDIENTS

2 PINTS OF VANILLA ICE CREAM
(SEE PAGE 152 FOR HOMEMADE)

4 (12 OZ.) BOTTLES OF QUALITY
ROOT BEER

WHIPPED CREAM (SEE PAGE 53),
FOR GARNISH

DIRECTIONS

1. Place 2 scoops of ice cream in the bottom of 4 tall glasses.

2. Slowly pour a bottle of root beer into each glass, top with the Whipped Cream, and serve.

Toasted Marshmallow Milkshakes

YIELD: **4 SERVINGS**

ACTIVE TIME: **10 MINUTES**

TOTAL TIME: **10 MINUTES**

INGREDIENTS

16 MARSHMALLOWS (SEE PAGE 180 FOR HOMEMADE)

2 PINTS OF VANILLA ICE CREAM (SEE PAGE 152 FOR HOMEMADE)

¾ CUP WHOLE MILK

1 TEASPOON SALT

1 TEASPOON PURE VANILLA EXTRACT

DIRECTIONS

1. Toast the marshmallows to desired color over an open flame. Either a grill or a burner on a gas stovetop will work for this task.

2. Place the toasted marshmallows in a blender with the remaining ingredients and puree until smooth.

3. Pour into tall glasses and serve.

Royal Dessert Pizza

YIELD: **6 TO 8 SERVINGS**

ACTIVE TIME: **15 MINUTES**

TOTAL TIME: **30 MINUTES**

INGREDIENTS

5 TABLESPOONS UNSALTED BUTTER, AT ROOM TEMPERATURE

½ CUP CASTER SUGAR

1 EGG

1 CUP SELF-RISING FLOUR, PLUS MORE FOR DUSTING

SEEDS OF ½ VANILLA BEAN

1 BALL OF TART PASTRY SHELL DOUGH (SEE PAGE 38)

2 TABLESPOONS PASTRY CREAM (SEE PAGE 50)

1 ROYAL GALA APPLE, CORED AND SLICED INTO THIN HALF-MOONS

1 TABLESPOON DARK BROWN SUGAR

1 HANDFUL OF COTTON CANDY (OPTIONAL)

2 TABLESPOONS CARAMEL (SEE PAGE 57), WARMED

DIRECTIONS

1. Preheat the oven to 425°F.

2. Place the butter and sugar in the mixing bowl of a stand mixer fitted with the paddle attachment. Beat on medium for 1 minute, add the egg, and beat for another minute. Scrape the mixing bowl as needed.

3. Add the flour and vanilla seeds, reduce the speed to low, and beat for 1 minute. Raise speed to medium and beat until the mixture is well combined.

4. Place the dough on a lightly floured surface and roll it into a 10" circle that is approximately ½" thick. Transfer the dough to a greased pizza pan or baking sheet, spread the butter-and-sugar mixture over the dough, and then gently spread the pastry cream on top.

5. Distribute the apple slices and sprinkle them with the brown sugar. Place the pizza in the oven and cook until the crust is golden brown, 12 to 15 minutes.

6. Remove from the oven, slice into eight pieces, and place the cotton candy in the center, if using. Drizzle the caramel over the pizza and serve.

Pound Cake with Vanilla & Peach Compote

YIELD: **4 SERVINGS**

ACTIVE TIME: **5 MINUTES**

TOTAL TIME: **30 MINUTES**

INGREDIENTS

12 PEACHES, PEELED AND CHOPPED

¼ CUP GRANULATED SUGAR

SEEDS OF ½ VANILLA BEAN

2 TEASPOONS ROSE WATER

POUND CAKE (SEE PAGE 41), SLICED

DIRECTIONS

1. Place the peaches, sugar, vanilla, and half of the rose water in a saucepan and simmer for 10 minutes over medium heat.

2. Remove the saucepan from heat, add the remaining rose water, and stir to incorporate. Transfer the mixture to a small bowl and let cool completely.

3. When the compote is cool, drizzle over the slices of Pound Cake.

Ricotta Cakes with Vanilla Roasted Cherries

YIELD: **6 SERVINGS**

ACTIVE TIME: **35 MINUTES**

TOTAL TIME: **24 HOURS**

INGREDIENTS

FOR THE CHERRIES

48 CHERRIES, WITH PITS

¼ CUP DEMERARA SUGAR

½ TEASPOON SALT

½ CUP BRANDY

SEEDS OF ½ VANILLA BEAN

FOR THE CAKES

⅔ CUP ALL-PURPOSE FLOUR

½ TEASPOON BAKING SODA

½ TEASPOON SALT

1 CUP RICOTTA CHEESE

YOLKS OF 2 LARGE EGGS

⅓ CUP WHOLE MILK

SEEDS OF ½ VANILLA BEAN

2 TABLESPOONS UNSALTED BUTTER, MELTED

WHITES OF 4 LARGE EGGS

¼ CUP GRANULATED SUGAR

1 TABLESPOON VEGETABLE OIL

DIRECTIONS

1. To prepare the cherries, place all of the ingredients in a bowl, stir to combine, and marinate overnight.

2. Preheat oven to 400°F. Strain the cherries and reserve the liquid. Place the cherries on a baking sheet, place them in the oven, and bake for 5 minutes. Remove, add half of the reserved liquid, and gently stir the cherries. Return to the oven and bake for another 5 minutes. Remove, add the remaining reserved liquid, and gently stir. Return to the oven and bake for 5 more minutes. Remove from the oven, let cool, and reduce the oven temperature to 200°F. When the cherries are cool enough to handle, pit the cherries and set them aside.

3. Place a wire rack in a rimmed baking sheet and place it in the oven. Place the flour, baking soda, and salt in a mixing bowl, whisk to combine, and make well in center. Place the ricotta, egg yolks, milk, and vanilla in the well and then whisk until combined. Add the butter and gently stir to incorporate.

4. Place the egg whites in the mixing bowl of a stand mixer fitted with the whisk attachment. Beat on medium-low until foamy and then increase speed to medium-high and beat until soft, billowy mounds form. Gradually add the sugar and whip until glossy, soft peaks form. Add one-third of egg white mixture to the batter and whisk gently to incorporate. Fold in the remaining egg white mixture.

5. Place 1 teaspoon of the oil in a 12" cast-iron skillet and warm over medium heat. When it starts to shimmer, add three ¼-cup portions of the batter to the skillet and cook until the edges are set and the bottom is golden brown, about 2 minutes. Flip with a wide, thin spatula and cook until the other side is golden brown, about 2 minutes. Transfer cooked cakes to the wire rack in the oven and repeat until all the batter has been used. If the skillet starts to look a little dry, add more of the vegetable oil as needed.

6. Place two cakes on each serving plate and ladle the cherries and their juices over them.

NOTE: It is crucial to wait until the cherries have been roasted to pit them, as it allows them to hold their shape.

Killer Vanilla Bread Pudding

YIELD: **4 TO 6 SERVINGS**

ACTIVE TIME: **20 MINUTES**

TOTAL TIME: **1 HOUR AND 45 MINUTES**

INGREDIENTS

4 TABLESPOONS UNSALTED BUTTER

4 CUPS CROISSANT OR BAGUETTE PIECES

2 EGGS

1 TEASPOON PURE VANILLA EXTRACT

2 PINTS OF VANILLA ICE CREAM (SEE PAGE 152 FOR HOMEMADE), AT ROOM TEMPERATURE

DIRECTIONS

1. Place a cast-iron skillet over low heat and add the butter. When it is melted, add the croissant or baguette pieces and shake the skillet until they are coated. Transfer the pieces of bread into a large baking dish.

2. Place the eggs and vanilla extract in a mixing bowl and whisk until combined. Add the softened ice cream and stir until just combined. Pour the mixture over the bread and shake the baking dish to evenly distribute. Cover the dish with tin foil and let stand in a cool place for 30 minutes.

3. Preheat the oven to 350°F.

4. Remove the foil, place the dish in the oven, and bake until the pudding is set and browned at the edges, about 45 minutes. Remove from the oven and let cool for 5 to 10 minutes before transferring to a serving dish.

Vegan Rice Pudding

YIELD: **6 TO 8 SERVINGS**

ACTIVE TIME: **30 MINUTES**

TOTAL TIME: **35 TO 40 MINUTES**

INGREDIENTS

3 (14 OZ.) CANS OF COCONUT MILK

1 CUP ARBORIO RICE

½ CUP GRANULATED SUGAR

3 STRIPS OF ORANGE ZEST

1 TEASPOON CINNAMON

½ TEASPOON GRATED NUTMEG

SEEDS AND POD OF 1 VANILLA BEAN

½ TEASPOON SALT

DIRECTIONS

1. Place all of the ingredients in a saucepan and bring to a gentle boil over medium-low heat. Reduce heat to low and simmer, while stirring occasionally, until the rice is tender and the mixture is thick, about 25 minutes.

2. Remove from heat and remove the orange zest and the vanilla pod. Let stand for 5 minutes. Serve warm or place in the refrigerator to chill for 5 minutes.

VARIETIES OF VANILLA

As those who are devotees of the vanilla bean know, there is plenty of variation within this flavor that many unfairly brand as bland. Here's a look at the varieties of vanilla beans and extracts you're most likely to encounter:

Madagascar Bourbon: These beans have nothing to do with American whiskey—though, to be fair, it's an understandable mistake given that many bourbons do carry strong notes of vanilla. Instead, it refers to Bourbon Island (now known as Reunion), an island east of Madagascar in the Indian Ocean after which the vanilla that grows in the region was named. The sweet, creamy flavor of these beans is what comes to mind when most think of vanilla, as its incredible versatility has made it ubiquitous.

Mexican: This vanilla adds a bit of nutmeg-y spice to the famously sweet and creamy quality. Because of this piquant quality, Mexican vanilla goes wonderfully with those cinnamon- and nutmeg-heavy desserts that show up around the holidays, and can also be used to dress up a barbecue sauce.

Indonesian: These beans carry a smoky, woody flavor and aroma that is particularly welcome in cookies and chocolate-rich desserts.

Tahitian: A fruity, floral flavor that carries hints of stone fruit and anise makes Tahitian vanilla a perfect match for fruit-based desserts, as well as ice creams and custards. It is interesting to note that Tahitian vanilla is a different species of orchid than the one that produces the other three, and its beans are noticeably plumper.

Vanilla Pudding

YIELD: **6 TO 8 SERVINGS**

ACTIVE TIME: **20 MINUTES**

TOTAL TIME: **2 HOURS AND 20 MINUTES**

INGREDIENTS

YOLKS OF 2 LARGE EGGS

⅓ CUP GRANULATED SUGAR

2 TABLESPOONS CORNSTARCH

¼ TEASPOON SALT

2 CUPS WHOLE MILK

2 TABLESPOONS UNSALTED
BUTTER, AT ROOM TEMPERATURE

SEEDS OF 2 VANILLA BEANS

DIRECTIONS

1. Place the egg yolks in a bowl and beat until combined.

2. Place the sugar, cornstarch, and salt in a saucepan, stir to combine, and warm over medium heat. Slowly add the milk and whisk constantly as the mixture comes to a boil.

3. Remove the saucepan from heat and stir approximately one-third of the warm mixture into the beaten egg yolks while whisking constantly. Pour the tempered eggs into the saucepan, place it back over medium heat, and cook for 1 minute while stirring constantly. Remove from heat.

4. Stir in the butter and vanilla seeds. Transfer the pudding into the serving dishes and place plastic wrap directly on the surface of each one to prevent a skin from forming. Place the pudding in the refrigerator and chill for 2 hours before serving.

Crème Brûlée

YIELD: **6 SERVINGS**

ACTIVE TIME: **1 HOUR**

TOTAL TIME: **3 HOURS AND 30 MINUTES**

INGREDIENTS

4 CUPS HEAVY CREAM

SEEDS AND POD OF 1 VANILLA
BEAN

1 CUP GRANULATED SUGAR

YOLKS OF 6 LARGE EGGS

8 CUPS HOT WATER (120°F)

DIRECTIONS

1. Preheat the oven to 325°F.

2. Place the cream and vanilla seeds and pod in a saucepan and bring to a boil over medium-high heat. Remove from heat, cover the pan, and let sit for 15 minutes.

3. Remove the vanilla pod and discard. Place ½ cup of the sugar and the egg yolks in a bowl and whisk until combined. While whisking constantly, add the cream mixture in ¼-cup increments. When all of the cream mixture has been incorporated, divide the mixture between six 8 oz. ramekins.

4. Transfer the ramekins to a 9 x 13-inch baking dish. Add the hot water until it comes halfway up the sides of the ramekins, place the dish in the oven, and bake until the custard is just set, about 40 minutes. Remove from the oven, transfer the ramekins to the refrigerator, and chill for 2 hours.

5. Remove the ramekins 30 minutes before you are ready to serve them and allow them to come to room temperature. Divide the remaining sugar between the ramekins and spread evenly on top. Use a kitchen torch to caramelize the sugar, let the crème brulee sit for 5 minutes, and then serve.

Tapioca Pudding

YIELD: **6 SERVINGS**

ACTIVE TIME: **15 MINUTES**

TOTAL TIME: **4 HOURS AND 15 MINUTES**

INGREDIENTS

2 LARGE EGGS

1 CUP GRANULATED SUGAR

½ CUP INSTANT TAPIOCA

SEEDS AND POD OF 1 VANILLA BEAN

4 CUPS HALF-AND-HALF

½ TEASPOON SALT

¼ TEASPOON GRATED NUTMEG

DIRECTIONS

1. Place the eggs, sugar, tapioca, and vanilla seeds and pod in a saucepan and whisk until the mixture is frothy.

2. Add the half-and-half, whisk to combine, and bring to a simmer over medium-low heat while stirring constantly. Cook until the mixture is very thick, about 10 minutes, while taking care not to let it come to a boil.

3. Remove the pan from heat and remove the vanilla pod. Transfer the mixture to a bowl and stir in the salt and nutmeg. Place the pudding in the refrigerator and chill for 4 hours before serving.

Homemade Marshmallows

YIELD: **24 MARSHMALLOWS**

ACTIVE TIME: **30 MINUTES**

TOTAL TIME: **6 HOURS AND 30 MINUTES**

INGREDIENTS

1 CUP WATER

3 PACKETS OF GELATIN

1½ CUPS GRANULATED SUGAR

1 CUP LIGHT CORN SYRUP

SEEDS OF 2 VANILLA BEANS

CONFECTIONERS' SUGAR, FOR DUSTING

DIRECTIONS

1. Place ½ cup of the water in the bowl of a stand mixer. Sprinkle the gelatin into the water and let the gelatin dissolve.

2. Place the remaining water, sugar, and corn syrup in a saucepan and cook, while swirling the pan occasionally, over medium heat until the mixture is 240°F. Remove the pan from heat and let stand for 1 minute.

3. Fit the stand mixer with the whisk attachment and run it at low speed while slowly pouring the contents of the saucepan down the side of the mixing bowl. Gradually increase the speed of the mixer until the mixture is white, fluffy, and glossy. Add the vanilla seeds and whisk to incorporate.

4. Sift the confectioners' sugar over a greased 9 x 13-inch baking dish until the dish is completely coated. Pour the mixture into the baking dish and use a greased rubber spatula to even out the surface. Let stand for 6 hours.

5. When ready to serve, dust a work surface, a knife, and your hands with confectioners' sugar. Transfer the block of marshmallow to the work surface, cut into cubes, and serve.

Rice Krispies Treats

YIELD: **24 BARS**

ACTIVE TIME: **10 MINUTES**

TOTAL TIME: **1 HOUR**

INGREDIENTS

5 TABLESPOONS UNSALTED BUTTER

1 LB. HOMEMADE MARSHMALLOWS (SEE PAGE 180)

1 (16 OZ.) BAG OF MINIATURE MARSHMALLOWS

½ TEASPOON PURE VANILLA EXTRACT

½ TEASPOON SALT

8 CUPS CRISPY RICE CEREAL

DIRECTIONS

1. Place the butter in a large saucepan and warm over medium heat until it is melted. Add the homemade and miniature marshmallows and cook, while stirring frequently, until marshmallows are also melted.

2. Add vanilla and salt and stir to incorporate. Add the cereal and stir gently until the cereal is evenly coated.

3. Remove the saucepan from heat and pour the mixture into greased 9 x 13-inch baking dish. Let the mixture cool.

4. When the mixture is cool enough to handle, press it into an even layer. Let stand for 30 minutes.

5. Cut the mixture into bars and serve.

Nougat

YIELD: **24 BARS**

ACTIVE TIME: **30 MINUTES**

TOTAL TIME: **1 HOUR AND 30 MINUTES**

INGREDIENTS

WHITES OF 3 LARGE EGGS

3 CUPS GRANULATED SUGAR

⅓ CUP LIGHT CORN SYRUP

1 CUP HONEY

1 CUP WATER

ZEST OF 1 LEMON

SEEDS OF 2 VANILLA BEANS

¾ TEASPOON SEA SALT

1 CUP SLIVERED ALMONDS, TOASTED

DIRECTIONS

1. Place the egg whites in the mixing bowl of a stand mixer and beat them until frothy. Set aside.

2. Place the sugar, corn syrup, honey, and water in a saucepan and bring to a boil over medium-high heat. Cook until the mixture is 300°F.

3. With the mixture running on low, add a splash of the hot syrup to the egg whites. When the eggs have been tempered, pour the rest of the hot syrup into the mixture and gradually increase the speed until the mixture is light and frothy. Add the lemon zest, vanilla seeds, salt, and slivered almonds and continue to run the mixer until the mixture has cooled considerably, about 15 to 20 minutes.

4. Pour the mixture onto a greased rimmed baking sheet and let cool completely before slicing into bars, about 1 hour.

NOT THAT NOUGAT

Anyone who is even slightly familiar with the world of candy bars has heard the term nougat.

But rest assured: this recipe, which is similar to the *torrone* that is a traditional part of the Christmas meal in Italy, is a far cry from that mysterious and ubiquitous filler. The nougat that inhabits everything from the Charleston Chew to the Zero Bar is a mixture of sucrose, corn syrup, and an aerating element such as egg white or gelatin.

CHAPTER 5

NUTTY

The title of this chapter refers to the flavor and/or the key ingredient of the preparations contained within. But it could also be used in reference to the feeling that framing nuts in a sweet package fosters in so many. The combination proves too much for many to resist, causing them to mindlessly reach for a peanut butter cup or a praline when the yen for something sugary arises.

This is more than just speculation: a 2016 look by Nielsen found that Reese's Peanut Butter Cups lapped the field in the American market, bringing in over $50 million in sales during an average week, while no other candy even cracked $40 million in sales. While the Reese's Cup is no doubt deserving of such love, we wouldn't be doing our duty if we did not provide a recipe for you to turn out a delicious version at home (see page 191).

THE DYNAMIC DUO

As mentioned on the previous page, the peanut butter cup's bid to be recognized as the ultimate confection has some serious money supporting it.

But what is it, other than the taste, that allows this sum to be much more than its parts? According to Gregory Ziegler, a professor of food science at Penn State University, the pleasure the pairing provides is due to a phenomenon known as "dynamic sensory contrast," with the smooth texture and rich taste of melted chocolate and the sweet and salty taste of peanut butter providing an opposition that our taste buds, which live for such juxtapositions, prove to be powerless against.

Homemade Peanut Butter Cups

YIELD: **12 CUPS**

ACTIVE TIME: **15 MINUTES**

TOTAL TIME: **1 HOUR AND 15 MINUTES**

INGREDIENTS

1 CUP CREAMY PEANUT BUTTER

½ CUP CONFECTIONERS' SUGAR

½ TEASPOON SALT

¼ TEASPOON PURE VANILLA
EXTRACT

¾ LB. QUALITY SEMISWEET OR
DARK CHOCOLATE CHIPS

12 MUFFIN LINERS

DIRECTIONS

1. Place the peanut butter, sugar, salt, and vanilla in a mixing bowl and stir to combine. If you need to soften the peanut butter, microwave for 15 to 30 seconds.

2. Place the chocolate chips in a microwave-safe bowl. Melt in the microwave on medium, removing to stir every 20 seconds.

3. Spray the muffin liners with nonstick cooking spray and place them in a muffin tin.

4. Place a spoonful of the melted chocolate in each muffin liner and then use spoon to drag chocolate halfway up the sides. When you have done this for each liner, place in refrigerator and let chill until chocolate has hardened, 15 to 20 minutes.

5. Remove from the refrigerator, scoop the peanut butter mixture into each chocolate shell and smooth with a rubber spatula. Return to the refrigerator and chill for 10 to 15 minutes.

6. Remove from the refrigerator, top each filled shell with another spoonful of melted chocolate, and smooth the top with a rubber spatula. Return to the refrigerator and chill for 25 to 30 minutes before serving.

Honey Nut Truffles

YIELD: **16 TO 20 TRUFFLES**

ACTIVE TIME: **10 MINUTES**

TOTAL TIME: **2 HOURS**

INGREDIENTS

½ CUP PEANUT BUTTER

¼ CUP HONEY

¼ TEASPOON SALT

1 CUP QUALITY SEMISWEET
CHOCOLATE CHIPS

DIRECTIONS

1. Place the peanut butter, honey, and salt in a bowl and stir until well combined. Place teaspoon-sized balls of the mixture on a parchment-lined baking sheet and then place in the refrigerator for 1 hour.

2. Remove the baking sheet from the refrigerator. Place the chocolate chips in microwave-safe bowl. Microwave on medium until melted, removing to stir every 20 seconds.

3. Dip the balls into the melted chocolate until completely covered. Place them back on the baking sheet. When all of the truffles have been coated, place them in the refrigerator and chill until the chocolate is set.

Muddy Buddies

YIELD: **8 TO 10 SERVINGS**

ACTIVE TIME: **5 MINUTES**

TOTAL TIME: **50 MINUTES**

INGREDIENTS

1 CUP SEMISWEET CHOCOLATE CHIPS

¾ CUP CREAMY PEANUT BUTTER

1 TEASPOON PURE VANILLA EXTRACT

9 CUPS RICE CHEX

1½ CUPS CONFECTIONERS' SUGAR

DIRECTIONS

1. Place the chocolate chips and peanut butter in a microwave-safe bowl and microwave on medium for 30 seconds. Remove from the microwave, add the vanilla, and stir until the mixture is smooth.

2. Place the Chex in a large mixing bowl and pour the peanut butter-and-chocolate mixture over the cereal. Carefully stir until all of the Chex are coated.

3. Place the mixture into a large resealable plastic bag and add the confectioners' sugar. Seal bag and shake until each piece is coated with sugar.

4. Pour the mixture onto a parchment-lined baking sheet. Place the sheet in the refrigerator and chill for 45 minutes.

Pralines

YIELD: **24 PRALINES**

ACTIVE TIME: **15 MINUTES**

TOTAL TIME: **50 MINUTES**

INGREDIENTS

1 CUP PACKED DARK BROWN SUGAR

1 CUP GRANULATED SUGAR

½ CUP EVAPORATED MILK

1 CUP PECAN HALVES OR PIECES

2 TABLESPOONS UNSALTED BUTTER

1½ TEASPOONS PURE VANILLA EXTRACT

DIRECTIONS

1. Place the sugars and evaporated milk in a Dutch oven and cook, while stirring constantly, until the sugars have dissolved. Continue cooking, while stirring frequently, until the mixture reaches 225°F.

2. Add the pecans and butter, stir until the butter melts, and then remove from heat.

3. Stir in the vanilla and let cool while stirring occasionally. When the mixture starts to thicken, place tablespoons of the mixture on a piece of parchment paper. They will settle into thin patties as they cool. Let stand for 30 minutes and wrap each praline in wax paper.

THE ORIGINAL STREET TREAT

Originating in France and initially containing almonds, the praline came into its own in Louisiana, where the plentiful pecan lent its natural sweetness to the treat. The transformation proved to be addictive, becoming so popular that they were being hawked on the streets of New Orleans as far back as the 1860s, a time when markets and vendors were largely concerned with providing the necessities of everyday life.

YIELD: **8 TO 10 SERVINGS**

ACTIVE TIME: **20 MINUTES**

TOTAL TIME: **1 HOUR AND 30 MINUTES**

Pecan Pie

INGREDIENTS

1 CUP LIGHT CORN SYRUP

1 CUP PACKED DARK BROWN SUGAR

3 EGGS, LIGHTLY BEATEN

⅓ CUP UNSALTED BUTTER, MELTED

½ TEASPOON SALT

1 CUP PECAN HALVES

1 BALL OF LEAF LARD PIECRUST DOUGH (SEE PAGE 33)

ALL-PURPOSE FLOUR, FOR DUSTING

DIRECTIONS

1. Preheat the oven to 350°F.

2. Place all of the ingredients, except for the pie dough and flour, in a large mixing bowl and stir to combine. Set the mixture aside.

3. Place the ball of dough on a lightly floured work surface and roll out to a 12" circle. Place the dough in a greased 9" pie plate, trim the edges, and then crimp the crust. Place the crust in the refrigerator for 15 minutes.

4. Pour the filling into crust. Place the pie in the oven and bake until the crust is golden brown and the filling is set, 45 to 50 minutes. Remove from the oven and let cool completely before serving.

Walnut Pie

YIELD: **8 TO 10 SERVINGS**

ACTIVE TIME: **20 MINUTES**

TOTAL TIME: **2 HOURS**

INGREDIENTS

2½ CUPS MINCED WALNUTS

¼ CUP PACKED DARK BROWN SUGAR

2 TABLESPOONS GRANULATED SUGAR

1½ TEASPOONS CINNAMON

1 BALL OF LEAF LARD PICECRUST DOUGH (SEE PAGE 33)

ALL-PURPOSE FLOUR, FOR DUSTING

1 STICK UNSALTED BUTTER, MELTED

¾ CUP HONEY

1 TABLESPOON FRESH LEMON JUICE

DIRECTIONS

1. Preheat the oven to 325°F.

2. Place the walnuts, brown sugar, granulated sugar, and the cinnamon in a mixing bowl and stir to combine.

3. Place the ball of dough on a lightly floured work surface and roll out to a 12″ circle. Place the dough in a greased 9″ pie plate, trim the edges, and then crimp the crust. Pour half of the melted butter over the crust and then spread the walnut mixture evenly on top. Pour the remaining butter over the walnut mixture, place the pie in the oven, and bake until the crust is golden brown, about 30 minutes. Remove from the oven and let cool.

4. Place the honey and lemon juice in a small saucepan and warm, while stirring constantly, over medium heat until the mixture is almost watery in consistency. Drizzle the mixture over the pie and let the pie cool completely before serving.

Peanut Butter Pie

YIELD: **8 TO 10 SERVINGS**

ACTIVE TIME: **15 MINUTES**

TOTAL TIME: **1 HOUR AND 30 MINUTES**

INGREDIENTS

3 EGGS

1 CUP DARK CORN SYRUP

½ CUP GRANULATED SUGAR

1½ CUPS CREAMY ALL-NATURAL
PEANUT BUTTER WITH NO ADDED
SUGAR

½ TEASPOON PURE VANILLA
EXTRACT

1 GRAHAM CRACKER CRUST
(SEE PAGE 34)

1 CUP SEMISWEET CHOCOLATE
CHIPS

DIRECTIONS

1. Preheat the oven to 350°F.

2. Place the eggs in a large bowl and whisk until thoroughly combined. Add the corn syrup and sugar and whisk until the sugar has dissolved.

3. Add the peanut butter and vanilla and whisk until the mixture is smooth and just combined.

4. Pour the mixture into the Graham Cracker Crust. Place the pie in the oven and bake until a knife inserted in the center comes out clean, about 1 hour. Remove from the oven and allow to cool completely.

5. Place the chocolate chips in a microwave-safe bowl. Microwave on medium until melted, removing to stir every 20 seconds. Drizzle the melted chocolate over the pie and chill in the refrigerator until the chocolate has hardened, about 45 minutes.

Red Velvet Cake with Pralines

YIELD: **6 TO 8 SERVINGS**

ACTIVE TIME: **30 MINUTES**

TOTAL TIME: **1 HOUR AND 30 MINUTES**

INGREDIENTS

2½ CUPS ALL-PURPOSE FLOUR

1½ CUPS GRANULATED SUGAR

1 TEASPOON BAKING SODA

1 TEASPOON SALT

1 TEASPOON COCOA POWDER

1½ CUPS VEGETABLE OIL

1 CUP BUTTERMILK, AT ROOM TEMPERATURE

2 LARGE EGGS, AT ROOM TEMPERATURE

2 TABLESPOONS RED FOOD COLORING

1 TEASPOON PURE VANILLA EXTRACT

1½ CUPS CHOPPED PRALINES (SEE PAGE 196)

CREAM CHEESE FROSTING (SEE PAGE 46)

DIRECTIONS

1. Preheat the oven to 350°F.

2. Sift the flour, sugar, baking soda, salt, and cocoa powder into a large mixing bowl. Place the oil, buttermilk, eggs, food coloring, and vanilla in another large mixing bowl and whisk to combine. Add the dry mixture to the wet mixture and stir until it is a smooth batter. Add the chopped Pralines and fold to incorporate.

3. Divide the batter evenly between three greased round 9″ cake pans. Place the pans in the oven and bake, while rotating the pans halfway through, until the cakes pull away from the edges of the pans and a toothpick inserted in the centers of the cakes comes out clean, about 30 minutes. Remove from the oven, remove the cakes from the pans, and let them cool completely on wire racks.

4. When the cakes have completely cooled, spread the frosting on top of one of the cakes. Gently place another cake on top, flat-side up, and spread more of the frosting on top of this cake. Place the third cake on top, flat-side up, and either frost the top or frost the entire cake.

Almond Meringues

YIELD: **48 COOKIES**

ACTIVE TIME: **15 MINUTES**

TOTAL TIME: **3 HOURS**

INGREDIENTS

WHITES OF 4 LARGE EGGS

½ TEASPOON PURE ALMOND EXTRACT

PINCH OF SALT

2 TEASPOONS CORNSTARCH

¾ CUP GRANULATED SUGAR

⅓ CUP CHOPPED ALMONDS, TOASTED

DIRECTIONS

1. Preheat the oven to 225°F and line two baking sheets with parchment paper. As timing is crucial, place a piping bag near your work station and fit the stand mixer with the whisk attachment.

2. Place the egg whites, almond extract, and salt in the mixing bowl of the stand mixer and beat on high until soft peaks form.

3. Add the cornstarch and sugar, reduce the speed to medium, and beat until incorporated. Raise speed to high and beat until stiff peaks start to form. Transfer the mixture to your piping bag and pipe onto the parchment-lined baking sheets. Sprinkle with the toasted almonds, place on separate racks in the oven and bake for 1 hour, while rotating the baking sheets halfway through. Turn off the oven, leave the meringues in the oven, and let them cool for another hour.

4. Remove from the oven and let cool to room temperature before serving.

NOTE: If you do not have a piping bag, simply fill a large resealable bag with the mixture, cut off one of the corners, and squeeze.

Macarons

INGREDIENTS

WHITES OF 3 EGGS

¼ CUP GRANULATED SUGAR

1⅔ CUPS CONFECTIONERS' SUGAR

1 CUP FINELY GROUND ALMONDS

2 TO 3 DROPS OF PREFERRED GEL
FOOD COLORING

DIRECTIONS

1. Line a baking sheet with parchment paper.

2. Place the egg whites in the bowl of a stand mixer fitted with a whisk attachment. Beat until foamy, add the granulated sugar, and continue to beat until the mixture is glossy, fluffy, and holds soft peaks.

3. Sift the confectioners' sugar and the ground almonds into a separate bowl. Add this mixture and the gel food coloring into the egg white mixture and fold until incorporated, taking care not to overmix the batter.

4. Transfer the batter into a resealable plastic bag with one corner removed. Pipe a 1½" disk of batter onto the parchment-lined baking sheet. If the disk holds a peak instead of flattening immediately, gently fold the batter a few more times and retest. Repeat until the disk flattens into an even disk. Transfer the batter into a piping bag.

5. Pipe the batter onto the parchment-lined baking sheet. Let stand at room temperature until a skin forms on top, about 1 hour.

6. Preheat the oven to 275°F. Place the cookies in the oven and bake until they are set but not browned, about 10 minutes. Remove and let cool completely before filling.

IT'S WHAT'S INSIDE THAT COUNTS

The impossibly delicate texture and dynamic coloring of the macaron only partly explains its surge in popularity. Another attribute leading to its rise is its adaptability, as the macaron can accommodate a large number of fillings, and thus appeal to a wide spectrum of palates. While you shouldn't be afraid to be bold with your filling decisions, always remember to err on the dry side, as wetter fillings, such as whipped cream, will dissolve the cookie. To get your mind working, here are five standard fillings.

Chocolate Ganache: Heat ½ cup heavy cream in a saucepan and bring to a simmer. Stir in ¼ lb. of chopped dark chocolate and continue stirring until the chocolate is melted. Add 2 tablespoons of unsalted butter, stir until the mixture is smooth, and chill in the refrigerator until thick and cool.

Vanilla Buttercream Frosting: See page 49.

Raspberry Buttercream: Add ¼ cup of seedless raspberry jam to the Vanilla Buttercream Frosting and beat until incorporated.

Lemon Curd: See page 387.

Cream Cheese Frosting: See page 46.

Peanut Butter & Jam Thumbprints

YIELD: **24 COOKIES**

ACTIVE TIME: **20 MINUTES**

TOTAL TIME: **1 HOUR**

INGREDIENTS

¾ CUP PACKED LIGHT BROWN SUGAR

1 STICK UNSALTED BUTTER, AT ROOM TEMPERATURE

1 CUP CREAMY PEANUT BUTTER

1 LARGE EGG, AT ROOM TEMPERATURE

½ TEASPOON PURE VANILLA EXTRACT

1 TEASPOON BAKING SODA

⅛ TEASPOON SALT

1 CUP ALL-PURPOSE FLOUR

1½ CUPS SEEDLESS RASPBERRY JAM

DIRECTIONS

1. Preheat the oven to 375°F and line two baking sheets with parchment paper. Combine the brown sugar, butter, and peanut butter in the mixing bowl of a stand mixer and beat at low speed until combined. Increase the speed to high and beat until the mixture is light and fluffy.

2. Add the egg, vanilla, baking soda, and salt and beat for 1 minute. Slowly add the flour and beat until a soft dough forms.

3. Remove tablespoons of the dough and roll them into balls. Place the balls on the baking sheets, 1½" apart. Use your index finger to make a large depression in the center of each ball. Place the cookies into the oven and bake for 10 to 12 minutes, until the edges are brown. Remove, let cool for 2 minutes, and then transfer to wire racks to cool completely.

4. While the cookies are cooling, place the raspberry jam in a saucepan and cook over medium heat. Bring to a boil, while stirring frequently, and cook until the jam has been reduced by one-quarter. Spoon a teaspoon of the jam into each cookie and allow it to set.

Baklava

YIELD: **48 PIECES**

ACTIVE TIME: **30 MINUTES**

TOTAL TIME: **1 HOUR**

INGREDIENTS

3½ CUPS WALNUTS, TOASTED

2½ CUPS GRANULATED SUGAR

1 TEASPOON CINNAMON

¼ TEASPOON GROUND CLOVES

1 (16 OZ.) PACKAGE OF FROZEN PHYLLO SHEETS, THAWED

3 STICKS UNSALTED BUTTER, MELTED

1½ CUPS WATER

½ CUP HONEY

½ LEMON, SLICED THIN

1 CINNAMON STICK

PISTACHIOS, CHOPPED, FOR GARNISH (OPTIONAL)

DIRECTIONS

1. Preheat the oven to 375°F.

2. Place the walnuts, ½ cup of the sugar, cinnamon, and cloves in a food processor. Pulse until very fine and set the mixture aside.

3. Preheat the oven temperature to 375°F and grease a 12 x 16-inch rimmed baking sheet. Place the phyllo sheets on a plate and cover with plastic wrap or a damp paper towel to keep them from drying out. Place 1 sheet of phyllo on the baking sheet and brush with some of the melted butter. Repeat with 7 more sheets, and spread one-third of the walnut mixture on top. Place 4 more sheets of phyllo dough on top, brushing each with butter. Spread half of the remaining walnut mixture on top, and then repeat. Top the last of the walnut mixture with the remaining sheets of phyllo dough, brushing each one with butter. Trim the edges to make a neat rectangle.

4. Cut pastry into squares or triangles, taking care not to cut through the bottom crust. Place in the oven and bake for 25 to 30 minutes, until the top layer of phyllo is brown.

5. While the pastry is cooking, combine the remaining sugar, water, honey, lemon, and cinnamon stick in a saucepan. Bring to a boil over medium heat while stirring occasionally. Reduce heat to low and simmer for 5 minutes. Strain syrup and keep it hot while the pastry finishes baking.

6. Remove the baking sheet from the oven and pour the hot syrup over the pastry. Place the pan on a wire rack, allow to cool to room temperature, and then cut through the bottom crust. If desired, garnish with pistachios before serving.

Almond Cookies

YIELD: **18 COOKIES**

ACTIVE TIME: **15 MINUTES**

TOTAL TIME: **1 HOUR**

INGREDIENTS

¼ CUP ALL-PURPOSE FLOUR

½ CUP CONFECTIONERS' SUGAR

½ CUP GRANULATED SUGAR

WHITES OF 2 EGGS

½ LB. UNSWEETENED ALMOND PASTE

½ CUP SLIVERED ALMONDS

DIRECTIONS

1. Preheat the oven to 350°F and line two baking sheets with parchment paper.

2. Place the flour, confectioners' sugar, granulated sugar, egg whites, and almond paste in a large mixing bowl and use your hands to combine. The dough will be very sticky.

3. Place the almonds in a bowl. Place teaspoons of the dough in the bowl of almonds and roll the pieces of dough until completely coated. Place on the baking sheets.

4. Place in the oven and bake until golden brown, 15 to 20 minutes. Remove and let cool on the baking sheets for a few minutes before transferring to a wire rack to cool completely.

MARZ ATTACKS

When shopping for the ingredients for these cookies, make sure that you select almond paste and not marzipan. The latter is smoother and sweeter, and will leave you with bars that are closer to hunks of rich frosting than the light, slightly chewy cookies that result from the coarser almond paste, which features almost twice the amount of almonds and far less sugar than its cousin.

Nutella Dumplings

YIELD: **36 DUMPLINGS**

ACTIVE TIME: **45 MINUTES**

TOTAL TIME: **45 MINUTES**

INGREDIENTS

3 CUPS ALL–PURPOSE FLOUR, PLUS MORE AS NEEDED

½ TEASPOON SALT, PLUS MORE TO TASTE

4 TABLESPOONS UNSALTED BUTTER

1 LARGE EGG, BEATEN

2 TABLESPOONS WATER

1½ CUPS NUTELLA

2 CUPS VEGETABLE OIL

CONFECTIONERS' SUGAR, FOR DUSTING

CINNAMON, FOR DUSTING

DIRECTIONS

1. Place the flour and salt in a large mixing bowl and stir to combine. Add the butter and beat on medium speed with a handheld mixer until the dough looks crumbly.

2. Add the beaten egg and water and beat until a smooth dough forms. You should be able to touch the dough with a hand without sticking. If it's too sticky, incorporate flour in 1-teaspoon increments until the dough is smooth and not sticky.

3. Transfer the dough to a lightly floured work surface and roll out to ⅛" thick. Using a biscuit or cookie cutter, cut the dough into as many 3" rounds as possible. Place the rounds on a lightly floured parchment-lined baking sheet and make sure they don't touch. When you have as many as you can fit in a single layer, cover them with another piece of parchment, sprinkle with flour, and keep arranging the rounds in the same manner.

4. Place a round in the palm of a slightly cupped hand and hold it so that it takes the shape of a taco. Place 1 teaspoon of Nutella in the center. Using your thumb and index finger, firmly pinch the edges together to form a tight seal. You want this seal (or seam) to be approximately ¼" wide. Pat the sealed dumpling gently to evenly distribute the filling. Check for holes (patch them with a little bit of dough) and make sure the seal is tight. Repeat until all of the wrappers have been filled and sealed.

5. Place the vegetable oil in a Dutch oven and heat to 350°F.

6. Working in batches of 3 to 4 dumplings, place them in the pot and cook for 2 to 3 minutes, until golden brown. Remove cooked dumplings from the oil and drain on a paper towel-lined wire rack. When dry but still warm, dust with confectioners' sugar and cinnamon.

Crispy Nutella Bars

YIELD: **24 BARS**

ACTIVE TIME: **10 MINUTES**

TOTAL TIME: **40 MINUTES**

INGREDIENTS

2 STICKS UNSALTED BUTTER

2 LBS. HOMEMADE
MARSHMALLOWS (SEE PAGE 180)

1 TEASPOON SALT

2 CUPS NUTELLA

12 CUPS CRISPY RICE CEREAL

DIRECTIONS

1. Place the butter in a large saucepan and cook over medium heat until melted. Add the marshmallows and salt and cook, while stirring, until the marshmallows are melted. Stir in the Nutella.

2. Add the cereal in two batches and stir until the cereal is evenly coated.

3. Pour the mixture into a greased 9 x 13-inch baking dish and let it cool briefly. When cool enough to handle, grease your hands and press the mixture into an even layer. Let stand for 30 minutes before cutting into bars.

Chewy Peanut Butter & Oat Bars

YIELD: **12 BARS**

ACTIVE TIME: **15 MINUTES**

TOTAL TIME: **45 MINUTES**

INGREDIENTS

¾ CUP WHOLE MILK

1 CUP GRANULATED SUGAR

¼ TEASPOON SALT

4 OZ. DARK CHOCOLATE, CHOPPED

1 TEASPOON PURE VANILLA
EXTRACT

½ CUP CREAMY PEANUT BUTTER

1 CUP ROLLED OATS

DIRECTIONS

1. Place the milk, sugar, and salt in a small saucepan and whisk to combine. Cook over medium heat until mixture comes to a boil and thickens, approximately 10 minutes. Remove pan from heat.

2. Place the chocolate in a microwave-safe bowl. Microwave on medium until melted, removing to stir every 20 seconds.

3. Add the vanilla, one-quarter of the melted chocolate, and the peanut butter to pan and mix until well combined. Fold in the oats and stir until they are completely coated.

4. Line a square 8" cake pan with parchment paper and pour the contents of the saucepan into it. Press into an even layer, spread the remaining melted chocolate over the top, and let sit for 30 minutes. Cut into little bars and serve immediately, or store in the refrigerator until ready to serve.

Vegan Pistachio Ice Cream

YIELD: **3 CUPS**

ACTIVE TIME: **20 MINUTES**

TOTAL TIME: **24 HOURS**

INGREDIENTS

1 (14 OZ.) CAN OF UNSWEETENED COCONUT MILK

1 CUP ALMOND MILK

¼ CUP AGAVE NECTAR

½ TEASPOON PURE ALMOND EXTRACT

2 CUPS PISTACHIOS, SHELLED AND CHOPPED

DIRECTIONS

1. Place the coconut milk, almond milk, agave nectar, almond extract, and half of the pistachios in a blender. Blend on high for three minutes and then place in the refrigerator to chill overnight.

2. Pour the mixture into an ice cream maker and churn until the desired texture is achieved, adding the remaining pistachios toward the end of the churning. Place in the freezer for 6 hours before serving.

Peanut Butter Cup Milkshakes

YIELD: **4 SERVINGS**

ACTIVE TIME: **2 MINUTES**

TOTAL TIME: **2 MINUTES**

INGREDIENTS

2 PINTS OF CHOCOLATE ICE CREAM (SEE PAGE 115 FOR HOMEMADE)

4 BANANAS, PEELED AND FROZEN

1 CUP CREAMY PEANUT BUTTER

½ CUP WHOLE MILK

6 TABLESPOONS CHOCOLATE SYRUP

½ TEASPOON SEA SALT

DIRECTIONS

1. Place all of the ingredients in a blender and puree until smooth.

2. Pour into tall glasses.

Fried Angel Hair Nests with Honey, Dates & Pistachios

YIELD: **4 TO 6 SERVINGS**

ACTIVE TIME: **15 MINUTES**

TOTAL TIME: **30 MINUTES**

INGREDIENTS

SALT, TO TASTE

SUGAR, TO TASTE

½ LB. ANGEL HAIR PASTA

1 TABLESPOON SESAME OIL

⅓ CUP HONEY

3 TABLESPOONS MINCED DATES

VEGETABLE OIL, FOR FRYING

PISTACHIOS, CHOPPED,
FOR GARNISH

CINNAMON, FOR DUSTING

DIRECTIONS

1. Bring a large pot of water to a boil. When the water is boiling, season it with salt and sugar and stir. Add the pasta and cook for 2 minutes less than the directed time. Drain the pasta, rinse under cold water, and drain again. Transfer to a bowl, add the sesame oil, and toss to coat.

2. While the pasta cooks, place the honey in a microwave-safe bowl and microwave on high until it liquefies and becomes easy to pour, 20 to 30 seconds. Remove from the microwave and stir in the dates.

3. Add vegetable oil to a Dutch oven until it is ¼" deep. Warm over medium-high heat. When the oil begins to shimmer, twirl the pasta around a fork to create small nests. Carefully place them in the hot oil and cook until golden and crisp at the edges, 30 to 60 seconds on each side. Transfer the crisp nests to a paper towel-lined plate to drain. Repeat until all of the pasta has been fried.

4. Arrange the crisp pasta nests on serving plates. Drizzle with the honey-and-date mixture and garnish with pistachios and cinnamon.

Kataifi Pudding

YIELD: **8 SERVINGS**

ACTIVE TIME: **15 MINUTES**

TOTAL TIME: **1 HOUR AND 30 MINUTES**

INGREDIENTS

SALT, TO TASTE

½ LB. ANGEL HAIR PASTA

7 TABLESPOONS UNSALTED BUTTER

1 TEASPOON CINNAMON

¾ CUP SLIVERED ALMONDS

¾ CUP RAISINS

¾ CUP CHOPPED PISTACHIOS

¾ CUP CASTER SUGAR

¼ CUP ICE-COLD WATER

WHIPPED CREAM (SEE PAGE 53), FOR GARNISH

DIRECTIONS

1. Preheat the oven to 300°F and grease a square 8″ cake pan with nonstick cooking spray.

2. Bring a large pot of water to a boil. When the water is boiling, add salt and stir. Add the pasta and cook for 3 minutes less than the directed time. Reserve ¼ cup of the pasta water, drain the pasta, and set aside. Return the empty pot to the stove. Immediately turn the heat to high and add 4 tablespoons of the butter and the reserved pasta water. Add the drained pasta and cook. Add the cinnamon and cook, while tossing to coat, for 1 to 2 minutes. Remove from heat.

3. Transfer one-third of the cooked pasta to the prepared pan. Sprinkle half of the almonds, raisins, pistachios, and ¼ cup of the sugar on top. Add half of the remaining pasta and sprinkle with the remaining almonds, raisins, pistachios, and another ¼ cup of the sugar. Top with the remaining pasta. Cut the remaining butter into small pieces and dot the pasta with them. Place on the center rack of the oven and bake for 25 minutes.

4. While it bakes, put the remaining sugar in a small saucepan over low heat and stir until it melts and turns golden brown. Remove from heat and very slowly and carefully (the mixture will splatter a bit) add the water. Return the pan to the heat and stir until the mixture thickens, about 4 minutes.

5. After 25 minutes, remove the dish from the oven and pour the sauce evenly over the top. Return to the oven to bake until the top is golden brown, about 5 minutes. Top with Whipped Cream and serve.

Butter Pecan Bread Pudding

YIELD: **4 TO 6 SERVINGS**

ACTIVE TIME: **45 MINUTES**

TOTAL TIME: **2 HOURS**

INGREDIENTS

½ CUP CHOPPED PECANS

½ CUP BROWN SUGAR

1 STICK UNSALTED BUTTER

4 CUPS DAY-OLD BREAD PIECES

2 CUPS HEAVY CREAM

1 TEASPOON PURE VANILLA
EXTRACT

½ CUP GRANULATED SUGAR

CARAMEL (SEE PAGE 57), WARMED

DIRECTIONS

1. Warm a cast-iron skillet over medium-high heat. When the skillet is hot, add the pecans and shake the skillet for 1 to 2 minutes as they toast. When the pecans are fragrant, transfer them to a bowl with the brown sugar and half of the butter. Toss to coat and set the mixture aside.

2. Place the remaining butter in the skillet and warm over low heat. When it is melted, add the pieces of bread and shake the skillet until they are coated. Transfer the pieces of bread into a large baking dish.

3. Place the heavy cream, vanilla, and granulated sugar in a mixing bowl and whisk until combined. Pour the mixture over the bread and shake the baking dish to evenly distribute. Cover the dish with aluminum foil and let stand in a cool place for 30 minutes.

4. Preheat the oven to 350°F.

5. Remove the foil, place the dish in the oven, and bake until the pudding is set and browned at the edges, about 45 minutes. Remove from the oven and let cool for 5 to 10 minutes before generously drizzling the caramel over the top.

Almond Croissants

INGREDIENTS

FOR THE POOLISH

1¾ CUPS ALL-PURPOSE FLOUR

1 TEASPOON INSTANT YEAST

1⅓ CUPS LUKEWARM WATER (90°F)

¾ CUP WHOLE WHEAT FLOUR

FOR THE CROISSANTS

5⅔ CUPS ALL-PURPOSE FLOUR, PLUS MORE FOR DUSTING

½ CUP GRANULATED SUGAR

1 TABLESPOON SALT

1¼ TEASPOONS INSTANT YEAST

1 CUP WHOLE MILK

3 TABLESPOONS UNSALTED BUTTER

YOLK OF 1 EGG

1 TEASPOON HEAVY CREAM

FOR THE LAMINATION LAYER

4½ STICKS UNSALTED BUTTER

FOR THE ALMOND FILLING

1 CUP SLIVERED ALMONDS

½ CUP UNSALTED BUTTER, MELTED

5 TABLESPOONS CONFECTIONERS' SUGAR

YOLK OF 1 EGG

SEEDS OF ½ VANILLA BEAN

DIRECTIONS

1. To make the poolish, place the all-purpose flour, ½ teaspoon of the yeast, and 1 cup of the water in a mixing bowl, stir to combine, and transfer the mixture to the refrigerator for 8 hours. Place the whole wheat flour, remaining yeast, and remaining water in a separate bowl and stir to combine. Let stand at room temperature for 1 hour and then place in the refrigerator for 8 hours.

2. To make the croissant dough, add the flour, sugar, salt, yeast, milk, and butter to the mixing bowl of a stand mixer. Add both poolish mixtures and beat on low speed until the mixture is just combined, about 2 minutes. Let rest for 20 minutes and then mix for 2 minutes on low speed. Transfer the dough to a separate bowl, cover with plastic wrap, and let stand at room temperature for 1 hour.

3. Place the butter for the lamination in a mixing bowl and beat until it is smooth and free of lumps. Transfer the butter onto a piece of parchment paper and smash until it is a 6½ x 9-inch rectangle of even thickness. Place the butter in the refrigerator when the dough has 20 minutes left to stand.

4. Place the dough on a floured work surface and roll out into a 13 x 9-inch rectangle. Remove the butter from the refrigerator and place it on the right half of the dough. Fold the left side of the dough over the butter, making sure that the dough completely covers the butter. Essentially, you want to make a "butter sandwich."

5. Roll the dough out to a 12 x 27-inch rectangle, fold it in half, and then fold it in half again. Wrap the dough in plastic, place in the refrigerator, and chill for 1 hour.

6. While the dough is chilling, prepare the filling. Place all of the ingredients in a food processor and blitz until the mixture is a smooth paste.

7. Place the dough on a floured work surface and gently roll it out into a 12 x 30-inch rectangle. Cut the rectangle into 4" squares and then cut each square into two triangles. Spread some of the almond filling in the center of each triangle.

8. Roll up the croissants, starting at the 90° angle and working toward the wide side (aka the hypotenuse). Place the croissants on parchment-lined baking sheets, making sure not to crowd the sheet. Cover with a kitchen towel at let them stand at room temperature for 4 hours. The croissants can be refrigerated until the next day after this period of rest.

9. When you are ready to bake the croissants, preheat the oven to 420°F. Place the egg yolk and heavy cream in a mug and stir to combine. Brush the egg wash on the tops of the croissants, place them in the oven, and bake until golden brown, 20 to 25 minutes.

CHAPTER 6

STONE FRUITS

The brevity of the season. The burst of juice that sets off a million pleasant sensations in your mouth. The versatility that allows them to shine whether enjoyed on their own, placed on a hot grill, or tucked into a light, flaky dough.

Stone fruits (cherries, peaches, plums, and coffee—yes, coffee) lend these immense talents to a number of classic desserts. While their growing season is far too short lived considering their unparalleled flavor and sweetness, the joy of making one's way through a cherry pie or a grill-seared peach is large enough to linger for the entire year.

AT THE PINNACLE

While the cherry is loved in general, the support for the Rainier cherry borders on reverence. After drawing people in with the sunset hues of its skin, the Rainier pays off that intrigue with amazingly creamy flesh and unparalleled sweetness.

That next-level existence is hard won. The Rainier is incredibly delicate, requiring considerable patience and a pioneering spirit of anyone who chooses to cultivate it. A gust of wind or a heavy rainfall can damage the cherry's fragile skin, and if the temperature hits 90, the cherry loses a day of life. If one can weather those swings, a crop of perfect cherries will result–for two months. The brevity of the season sends cherry lovers into a tizzy, resulting in high prices that can make the delicate fruit seem well worth the gamble it requires.

Named for the truly awesome mountain that looms large on the Seattle skyline, the Rainier is a cross between two varieties of sweet red cherries—a Bing and a Van—that Harold Fogle, a professor at Washington State University, produced in 1952. Fogle's matchmaking was spot on in this instance, as he produced a cherry that occasionally goes for $1 a piece in Japan.

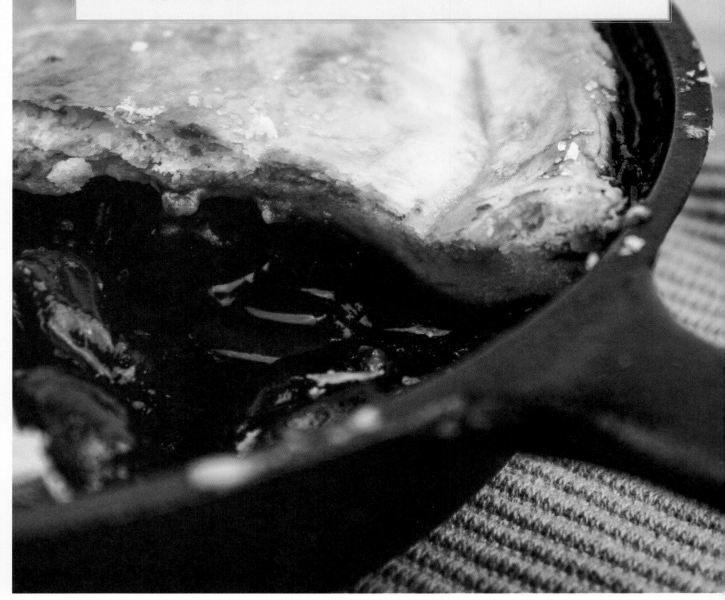

Cherry Pie

YIELD: **4 TO 6 SERVINGS**

ACTIVE TIME: **30 MINUTES**

TOTAL TIME: **1 HOUR AND 30 MINUTES**

INGREDIENTS

4 CUPS RAINIER CHERRIES, PITTED

2 CUPS GRANULATED SUGAR

2 TABLESPOONS FRESH LEMON JUICE

3 TABLESPOONS CORNSTARCH

1 TABLESPOON WATER

¼ TEASPOON PURE ALMOND EXTRACT

2 LEAF LARD PIECRUSTS (SEE PAGE 33)

1 EGG, BEATEN

DIRECTIONS

1. Preheat oven to 350°F. Place the cherries, sugar, and lemon juice in a saucepan and cook, while stirring occasionally, over medium heat until the mixture is syrupy.

2. Combine the cornstarch and water in a small bowl and stir this mixture into the saucepan. Reduce heat to low and cook, while stirring, until the mixture is thick. Remove from heat, add the almond extract, and let cool.

3. When the cherry mixture has cooled, place the bottom crust in a greased 9" pie plate and pour the cherry mixture into the crust. Top with the other crust, make a few slits in the top, and brush the top crust with the beaten egg.

4. Place the pie in the oven and bake until the top crust is golden brown, about 45 minutes. Remove and let cool before serving.

Cherry Crumb Pie

YIELD: **8 TO 10 SERVINGS**

ACTIVE TIME: **15 MINUTES**

TOTAL TIME: **1 HOUR**

INGREDIENTS

FOR THE PIE

6 CUPS CHERRIES, PITTED

⅔ CUP GRANULATED SUGAR

2 TABLESPOONS CORNSTARCH

PINCH OF SALT

1 TEASPOON PURE ALMOND
EXTRACT

1 LEAF LARD PIECRUST
(SEE PAGE 33), BLIND BAKED

FOR THE CRUMB TOPPING

1 CUP ALL-PURPOSE FLOUR

⅔ CUP CHOPPED ALMONDS,
TOASTED

¾ CUP PACKED LIGHT BROWN
SUGAR

ZEST OF 1 SMALL LEMON

¼ TEASPOON SALT

3 TABLESPOONS UNSALTED
BUTTER, MELTED

DIRECTIONS

1. Preheat the oven to 350°F.

2. Place the cherries, sugar, cornstarch, salt, and almond extract in a mixing bowl and stir to combine. Pour the mixture into the baked crust and evenly distribute.

3. To prepare the crumb topping, place the flour, almonds, sugar, lemon zest, and salt in the mixing bowl of a stand mixer fitted with the paddle attachment. Beat until combined and then, with the mixer running, slowly pour in the melted butter and beat until the mixture is moist and crumbly.

4. Sprinkle the topping over the cherry filling. Place the pie in the oven and bake until the crust is golden brown and the filling is bubbling around the edges. Remove and allow to cool before slicing and serving.

Cherry & Apple Pie

YIELD: **6 TO 8 SERVINGS**

ACTIVE TIME: **15 MINUTES**

TOTAL TIME: **45 MINUTES**

INGREDIENTS

3 LARGE APPLES, PEELED, CORED, AND SLICED

1 TABLESPOON UNSALTED BUTTER

1 TABLESPOON FRESH LEMON JUICE

¼ TEASPOON GROUND GINGER

2 CUPS CHERRIES, PITTED AND PUREED

1 LEAF LARD PIECRUST (SEE PAGE 33), BLIND BAKED

DIRECTIONS

1. Preheat the oven to 350°F.

2. Place the apples and butter in a skillet and cook over medium heat, while stirring, until the apples start to soften, about 10 minutes.

3. Transfer apple pieces to a large bowl and add the lemon juice, ground ginger, and the cherry puree. Stir to combine, place the mixture in the piecrust, and evenly distribute.

4. Place the pie in the oven and bake until the filling is heated through and set, about 20 minutes. Remove from the oven and let cool before serving.

Cherry & Watermelon Soup

YIELD: **4 SERVINGS**

ACTIVE TIME: **20 MINUTES**

TOTAL TIME: **24 HOURS**

INGREDIENTS

2½ CUPS WATERMELON CUBES

1 TABLESPOON KIRSCH

ZEST AND JUICE OF 1 LIME

SEEDS AND POD OF ½ VANILLA BEAN

¾ CUP CHERRIES, PITTED

1 CUP RIESLING

1 CUP CHAMPAGNE

DIRECTIONS

1. Place 1 cup of the watermelon cubes, the kirsch, lime zest, lime juice, and vanilla seeds and pod in a mixing bowl, stir to combine, and chill in the refrigerator for 1 hour.

2. Spread the mixture evenly over a rimmed baking sheet, place in the freezer, and freeze overnight.

3. Place the remaining watermelon, the cherries, and the Riesling in a food processor and puree until smooth. Strain through a fine sieve and place the puree in the refrigerator until ready to serve.

4. Remove the baking tray from the freezer and cut the mixture into cubes. Add these cubes and the Champagne to the puree and ladle into bowls.

TALES FROM THE BLACK FOREST

Kirsch is a clear fruit brandy that is made from double distilling the fermented fruit and pits of the Morello cherry, a dark, sour variety. German for "cherry water," kirsch is not sweet like most cherry brandies, but instead carries a fruit-forward and slightly bitter flavor that contains notes of almond.

This dry, nutty, and bitter quality makes it a natural to incorporate in desserts such as cherries jubilee and black forest cake, where it can add considerable depth.

A LOVELY, CHILD-LIKE QUALITY

Clafoutis is one of those dishes that perfectly captures the best features of French cuisine: fresh, quality ingredients being simply prepared to produce a rich, flavorful result. And, like so many of the culinary gifts the world has received from the French, Clafoutis was introduced to a wider audience by Julia Child.

Child is the reason the pits remain in the cherries in this recipe, as she believed that they added a nutty flavor and prevented the cherries' juices from staining the custard.

Cherry Clafoutis

YIELD: **4 TO 6 SERVINGS**

ACTIVE TIME: **20 MINUTES**

TOTAL TIME: **45 MINUTES**

INGREDIENTS

1 STICK UNSALTED BUTTER, MELTED

1 CUP GRANULATED SUGAR, PLUS 2 TEASPOONS

⅔ CUP ALL-PURPOSE FLOUR

½ TEASPOON SALT

1 TEASPOON PURE VANILLA EXTRACT

3 EGGS, BEATEN

1 CUP WHOLE MILK

3 CUPS CHERRIES, WITH PITS

CONFECTIONERS' SUGAR, FOR TOPPING

DIRECTIONS

1. Preheat the oven to 400°F. Place 6 tablespoons of the butter, ½ cup of the granulated sugar, the flour, salt, vanilla, eggs, and milk in a large mixing bowl and stir until the mixture is well combined and smooth. Set the mixture aside.

2. Grease a cast-iron skillet with the remaining butter and put the skillet in the oven to warm up.

3. When the skillet is warm, remove from the oven, place ½ cup of the granulated sugar in the skillet, and shake to distribute it evenly. Distribute the cherries in the skillet and then pour the batter into the skillet. Sprinkle the remaining granulated sugar on top, place the skillet in the oven, and bake until the custard is golden brown and set in the middle, about 30 minutes.

4. Remove from the oven, sprinkle with the confectioners' sugar, and serve immediately, making sure to remind everyone that the cherries still have their pits.

Peach Pie

YIELD: **6 TO 8 SERVINGS**

ACTIVE TIME: **15 MINUTES**

TOTAL TIME: **1 HOUR AND 15 MINUTES**

INGREDIENTS

1 TABLESPOON UNSALTED BUTTER

2 LEAF LARD PIECRUSTS
(SEE PAGE 33)

4 CUPS PEELED, PITTED, AND
SLICED PEACHES

1 TEASPOON FRESH LEMON JUICE

¾ CUP GRANULATED SUGAR,
PLUS 2 TABLESPOONS

¼ CUP ALL-PURPOSE FLOUR

WHITE OF 1 EGG

DIRECTIONS

1. Preheat the oven to 350°F. Butter a 9″ pie plate and place one of the piecrusts in it.

2. Place the slices of peach, lemon juice, ¾ cup of sugar, and flour in a mixing bowl and stir until the peach slices are evenly coated.

3. Fill the piecrust with the mixture and evenly distribute. Place the other piecrust over the mixture and crimp the edges to seal.

4. Brush the top crust with the egg white and sprinkle the remaining sugar over it. Cut 4 or 5 slits in the center of the crust, place the pie in the oven, and bake until the crust is golden brown and the filling is bubbling, 1 hour. Remove and let cool before serving.

NOTE: A dollop of bourbon-spiked whipped cream is outstanding on top of this pie. Just add 1 tablespoon of bourbon to the ingredients for the Whipped Cream on page 53 and proceed as directed.

Peach Cobbler

YIELD: **4 TO 6 SERVINGS**

ACTIVE TIME: **30 MINUTES**

TOTAL TIME: **1 HOUR**

INGREDIENTS

FOR THE BISCUITS

2 CUPS ALL-PURPOSE FLOUR, PLUS MORE FOR DUSTING

1 TEASPOON GRANULATED SUGAR

1 TEASPOON SALT

1 TABLESPOON BAKING POWDER

6 TABLESPOONS UNSALTED BUTTER, CUT INTO SMALL PIECES

½ CUP BUTTERMILK, PLUS MORE AS NEEDED

FOR THE FILLING

5 OR 6 PEACHES, PITTED AND SLICED

¼ CUP GRANULATED SUGAR

1 TO 2 TABLESPOONS ALL-PURPOSE FLOUR

1 TEASPOON CINNAMON

WHIPPED CREAM (SEE PAGE 53), FOR SERVING (OPTIONAL)

VANILLA ICE CREAM (SEE PAGE 152 FOR HOMEMADE), FOR SERVING (OPTIONAL)

DIRECTIONS

1. Preheat the oven to 400°F.

2. To prepare the biscuits, place the flour, sugar, salt, and baking powder in a mixing bowl and stir to combine. Add the butter and work it into the mixture with a pastry blender. When a crumbly dough forms, add the buttermilk and work the mixture until a stiff dough forms. If the dough is not holding together, incorporate more buttermilk, adding 1 tablespoon at a time.

3. Place the dough on a flour-dusted work surface and press it out to a thickness of 1". Use a floured biscuit cutter or mason jar to cut the dough into rounds.

4. To prepare the filling, place the peaches, sugar, and flour in a bowl and stir to combine. The amount of flour you use will depend on how juicy the peaches are; more juice means more flour. Remove the skillet from the oven, transfer the mixture into the skillet, and bake for 10 minutes.

5. Remove the skillet from the oven and place the biscuits on top of the filling, making sure they are evenly distributed. Sprinkle the cinnamon on top and return the skillet to the oven. Bake until the biscuits are golden brown and the filling is bubbling, about 12 minutes. Make sure not to burn the topping. Remove from the oven, let cool briefly, and serve with Whipped Cream or ice cream.

Peach Galette

YIELD: **6 TO 8 SERVINGS**

ACTIVE TIME: **15 MINUTES**

TOTAL TIME: **45 MINUTES**

INGREDIENTS

1 BALL OF LEAF LARD PIECRUST DOUGH (SEE PAGE 33)

ALL-PURPOSE FLOUR, FOR DUSTING

3 CUPS PEELED AND SLICED PEACHES

½ CUP GRANULATED SUGAR, PLUS 1 TABLESPOON

JUICE OF ½ LEMON

3 TABLESPOONS CORNSTARCH

PINCH OF SALT

1 TEASPOON AMARETTO LIQUEUR (OPTIONAL)

2 TABLESPOONS PEACH JAM

1 EGG, BEATEN

DIRECTIONS

1. Preheat the oven to 400°F.

2. Place the ball of dough on a flour-dusted work surface and roll it out into a 9" circle. Place the dough on a parchment-lined baking sheet.

3. Place the peaches, ½ cup sugar, lemon juice, cornstarch, and salt in a mixing bowl and stir until the peaches are evenly coated.

4. If using the Amaretto, place it in a bowl, add the jam, and stir to combine. Spread the jam mixture (or just the jam) over the dough, making sure to leave 1½" of dough at the edge. Spread the filling over the jam and fold the uncovered crust up over the filling.

5. Brush the crust with the egg and sprinkle the remaining sugar over it. Place the galette in the oven and bake until the crust is golden brown and the filling is bubbling, about 35 minutes. Remove from the oven and let cool before serving.

Caramelized Peach Custard Tart

YIELD: **6 TO 8 SERVINGS**

ACTIVE TIME: **25 MINUTES**

TOTAL TIME: **1 HOUR**

INGREDIENTS

2 TABLESPOONS UNSALTED BUTTER

2 LARGE PEACHES, PITTED AND SLICED

7 TABLESPOONS GRANULATED SUGAR

¼ TEASPOON CINNAMON

2 TABLESPOONS BRANDY

½ CUP WHOLE MILK

½ CUP HEAVY CREAM

2 EGGS

YOLK OF 1 EGG

½ TEASPOON PURE VANILLA EXTRACT

¼ TEASPOON SALT

1 TART PASTRY SHELL (SEE PAGE 38)

DIRECTIONS

1. Place the butter in a skillet and melt over medium-high heat. Add the peaches to the melted butter and cook, turning the slices as they cook, until they are brown on all sides.

2. Sprinkle 3 tablespoons of the sugar and all of the cinnamon over the peaches and shake the pan until they are evenly coated. Cook until the peaches start to caramelize.

3. Tilt the pan away from you, add the brandy, and use a long match or wand lighter to light the brandy. Shake the pan until the alcohol cooks off and then pour the mixture into a heatproof mixing bowl. Let the mixture cool.

4. Preheat the oven to 300°F. When the flambéed peaches are close to cool, place the milk, heavy cream, eggs, egg yolk, remaining sugar, vanilla, and salt in a mixing bowl and whisk to combine.

5. Place the flambéed peaches in the pastry shell, evenly distribute, and then strain the custard over the top. Place the tart in the oven and bake until the custard is just set, 20 to 25 minutes. Remove from the oven and let cool before serving.

Peachy Keen Cake

YIELD: **8 SERVINGS**

ACTIVE TIME: **20 MINUTES**

TOTAL TIME: **1 HOUR AND 30 MINUTES**

INGREDIENTS

2½ CUPS CAKE FLOUR, PLUS MORE FOR DUSTING

1¼ TEASPOONS BAKING POWDER

¼ TEASPOON BAKING SODA

¾ TEASPOON SALT

1¾ CUPS GRANULATED SUGAR

2 STICKS UNSALTED BUTTER, MELTED

2 TEASPOONS PURE VANILLA EXTRACT

3 TABLESPOONS VEGETABLE OIL

YOLKS OF 6 LARGE EGGS, AT ROOM TEMPERATURE

WHITES OF 3 LARGE EGGS, AT ROOM TEMPERATURE

½ LB. FRESH PEACHES, PITTED AND SLICED

½ CUP LIGHT BROWN SUGAR

DIRECTIONS

1. Preheat the oven to 350°F.

2. Place the flour, baking powder, baking soda, salt, and 1½ cups of the granulated sugar in a large mixing bowl and whisk until combined. Place 1 stick of butter, vanilla, vegetable oil, and egg yolks in a separate mixing bowl and whisk until combined.

3. Place the egg whites in a bowl and beat until foamy. Gradually add the remaining granulated sugar and beat until stiff peaks begin to form. Set aside.

4. Gradually add the butter-and-vanilla mixture to the flour mixture and whisk until the mixture is smooth. Add the beaten egg white mixture and fold until incorporated. Set the batter aside.

5. Place the remaining butter, the peaches, and brown sugar in a large cast-iron skillet. Cook over medium heat until the butter starts to bubble. Turn off the burner and pour the batter over the peaches.

6. Place the cake in the oven and bake for 35 to 40 minutes, until the cake is golden brown and a toothpick inserted into the center comes out clean. Remove from the oven and let cool.

7. When the cake has cooled, place a large serving plate on the counter and use a pot holder or oven mitt to lift the skillet. Flip the skillet over and invert the cake onto the plate.

Grilled Peaches with Bourbon Caramel

YIELD: **6 SERVINGS**

ACTIVE TIME: **20 MINUTES**

TOTAL TIME: **20 MINUTES**

INGREDIENTS

½ CUP GRANULATED SUGAR

¼ CUP BOURBON, PLUS 2 TABLESPOONS

¼ CUP HEAVY CREAM, WARMED

1 TABLESPOON UNSALTED BUTTER

1 TEASPOON SALT

6 PEACHES, PITTED AND HALVED

2 PINTS OF VANILLA ICE CREAM (SEE PAGE 152 FOR HOMEMADE), FOR SERVING

DIRECTIONS

1. Preheat your gas or charcoal grill to 400°F.

2. Place the sugar and ¼ cup of bourbon in a small saucepan and cook over medium heat until the sugar has dissolved. Reduce the heat and add the heavy cream, stirring constantly to incorporate. Add the remaining bourbon, the butter, and salt, remove from heat, and pour into a heatproof mixing bowl.

3. When the grill is ready, place the peaches, cut-side down, on the grill and cook until the flesh becomes tender and starts to caramelize, about 5 minutes. Turn the peaches over and cook for another 4 to 5 minutes. Place 2 to 3 peach halves in each bowl, drizzle the bourbon caramel over the peaches, and top with vanilla ice cream.

Tiramisu

YIELD: **8 TO 10 SERVINGS**

ACTIVE TIME: **20 MINUTES**

TOTAL TIME: **3 HOURS AND 30 MINUTES**

INGREDIENTS

2 CUPS FRESHLY BREWED ESPRESSO

½ CUP GRANULATED SUGAR,
PLUS 1 TABLESPOON

3 TABLESPOONS KAHLUA

YOLKS OF 4 LARGE EGGS

2 CUPS MASCARPONE CHEESE

1 CUP HEAVY CREAM

36 LADYFINGERS

2 TABLESPOONS UNSWEETENED
COCOA POWDER

DIRECTIONS

1. Place the espresso, 1 tablespoon of sugar, and Kahlua in a bowl and stir to combine. Set the mixture aside.

2. Place 1" of water in a saucepan and bring to a simmer. Place the remaining sugar and egg yolks in a metal mixing bowl and set the bowl over the simmering water. Whisk the mixture continually until it has nearly tripled in size, approximately 10 minutes. Remove from heat, add the mascarpone, and fold to incorporate.

3. Pour the heavy cream into a separate bowl and whisk until soft peaks start to form. Gently fold the whipped cream into the mascarpone mixture.

4. Place the ladyfingers in the espresso mixture and briefly submerge them. Place an even layer of the soaked ladyfingers on the bottom of a 9 x 13-inch baking dish. This will use up approximately half of the ladyfingers. Spread half of the mascarpone mixture on top of the ladyfingers and then repeat until the ladyfingers and mascarpone have been used up.

5. Cover with plastic and place in the refrigerator for 3 hours. Sprinkle the cocoa powder over the top before serving.

THE PHILOSOPHER'S STONE

Many people will be surprised to see coffee-centered desserts sitting in a chapter with cherries and peaches, but the beverage that holds so many in thrall is in fact the product of a stone fruit. Coffee beans are the roasted pits of the red or purple fruit commonly referred to as the coffee cherry. This pit resembles a bean far more than it does a cherry or peach pit, which is part of the reason coffee's status as a stone fruit remains a blind spot for many.

Mocha Balls

YIELD: **24 BALLS**

ACTIVE TIME: **20 MINUTES**

TOTAL TIME: **1 HOUR**

INGREDIENTS

2 TABLESPOONS INSTANT ESPRESSO POWDER

2 TABLESPOONS BOILING WATER

1 STICK UNSALTED BUTTER, CUT INTO SMALL PIECES AND AT ROOM TEMPERATURE

⅓ CUP GRANULATED SUGAR

1 LARGE EGG, AT ROOM TEMPERATURE

½ TEASPOON PURE VANILLA EXTRACT

1¼ CUPS UNSWEETENED COCOA POWDER

1⅓ CUPS ALL-PURPOSE FLOUR

PINCH OF SALT

DIRECTIONS

1. Preheat the oven to 350°F.

2. Place the instant espresso powder and the water in a small bowl and stir until the powder has dissolved. Set aside and let cool.

3. Place the butter and sugar in a mixing bowl and beat at medium speed with a handheld mixer until light and fluffy. Add the egg and vanilla, beat until well combined, and then add ¼ cup of the cocoa powder and the espresso mixture. Beat until combined, scraping down the bowl as necessary. Reduce the speed to low, add the flour and salt, and beat until the dough just holds together.

4. Form tablespoons of the dough into balls and place them on parchment-lined baking sheets. Place in the oven and bake until firm, about 15 minutes.

5. Sift the remaining cocoa powder into a shallow bowl and use a spatula to transfer a few cookies at a time into the bowl. Roll the cookies around until well coated and then transfer them to wire racks to cool completely.

Irish Coffee

INGREDIENTS

½ CUP FRESHLY BREWED COFFEE

DASH OF GRANULATED SUGAR

1 OZ. IRISH WHISKEY

1 OZ. BAILEYS IRISH CREAM

WHIPPED CREAM (SEE PAGE 53),
FOR GARNISH

DIRECTIONS

1. Pour the coffee into a mug and add the sugar. Stir until the sugar has dissolved.

2. Add the whiskey and stir again. Top with Baileys Irish Cream. If you can, layer the cream on top rather than stirring it in. Garnish with a dollop of Whipped Cream.

THIRD STONE FROM THE SUN

Irish coffee might reign amongst the brunch set, but that doesn't mean it's the only acceptable way to dress up a cup of joe. If you're not a fan of whiskey, or you're just looking for something different, take one of the following variations out for a spin.

Ice Age: Place ½ cup iced coffee, 1 oz. bourbon, a splash of simple syrup, and a dash of Angostura Bitters in a rocks glass filled with ice and stir until chilled.

Cuban Coffee: Place ½ cup coffee, 1 oz. black rum, 1 teaspoon sugar, and a splash of Baileys Irish Cream in a mug and stir to combine.

Cancun Coffee: Place ½ cup coffee, 1 oz. tequila, 1 oz. Kahlua, and a splash of Baileys Irish Cream in a mug and stir to combine.

Pumpkin Pie Latte

YIELD: **1 SERVING**

ACTIVE TIME: **1 MINUTE**

TOTAL TIME: **1 MINUTE**

INGREDIENTS

½ CUP BREWED ESPRESSO OR VERY STRONG COFFEE

1 OZ. BAILEYS IRISH CREAM

1 OZ. WHOLE MILK, FROTHED

DASH OF PUMPKIN PIE SPICE

DIRECTIONS

1. Fill a mug about two-thirds of way with the espresso or coffee.

2. Add the Baileys Irish Cream and stir to combine. Top with the frothed milk and the dash of pumpkin pie spice.

Affogato

INGREDIENTS

1 PINT OF VANILLA ICE CREAM
(SEE PAGE 152 FOR HOMEMADE)

¼ CUP KAHLUA OR SAMBUCA

1 TEASPOON GRATED NUTMEG

1¼ CUPS BREWED ESPRESSO OR
VERY STRONG COFFEE

WHIPPED CREAM (SEE PAGE 53),
FOR GARNISH

CHOCOLATE SHAVINGS, FOR
GARNISH

DIRECTIONS

1. Scoop ice cream into five small glasses. Pour 1 tablespoon of preferred liqueur over each scoop. Sprinkle a bit of nutmeg over each scoop.

2. Pour the espresso or coffee over the ice cream. Top with Whipped Cream and chocolate shavings.

Plum Galette

YIELD: **4 TO 6 SERVINGS**

ACTIVE TIME: **20 MINUTES**

START TO FINISH: **1 HOUR**

INGREDIENTS

1 BALL OF LEAF LARD PIECRUST
DOUGH (SEE PAGE 33)

ALL-PURPOSE FLOUR, FOR
DUSTING

3 CUPS PITTED AND SLICED PLUMS

½ CUP GRANULATED SUGAR,
PLUS 1 TABLESPOON

JUICE OF ½ LEMON

3 TABLESPOONS CORNSTARCH

PINCH OF SALT

2 TABLESPOONS BLACKBERRY JAM

1 EGG, BEATEN

DIRECTIONS

1. Preheat the oven to 400°F. Place the ball of dough on a flour-dusted work surface, roll it out to 9″, and place it on a parchment-lined baking sheet.

2. Place the plums, the ½ cup of sugar, lemon juice, cornstarch, and salt in a mixing bowl and stir until the plums are evenly coated.

3. Spread the jam over the crust, making sure to leave 1½″ of dough around the edge. Place the filling on top of the jam and fold the crust over it. Brush the crust with the beaten egg and sprinkle it with the remaining sugar.

4. Put the galette in the oven and bake until the crust is golden brown and the filling is bubbly, about 35 to 40 minutes. Remove from the oven and allow to cool before serving.

Plum Cake

YIELD: **8 TO 10 SERVINGS**

ACTIVE TIME: **20 MINUTES**

TOTAL TIME: **1 HOUR**

INGREDIENTS

¾ CUP ALL-PURPOSE FLOUR, PLUS MORE FOR DUSTING

2 TABLESPOONS SEEDLESS RASPBERRY JAM

3 TABLESPOONS BRANDY

1 LB. PLUMS, HALVED AND PITTED

¾ CUP GRANULATED SUGAR

⅓ CUP SLIVERED ALMONDS

½ TEASPOON BAKING POWDER

¼ TEASPOON SALT

6 TABLESPOONS UNSALTED BUTTER, DIVIDED INTO TABLESPOONS AND AT ROOM TEMPERATURE

1 TEASPOON PURE VANILLA EXTRACT

1 LARGE EGG, AT ROOM TEMPERATURE

YOLK OF 1 LARGE EGG, AT ROOM TEMPERATURE

DIRECTIONS

1. Preheat the oven to 350°F. Grease a 9″ springform pan and dust it with flour.

2. Place the jam and brandy in a skillet and cook over medium heat until it is syrupy, 2 to 3 minutes.

3. Remove the skillet from heat and add the plums, cut-side down. Cook over medium heat, while stirring occasionally, until the plums release their juices, about 5 minutes. Remove from heat and let cool.

4. Place the sugar and almonds in a food processor and pulse until the mixture is finely ground. Add the flour, baking powder, and salt to the food processor and pulse until combined.

5. Add the pieces of butter and pulse until the mixture is a coarse meal. Add the vanilla, egg, and egg yolk and process until the batter is smooth. Transfer the batter to the springform pan and place the plum slices on top, skin-side down. Place the cake in the oven and bake until golden brown and a toothpick inserted into the center comes out clean, about 30 minutes. Remove from the oven and let it cool in the pan.

Caramelized Plums with Honey-Ginger Frozen Yogurt

YIELD: **4 SERVINGS**

ACTIVE TIME: **15 MINUTES**

TOTAL TIME: **4 HOURS AND 30 MINUTES**

INGREDIENTS

2½ CUPS GREEK YOGURT

½ CUP EVAPORATED MILK

¼ TEASPOON PURE VANILLA EXTRACT

1 TEASPOON GRATED GINGER

⅛ CUP LIGHT CORN SYRUP

½ TEASPOON SALT

⅓ CUP HONEY

½ CUP GRANULATED SUGAR

2 PLUMS, PITTED AND CHOPPED INTO ½" PIECES

4 TABLESPOONS UNSALTED BUTTER

DIRECTIONS

1. Place the yogurt, evaporated milk, vanilla, ginger, corn syrup, salt, and honey in a mixing bowl and stir to combine. Pour the mixture into an ice cream maker and churn until the desired texture has been reached. Transfer to the freezer and freeze for at least 4 hours.

2. When ready to serve, place the sugar in a bowl and dip the pieces of plum into it until they are completely coated.

3. Place the butter in a large skillet and melt over medium heat. Add the pieces of plum and cook until golden brown all over, about 5 minutes.

4. Scoop the frozen yogurt into bowls and top with the caramelized plums.

Apricots in a Moscato Reduction

YIELD: **6 TO 8 SERVINGS**

ACTIVE TIME: **15 MINUTES**

TOTAL TIME: **10 TO 12 HOURS**

INGREDIENTS

3 CUPS MOSCATO D'ASTI

20 DRIED APRICOTS, SLICED

⅓ CUP GRANULATED SUGAR

½ TEASPOON GRATED NUTMEG

2 SPRIGS OF FRESH THYME

16 FRESH APRICOTS, SLICED

SHORTBREAD (SEE PAGE 293), FOR SERVING

DIRECTIONS

1. Bring the Moscato to boil in a small saucepan. Remove from heat and add the dried apricots. Cover the pan and let stand for 10 hours. Strain through a fine sieve, reserve 1 cup of the liquid, and place the infused dried apricots in a bowl.

2. Place the reserved liquid and the sugar in a small saucepan and bring to a boil over medium-high heat while stirring. Once the sugar has dissolved, add the nutmeg and thyme and simmer for 10 minutes. Remove pan from heat and remove the thyme. Place the syrup in the refrigerator and chill until cool.

3. Slice the rehydrated apricots and place them in a mixing bowl with the fresh apricots. Pour the syrup over the fruit and toss to coat. Serve with Shortbread.

CHAPTER 7

BERRIES

————————

There are times when even those with a fierce sweet tooth want
a break from the incessant stream of rich, heavy desserts. That
is when berry-based confections come to the rescue, offering
a lightness not often seen in the world of desserts, while still
providing the sugary conclusion so many desire at the end of a day.

As anyone who has sat down and stuffed their face in a patch
at the height of strawberry season will tell you, Mother Nature
is unsurpassed as a producer of sweets. When working with
ingredients this perfect, it's important to stay out of the way and
keep it simple. By turning out classics like Strawberry Shortcake
(see page 283), Blueberry Pie (see page 300), and Black Raspberry
Ice Cream (see page 315), you'll help spread this crucial message.

Strawberry Shortcake

YIELD: **6 SERVINGS**

ACTIVE TIME: **30 MINUTES**

TOTAL TIME: **1 HOUR AND 15 MINUTES**

INGREDIENTS

2 LBS. STRAWBERRIES, HULLED AND HALVED

¼ CUP GRANULATED SUGAR, PLUS 2 TABLESPOONS

2 CUPS ALL-PURPOSE FLOUR, PLUS MORE FOR DUSTING

2 TEASPOONS BAKING POWDER

½ TEASPOON LEMON ZEST

¼ TEASPOON CINNAMON

1½ CUPS HEAVY CREAM

WHIPPED CREAM (SEE PAGE 53)

DIRECTIONS

1. Preheat the oven to 400°F.

2. Place the strawberries and ¼ cup of sugar in a large bowl and cover with plastic wrap. Let the mixture sit until the strawberries start to release their juice, about 45 minutes.

3. Place the flour, baking powder, remaining sugar, lemon zest, and cinnamon in a mixing bowl and whisk to combine. Add the heavy cream very slowly and beat with a handheld mixer until a smooth dough forms.

4. Transfer the dough to a lightly floured work surface and roll it out into a 9 x 6-inch rectangle that is approximately ¾" thick. Use a floured biscuit cutter or mason jar to cut six rounds from the dough. Place the rounds on a greased baking sheet, place the sheet in the oven, and bake until golden brown, about 12 minutes. Remove from the oven and let cool for 10 minutes.

5. Starting at the equator, cut each of the cakes in half. Place a dollop of the Whipped Cream on top of one of the halves, followed by a few scoops of the strawberries and their juices. Top with the other half and serve.

Strawberry & Oat Bars

YIELD: **16 BARS**

ACTIVE TIME: **10 MINUTES**

TOTAL TIME: **1 HOUR AND 10 MINUTES**

INGREDIENTS

1½ CUPS GRANULATED SUGAR

¼ CUP HONEY

½ TEASPOON SALT

½ CUP WHOLE MILK

1 STICK UNSALTED BUTTER

3 CUPS ROLLED OATS

1 TABLESPOON PURE VANILLA
EXTRACT

½ CUP STRAWBERRY JAM

DIRECTIONS

1. Place the sugar, honey, salt, milk, and butter in a
    saucepan and cook, while stirring, over medium heat.
    When the sugar has dissolved, cook for another 2
    minutes.

2. Remove the saucepan from heat and stir in the oats,
    vanilla extract, and jam. Let the mixture cool for 2
    minutes.

3. Scoop the mixture onto a parchment-lined baking sheet
    and use a rubber spatula to evenly distribute it. Place the
    baking sheet in the refrigerator and chill until set, about
    1 hour. Remove from the refrigerator, slice into bars, and
    serve.

Sunset Cake

YIELD: **8 TO 10 SERVINGS**

ACTIVE TIME: **30 MINUTES**

TOTAL TIME: **24 HOURS**

INGREDIENTS

2 CUPS FROZEN WHOLE
STRAWBERRIES

¾ CUP WHOLE MILK, AT ROOM
TEMPERATURE

WHITES OF 6 LARGE EGGS, AT
ROOM TEMPERATURE

2 TEASPOONS PURE VANILLA
EXTRACT

2¼ CUPS CAKE FLOUR, PLUS MORE
FOR DUSTING

1¾ CUPS GRANULATED SUGAR

4 TEASPOONS BAKING POWDER

1 TEASPOON SALT

1½ STICKS UNSALTED BUTTER,
DIVIDED INTO TABLESPOONS AND
AT ROOM TEMPERATURE

VANILLA BUTTERCREAM FROSTING
(SEE PAGE 49)

DIRECTIONS

1. Place the strawberries in a large mixing bowl and let
    them thaw overnight.

2. Preheat the oven to 350°F and grease two round 9″ cake
    pans with nonstick cooking spray.

3. Place the juice from the thawed strawberries in a small
    saucepan and bring to a boil over medium-high heat.
    Cook, while stirring occasionally, until the mixture is
    syrupy and has reduced by two-thirds, about 6 minutes.
    Remove from the heat and briefly let cool. Add the milk
    and stir to combine.

4. Place the strawberry juice-and-milk mixture, egg whites,
    and vanilla in a mixing bowl and whisk to combine. Set
    aside. Place the flour, sugar, baking powder, and salt in
    a mixing bowl and whisk to combine. Add the butter 1
    tablespoon at a time and work the mixture with a pastry
    blender until it is a coarse meal consisting of pea-sized
    pieces. Add half of the egg white mixture and beat until
    the batter is light and fluffy. Add the remaining egg white
    mixture and beat until incorporated.

5. Divide the batter between the cake pans, place in the
    oven, and bake for 20 minutes, until a toothpick inserted
    in the center of each comes out clean. Remove from
    the oven and cool in the pans for 10 minutes. Remove
    the cakes from the pans and place on wire racks to cool
    completely.

6. Pat the thawed strawberries dry. Spread some of the
    frosting on top of one of the cakes. Place the other cake
    on top, flat-side up, and cover the entire cake with the
    rest of the frosting. Arrange the whole strawberries on
    top and serve.

Roasted Strawberry Handpies with Cinnamon Glaze

YIELD: **8 SERVINGS**

ACTIVE TIME: **40 MINUTES**

TOTAL TIME: **2 HOURS**

INGREDIENTS

3 QUARTS OF FRESH STRAWBERRIES, HULLED AND SLICED

1 CUP GRANULATED SUGAR

2 TEASPOONS FRESH LEMON JUICE

1 TABLESPOON CORNSTARCH

½ TABLESPOON WATER

1 BALL OF LEAF LARD PIECRUST DOUGH (SEE PAGE 33)

2 EGGS, BEATEN

1½ CUPS SIFTED CONFECTIONERS' SUGAR

3 TO 4 TABLESPOONS WHOLE MILK

1 TEASPOON CINNAMON

DIRECTIONS

1. Preheat the oven to 400°F.

2. Place the strawberries on a baking sheet and bake in the oven until they start to darken and release their juice, about 20 to 30 minutes. If you prefer, you can bake them for up to an hour. Cooking the strawberries for longer will caramelize the sugars and lend them an even richer flavor.

3. Remove the strawberries from the oven and place them in a saucepan with the sugar and lemon juice. Bring to a simmer over medium heat and cook for 20 minutes, until the mixture has thickened slightly.

4. Place the cornstarch and water in a small cup and stir until there are no lumps in the mixture. Add to the saucepan and stir until the mixture is syrupy. Remove from heat.

5. Divide the ball of piecrust dough into two squares and then cut each square into quarters. Spoon some of the strawberry mixture into the center of each quarter.

6. Take a bottom corner of each pie and fold to the opposite top corner. Press down to ensure that none of the mixture leaks out and then use a fork to seal the edge. Place the pies on a baking sheet and brush them with the beaten egg. Place in the oven and bake until golden brown, about 20 to 30 minutes.

7. While the pies are cooking, place the confectioners' sugar, milk, and cinnamon in a bowl and stir until well combined.

8. Remove the pies from the oven, brush them with the sugar-and-cinnamon glaze, and allow to cool before serving.

YIELD: **6 TO 8 SERVINGS**

ACTIVE TIME: **40 MINUTES**

TOTAL TIME: **4 HOURS**

Strawberry Pie

INGREDIENTS

¾ CUP GRANULATED SUGAR

3 TABLESPOONS CORNSTARCH

½ CUP WATER

6 CUPS FRESH STRAWBERRIES, HULLED AND HALVED

1 LEAF LARD PIECRUST (SEE PAGE 33), BLIND BAKED

½ CUP UNSWEETENED STRAWBERRY PRESERVES

WHIPPED CREAM (SEE PAGE 53), FOR SERVING (OPTIONAL)

VANILLA ICE CREAM (SEE PAGE 152 FOR HOMEMADE), FOR SERVING (OPTIONAL)

DIRECTIONS

1. Place the sugar, cornstarch, and water in a saucepan and cook, while stirring, over medium heat. When the sugar and cornstarch have dissolved, stir in 1 cup of the strawberry pieces and cook, while stirring, until the mixture begins to thicken and come to a boil. Continue to cook and stir the mixture for 5 minutes. Remove from the heat and let cool for 20 minutes.

2. Place the remaining strawberry pieces in even layers in the baked piecrust. When the mixture in the saucepan has cooled, pour it over the strawberries.

3. Place the strawberry preserves in a microwave-safe bowl. Microwave on medium until just melted, about 20 seconds. Stir and drizzle over the pie.

4. Cover the pie with plastic wrap and place in the refrigerator for at least 3 hours before serving. Place a dollop of Whipped Cream or a scoop of ice cream on top of each slice.

Strawberry Consommé with Cardamom Panna Cotta

YIELD: **4 SERVINGS**

ACTIVE TIME: **30 MINUTES**

TOTAL TIME: **5 HOURS**

INGREDIENTS

FOR THE CONSOMMÉ

2 QUARTS OF STRAWBERRIES, HULLED AND CHOPPED

½ CUP GRANULATED SUGAR

SEEDS OF 1 VANILLA BEAN

1 CINNAMON STICK

1 STAR ANISE POD

JUICE AND ZEST OF 2 LEMONS

1 SPRIG OF MINT

2 TABLESPOONS GRAND MARNIER

FOR THE PANNA COTTA

¾ CUP BUTTERMILK

¾ CUP HEAVY CREAM

SEEDS AND POD OF ½ VANILLA BEAN

SEEDS OF 2 CARDAMOM PODS, CHOPPED

2 TABLESPOONS SUGAR

1¼ TEASPOONS GELATIN

SHORTBREAD (SEE RECIPE), FOR SERVING

DIRECTIONS

1. To prepare the consommé, place all of the ingredients in a metal mixing bowl, stir to combine, and cover with plastic wrap.

2. Bring 2 cups of water to boil in a saucepan. Place the bowl over the saucepan and reduce the heat so that the water simmers. Cook the consommé for 1 hour, turn off the burner, and let stand for 1 hour.

3. After 1 hour, strain the mixture through a fine sieve and place it in the refrigerator for 1 hour.

4. While the consommé is chilling in the refrigerator, prepare the panna cotta. Place half of the buttermilk in a bowl and set aside. Place the remaining buttermilk, heavy cream, vanilla seeds and pod, the cardamom seeds, and the sugar in a small saucepan and bring to a simmer over medium-low heat. Remove from heat and let stand for 10 minutes.

5. Place the gelatin in the bowl of cold buttermilk and stir quickly to combine. Bring the contents of the saucepan to a boil over medium heat and add the buttermilk-and-gelatin mixture. Remove the pan from heat and stir gently for 2 minutes. Strain through a fine sieve and chill in the refrigerator for 15 minutes, removing to stir every 5 minutes. Pour the panna cotta into the serving dishes and refrigerate for 1 hour.

6. To serve, ladle the consommé over the panna cotta and serve with pieces of the Shortbread.

SHORTBREAD

2½ STICKS UNSALTED BUTTER

10 TABLESPOONS GRANULATED SUGAR

2½ CUPS ALL-PURPOSE FLOUR

1 TEASPOON SALT

1. Grate the butter into a bowl and place it in the freezer for 30 minutes.

2. Preheat the oven to 325°F.

3. Place ½ cup of the sugar, the flour, salt, and the frozen butter in the mixing bowl of a stand mixer fitted with the paddle attachment and beat on low until the mixture is fine like sand. Transfer the mixture to a greased square 8" cake pan, place in the oven, and bake for 1 hour and 15 minutes.

4. Remove from the oven, sprinkle the remaining sugar on top, and let cool before slicing and serving.

Strawberry Mousse

YIELD: **4 TO 6 SERVINGS**

ACTIVE TIME: **30 MINUTES**

TOTAL TIME: **7 HOURS AND 30 MINUTES**

INGREDIENTS

2 LBS. STRAWBERRIES, HULLED AND SLICED

¼ CUP GRANULATED SUGAR

PINCH OF SALT

1¾ TEASPOONS GELATIN

4 OZ. CREAM CHEESE, CUT INTO SMALL PIECES AND AT ROOM TEMPERATURE

WHIPPED CREAM (SEE PAGE 53)

DIRECTIONS

1. Reserve a few strawberry slices for topping. Place the remaining strawberries, sugar, and the salt in a mixing bowl. Toss to combine and then let the mixture stand for 45 minutes, while stirring occasionally.

2. Strain the mixture through a fine sieve and reserve the juice. Place 3 tablespoons in a small bowl, add the gelatin, and stir to combine. Let the mixture sit until the gelatin has softened.

3. Place the remaining juice in a saucepan and cook over medium-high heat until it has reduced by half, about 10 minutes. Remove pan from heat, add the softened gelatin mixture, and stir until the gelatin has dissolved. Add the cream cheese and whisk until the mixture is smooth.

4. Place the coated strawberries in a blender or food processor and puree until smooth. Strain the puree through a fine sieve to remove the seeds and pulp. Discard the solids, add the puree to the mixture in the saucepan, and whisk until combined. Add the Whipped Cream, whisk until incorporated, and divide the mixture between the serving dishes. Place in the refrigerator and chill for 6 hours. Top with the reserved slices of strawberries before serving.

Strawberry & Lemon Curd Trifle

YIELD: **4 TO 6 SERVINGS**

ACTIVE TIME: **45 MINUTES**

TOTAL TIME: **45 MINUTES**

INGREDIENTS

2 QUARTS OF FRESH STRAWBERRIES, HULLED AND SLICED

JUICE OF 1 LEMON

3 TABLESPOONS GRANULATED SUGAR

1 TEASPOON CORNSTARCH

4 CUPS HEAVY CREAM

1 TABLESPOON CONFECTIONERS' SUGAR

1 TEASPOON PURE VANILLA EXTRACT

1 TEASPOON LIMONCELLO

1½ CUPS LEMON CURD (SEE PAGE 387)

POUND CAKE (SEE PAGE 41), SLICED

DIRECTIONS

1. Place the strawberries, lemon juice, sugar, and cornstarch in a medium saucepan and cook over medium heat until strawberries soften and begin to give up their juice, approximately 5 minutes. Remove from heat and let cool.

2. Place the cream, confectioners' sugar, vanilla, and limoncello in a bowl and beat until soft peaks form. Very gently fold the lemon curd into the whipped cream.

3. Cover the bottom of a trifle dish with the lemon whipped cream. Place a layer of Pound Cake slices on top and then scoop the strawberry mixture on top of the pound cake. Repeat until all of the strawberries and slices of cake have been used, giving you three or four layers. Top with remaining lemon whipped cream and place in the refrigerator until ready to serve.

Strawberry Sorbet

YIELD: **8 SERVINGS**

ACTIVE TIME: **30 MINUTES**

TOTAL TIME: **9 HOURS AND 30 MINUTES**

INGREDIENTS

1 CUP GRANULATED SUGAR

½ CUP WATER

3 PINTS OF FRESH STRAWBERRIES, HULLED

¼ CUP FRESH LEMON JUICE

½ TEASPOON SALT

1 TEASPOON LEMON ZEST

DIRECTIONS

1. Place the sugar and water in a saucepan and cook over medium heat, while stirring, until the sugar has dissolved. Remove from heat and let cool.

2. Place the strawberries, lemon juice, salt, and lemon zest in a food processor and puree until smooth. Add the cooled simple syrup and blitz to incorporate. Place the mixture in the refrigerator and chill for 3 hours.

3. Remove the mixture from the refrigerator and pour into an ice cream maker. Churn until the desired consistency has been achieved, transfer to the freezer, and freeze for 6 hours before serving.

Blueberry Pie

YIELD: **6 TO 8 SERVINGS**

ACTIVE TIME: **30 MINUTES**

TOTAL TIME: **1 HOUR AND 30 MINUTES**

INGREDIENTS

6 CUPS FRESH OR FROZEN BLUEBERRIES

1 TABLESPOON FRESH LEMON JUICE

1 TEASPOON LEMON ZEST

¾ CUP GRANULATED SUGAR, PLUS 2 TABLESPOONS

ALL-PURPOSE FLOUR, FOR DUSTING

2 BALLS OF LEAF LARD PIECRUST DOUGH (SEE PAGE 33)

WHITE OF 1 EGG

DIRECTIONS

1. Preheat the oven to 350°F.

2. Place the blueberries, lemon juice, lemon zest, and ¾ cup of the sugar in a large mixing bowl and stir to combine.

3. Place the balls of dough on a flour-dusted work surface and roll them out to fit a 9″ pie plate. Place one crust in a greased 9″ pie plate, trim away any excess, and fill with the blueberry mixture. Place the other crust over the mixture and crimp to seal.

4. Brush the top crust with the egg white and then sprinkle the remaining sugar over it. Cut 4 or 5 slits in the middle, place the pie in the oven, and bake until the crust is golden brown and the filling is bubbling, about 45 minutes. Remove from the oven and let cool completely before serving.

A DAY TO REMEMBER

Some people think any time is a good time for pie, but for many people it is associated with a specific holiday or time of year: apple pie in October, pumpkin and pecan pie on Thanksgiving, and strawberry rhubarb pie as the summer gets underway.

But a pie getting official recognition and being honored with a day of its own means that it resides on an entirely different level. The blueberry pie has been regarded as such, using its considerable charm to transcend mere tradition and claim April 28 as National Blueberry Pie Day. Interestingly, this is far too early for those who live in Maine—where blueberry pie is the official state dessert—to enjoy a slice made with fresh berries, as blueberry season in the New England state typically runs from July to September.

Blueberry Buckle

YIELD: **8 TO 10 SERVINGS**

ACTIVE TIME: **20 MINUTES**

TOTAL TIME: **2 HOURS**

INGREDIENTS

2 CUPS ALL-PURPOSE FLOUR

¾ CUP GRANULATED SUGAR

½ CUP PACKED LIGHT BROWN SUGAR

¼ TEASPOON CINNAMON

¾ TEASPOON SALT

14 TABLESPOONS UNSALTED BUTTER, CUT INTO SMALL PIECES AND AT ROOM TEMPERATURE

1½ TEASPOONS BAKING POWDER

½ TEASPOON LEMON ZEST

1½ TEASPOONS PURE VANILLA EXTRACT

2 LARGE EGGS, AT ROOM TEMPERATURE

1 QUART OF FRESH BLUEBERRIES

DIRECTIONS

1. Preheat the oven to 350°F and grease a round 9″ cake pan.

2. Place ½ cup of the flour, 2 tablespoons of the granulated sugar, the brown sugar, cinnamon, and a pinch of the salt in a mixing bowl and mix until combined. Add 4 tablespoons of the butter and work the mixture with a pastry blender until it resembles wet sand. Set aside.

3. Place the remaining flour and the baking powder in a small bowl and whisk to combine. Place the remaining butter, sugar, salt, and the lemon zest in a mixing bowl and beat until the mixture is light and fluffy. Add the vanilla, beat until incorporated, and then add the eggs one at a time. Beat until incorporated and then gradually add the flour mixture. Beat until all of the flour has been incorporated. Add the blueberries and then fold the batter until it is homogenous and the blueberries have been evenly distributed. Scrape down the bowl as needed while mixing the batter.

4. Transfer the batter to the cake pan and smooth the surface with a rubber spatula. Sprinkle the sugar-and-cinnamon mixture over the batter, place the cake in the oven, and bake until it is golden brown and a toothpick inserted into the center comes out clean, about 50 minutes. Remove from the oven and let cool in the pan for 15 minutes.

5. Remove from the pan, transfer to a wire rack, and let cool to room temperature.

Chilled Blueberry & Yogurt Soup

YIELD: **4 SERVINGS**

ACTIVE TIME: **5 MINUTES**

TOTAL TIME: **30 MINUTES**

INGREDIENTS

1 PINT OF FRESH BLUEBERRIES, PLUS MORE FOR GARNISH

4 CUPS PLAIN GREEK YOGURT

1 CUP ORANGE JUICE

1 CUP CHAMPAGNE

SEEDS OF 1 VANILLA BEAN

1 TEASPOON CINNAMON

GRANULATED SUGAR, TO TASTE

DIRECTIONS

1. Place all of the ingredients, except for the sugar, in a food processor and gently pulse until combined.

2. Add sugar to taste and place the mixture in the refrigerator for 15 minutes.

3. Pour the mixture into chilled bowls or champagne flutes. Garnish with additional blueberries before serving.

Black & Blue Galette

YIELD: **6 TO 8 SERVINGS**

ACTIVE TIME: **20 MINUTES**

TOTAL TIME: **1 HOUR AND 30 MINUTES**

INGREDIENTS

1 BALL OF LEAF LARD PIECRUST DOUGH (SEE PAGE 33)

ALL-PURPOSE FLOUR, FOR DUSTING

1½ CUPS FRESH BLUEBERRIES

1½ CUPS FRESH BLACKBERRIES

½ CUP LIGHT BROWN SUGAR

JUICE OF ½ LEMON

3 TABLESPOONS CORNSTARCH

PINCH OF SALT

1 EGG, BEATEN

1 TABLESPOON GRANULATED SUGAR

DIRECTIONS

1. Preheat the oven to 400°F.

2. Roll out the ball of dough to 9" on a flour-dusted work surface and then place it on a parchment-lined baking sheet.

3. Place the berries, brown sugar, lemon juice, cornstarch, and salt in a large mixing bowl and stir until the berries are evenly coated.

4. Spread the coated berries over the piecrust, making sure to leave 1½" of crust at the edge. Fold the crust over the filling, brush the folded crust with the beaten egg, and sprinkle the granulated sugar over it.

5. Place the galette in the oven and bake until the crust is golden brown and the filling is bubbly, about 35 to 40 minutes. Remove from the oven and let cool before serving.

Blueberry Varenyky

YIELD: **36 VARENYKY**

ACTIVE TIME: **1 HOUR**

TOTAL TIME: **1 HOUR AND 30 MINUTES**

INGREDIENTS

FOR THE FILLING

3½ CUPS FRESH BLUEBERRIES

1 TABLESPOON GRANULATED SUGAR

ZEST OF 1 LEMON

FOR THE DOUGH

3 CUPS ALL-PURPOSE FLOUR, PLUS MORE AS NEEDED

½ TEASPOON SALT, PLUS MORE TO TASTE

9 TABLESPOONS UNSALTED BUTTER

⅔ CUP SOUR CREAM, AT ROOM TEMPERATURE

1 LARGE EGG, BEATEN

WATER, AS NEEDED

1 TABLESPOON VEGETABLE OIL

CONFECTIONERS' SUGAR, FOR DUSTING

DIRECTIONS

1. To prepare the filling, place two-thirds of the blueberries in a medium saucepan. Add the sugar and lemon zest and stir to combine. Cook over medium heat, while stirring occasionally, until the blueberries burst and release their juice, about 4 minutes. Reduce the heat to low and simmer until the mixture is very thick, about 18 minutes. Stir in the remaining blueberries, remove the pan from heat, and let cool completely.

2. To prepare the dough, place the flour and salt in the mixing bowl of a stand mixer. Add 4 tablespoons of the butter and the sour cream and beat on medium speed until a crumbly dough forms, about 5 minutes.

3. Place the egg in a measuring cup and add just enough water for the mixture to measure ¾ cup. Beat until combined and pour into the mixing bowl. Beat on medium speed until the dough holds together and is no longer sticky. If the dough is sticky, incorporate more flour, 1 teaspoon at a time.

4. Place the dough on a flour-dusted work surface and roll out to ⅛" thick. Use a mason jar or cookie cutter to cut as many 3" rounds from the dough as possible. Place the rounds on a parchment-lined baking sheet and lightly dust with flour. When you have as many as you can fit in a single layer, cover with another piece of parchment.

5. To fill the varenyky, place a round in a slightly cupped hand and hold it so that it takes the shape of a taco. Place 1 teaspoon of the filling in the center. Using your thumb and index finger, firmly pinch the edges together to form a tight seal. You'll want this seal, or seam, to be approximately ¼" wide. Pat the sealed varenyky gently to evenly distribute the filling. Check for holes (patch them with a little bit of dough) and make sure the seal is tight. Reserve any leftover filling.

6. Bring a large pot of salted water to a boil. Once it's boiling, add the vegetable oil and stir. Working in batches, add the varenyky to the water and stir for 1 minute to keep them from sticking to the bottom. After the dumplings float to the surface, cook for another 3 minutes.

7. While the first batch of varenyky boils, melt the remaining butter in a microwave or in a skillet over low heat. Remove the varenyky from the water using a large slotted spoon and let them drain for a few seconds over the pot. Transfer to a warmed platter, top them with some of the melted butter, and gently toss. Tent loosely with aluminum foil to keep them warm while you cook the remaining dumplings.

8. To serve, dust the varenyky with the confectioners' sugar and top with any remaining filling.

Yogurt Custard Pie with Blueberry & Basil Jam

YIELD: **6 TO 8 SERVINGS**

ACTIVE TIME: **45 MINUTES**

TOTAL TIME: **3 HOURS**

INGREDIENTS

FOR THE JAM

2 PINTS OF FRESH BLUEBERRIES

¼ CUP BASIL LEAVES, MINCED

⅔ TEASPOON FRESH LEMON JUICE

⅔ CUP GRANULATED SUGAR

1 TABLESPOON WATER

FOR THE PIE

1 CUP PLAIN GREEK YOGURT

2 EGGS, LIGHTLY BEATEN

¼ CUP GRANULATED SUGAR

3 TABLESPOONS FRESH LEMON JUICE

1 TEASPOON PURE VANILLA EXTRACT

1 GRAHAM CRACKER CRUST (SEE PAGE 34)

1 CUP FRESH BLUEBERRIES, FOR GARNISH

DIRECTIONS

1. To prepare the jam, place all of the ingredients in a saucepan and bring to a boil over medium-high heat, while stirring frequently. Reduce the heat and simmer, while continuing to stir frequently, until the mixture has reduced by half and is starting to thicken. Remove from heat and let it thicken as it cools.

2. Preheat the oven to 350°F.

3. To prepare the pie, place the yogurt, eggs, sugar, lemon juice, and vanilla in a mixing bowl and stir to combine. Transfer the filling into the piecrust and use a rubber spatula to distribute it evenly and smooth the top.

4. Place the pie in the oven and bake until the filling is just set, about 25 minutes. A toothpick inserted at the edge of the pie will come out clean, but the center may look slightly undercooked. Remove from the oven and let the pie cool for 10 minutes.

5. Spread the cooled jam over the surface of the pie and arrange the blueberries on top. Place in the refrigerator and chill for 2 hours before serving. Place any leftover jam in a sterilized mason jar and store in the refrigerator for up to 1 week.

Raspberry Pie Bars

YIELD: **12 TO 24 BARS**

ACTIVE TIME: **15 MINUTES**

TOTAL TIME: **1 HOUR**

INGREDIENTS

2 BALLS OF LEAF LARD PIECRUST DOUGH (SEE PAGE 33)

⅔ CUP ALL-PURPOSE FLOUR, PLUS MORE FOR DUSTING

7 CUPS FRESH RASPBERRIES

2 CUPS GRANULATED SUGAR, PLUS MORE TO TASTE

2 TABLESPOONS FRESH LEMON JUICE

PINCH OF SALT

1 EGG, BEATEN

DIRECTIONS

1. Preheat the oven to 350°F and grease a rimmed 15 x 10-inch baking sheet.

2. Roll out one of the balls of dough on lightly floured work surface so that it fits the baking sheet. Place it in the pan, press down to ensure that it is even, and prick it with a fork. Roll out the other crust so that it is slightly larger than the sheet.

3. Place the raspberries, sugar, flour, lemon juice, and salt in a mixing bowl and stir until well combined. Spread this mixture evenly across the crust in the baking sheet.

4. Place the top crust over the filling and trim any excess. Brush the top crust with the egg and sprinkle additional sugar on top.

5. Place the bars in the oven and bake until golden brown, about 40 minutes. Remove from the oven and let cool before slicing.

SHADES OF BLACK

Rarely seen outside of the ice cream stand, most folks assume that the black raspberry is just another name for the blackberries they regularly encounter at the farmers market or grocery store.

But despite the similarities in appearance, there are a few crucial differences. The black raspberry is less tart than the blackberry and its red counterpart. The black raspberry is fruitier and also not as sweet as the blackberry, which has high levels of sugar. This diminished sweetness and tartness lend the flavor of the black raspberry a floral quality that shines in a rich, custardy ice cream.

That said, taste is not the only way to recognize the difference between the two: the black raspberry will have small hairs and will be hollow inside, since it comes directly off the bush, as opposed to the blackberry, which must be pulled from a stem.

Black Raspberry Ice Cream

YIELD: **4 CUPS**

ACTIVE TIME: **30 MINUTES**

TOTAL TIME: **24 HOURS**

INGREDIENTS

2½ CUPS HEAVY CREAM

1½ CUPS WHOLE MILK

1 CUP GRANULATED SUGAR

SALT, TO TASTE

YOLKS OF 6 LARGE EGGS

1 TEASPOON PURE VANILLA EXTRACT

5 CUPS BLACK RASPBERRIES

DIRECTIONS

1. Place the cream, milk, sugar, and salt in a saucepan, warm over medium heat until it starts to bubble, and remove from heat. Take care not to let the mixture come to a boil.

2. Place the egg yolks in a glass mixing bowl and whisk to combine. While whisking constantly, add one-third of the warm milk mixture to the egg yolks. When incorporated, whisk the tempered egg yolks into the saucepan.

3. Cook over medium-low heat, while stirring constantly, until the mixture is thick enough to coat the back of a wooden spoon, about 5 minutes. Take care not to let the mixture come to a boil. Strain through a fine mesh sieve and stir in the vanilla. Set the mixture aside.

4. Place the raspberries in a blender and puree until smooth. Strain through a fine sieve to remove the seeds and then stir the puree into the custard. Cover and place in the refrigerator to chill overnight.

5. Pour the mixture in an ice cream maker and churn until the desired consistency is achieved. Place in the freezer for 6 hours before serving.

Miniature Raspberry & Cream Tarts

YIELD: **12 TARTS**

ACTIVE TIME: **35 MINUTES**

TOTAL TIME: **2 HOURS**

INGREDIENTS

1 BALL OF TART PASTRY SHELL DOUGH (SEE PAGE 38)

ALL-PURPOSE FLOUR, FOR DUSTING

2¾ CUPS WHOLE MILK

⅛ TEASPOON SALT

⅔ CUP GRANULATED SUGAR

YOLKS OF 4 EGGS

¼ CUP CORNSTARCH

2 TABLESPOONS UNSALTED BUTTER

1 TEASPOON PURE VANILLA EXTRACT

1 CUP FRESH RASPBERRIES

CONFECTIONERS' SUGAR, FOR DUSTING

DIRECTIONS

1. Preheat the oven to 350°F and spray a muffin tin with nonstick cooking spray.

2. Roll the ball of dough out on a flour-dusted work surface to ¼" thickness. Using a floured biscuit cutter or mason jar, cut 12 rounds out of the dough and place them in the cups of the muffin tin. Place in the oven and bake until golden brown, about 25 minutes. Remove from the oven and let cool.

3. Place the milk, salt, and sugar in large saucepan and bring to a simmer over medium heat.

4. Place the egg yolks and cornstarch in a large bowl and whisk to combine. While whisking constantly, add the warm milk mixture to the egg mixture in ½-cup increments. When 2 cups of the milk mixture have been incorporated, add the tempered eggs to the saucepan, while whisking constantly to incorporate.

5. Cook the mixture over medium heat, while stirring constantly, until it starts to thicken. Stir in the butter and vanilla and spoon the mixture into the baked tart shells. Place in the refrigerator and chill until cool.

6. Remove from the refrigerator, top each tart with a few raspberries and a dusting of confectioners' sugar, and serve.

Raspberry Ice Cream Cake

YIELD: **8 TO 10 SERVINGS**

ACTIVE TIME: **20 MINUTES**

TOTAL TIME: **1 HOUR AND 20 MINUTES**

INGREDIENTS

1 LARGE PACKAGE OF LADYFINGERS

1 PINT OF VANILLA ICE CREAM
(SEE PAGE 152 FOR HOMEMADE)

1 (12 OZ.) JAR OF RASPBERRY
PRESERVES

1 PINT OF BLACK RASPBERRY
ICE CREAM (SEE PAGE 315 FOR
HOMEMADE)

1 PINT OF FRESH RASPBERRIES,
FOR TOPPING (OPTIONAL)

WHIPPED CREAM (SEE PAGE 53),
FOR TOPPING (OPTIONAL)

DIRECTIONS

1. Line the bottom of a 9″ springform pan with some of the ladyfingers.

2. Spread a layer of vanilla ice cream on top. Spread a thin layer of raspberry preserves on top of the vanilla ice cream and then add a layer of the black raspberry ice cream. Add another layer of raspberry preserves, top with ladyfingers, and repeat until you reach the top of the pan.

3. Place the pan in the freezer for at least 1 hour. When ready to serve, top each piece with fresh raspberries and a dollop of Whipped Cream, if desired.

Classic Summer Fruit Salad

YIELD: **8 TO 10 SERVINGS**

ACTIVE TIME: **5 MINUTES**

TOTAL TIME: **25 MINUTES**

INGREDIENTS

5 FRESH MINT LEAVES, MINCED

¼ CUP FRESH ORANGE JUICE

1 TEASPOON HONEY

1 PINT OF FRESH STRAWBERRIES, HULLED AND HALVED

1 PINT OF FRESH BLUEBERRIES

1 PINT OF FRESH RASPBERRIES

2 CUPS SEEDLESS GRAPES, HALVED

DIRECTIONS

1. Place the mint, orange juice, and honey in a bowl, stir to combine, and set aside.

2. In a large bowl, combine the strawberries, blueberries, raspberries, and grapes. Add dressing and toss to coat.

3. Place in refrigerator and chill for 20 minutes before serving.

Mixed Berry Pie

INGREDIENTS

1½ CUPS FRESH BLUEBERRIES

1 CUP FRESH BLACKBERRIES

1 CUP FRESH RASPBERRIES

1½ CUPS FRESH STRAWBERRIES, HULLED AND HALVED

1 TABLESPOON FRESH LEMON JUICE

½ CUP LIGHT BROWN SUGAR

2 TABLESPOONS CORNSTARCH

½ CUP UNSWEETENED RASPBERRY PRESERVES

2 BALLS OF LEAF LARD PIECRUST DOUGH (SEE PAGE 33)

ALL-PURPOSE FLOUR, FOR DUSTING

1 EGG, BEATEN

DIRECTIONS

1. Preheat the oven to 375°F and grease a 9" pie plate.

2. Place all of the berries and the lemon juice, brown sugar, and cornstarch in a large bowl and toss to combine. Transfer the fruit to a large saucepan and cook over medium heat until the berries start to break down, 7 to 10 minutes. Stir in the preserves, remove the pan from heat, and set the mixture aside.

3. Place the balls of dough on a flour-dusted work surface and roll them out to fit the prepared pie plate. Transfer one of the crusts to the pie plate and fill it with the berry mixture.

4. Cut the other crust into 1" thick strips. Lay some of the strips over the pie and trim the strips so that they fit. To make a lattice crust, lift every other strip and fold them back so you can place another strip across those strips that remain flat. Lay the folded strips back down over the cross-strip. Fold back the strips that you laid the cross-strip on top of, and repeat until the lattice covers the surface of the pie. Brush the strips with the beaten egg, taking care not to get any egg on the filling.

5. Place the pie in the oven and bake for 45 minutes, until the crust is golden brown and the filling is bubbling. Remove from the oven and let cool before serving.

Berry Compote

YIELD: **2 CUPS**

ACTIVE TIME: **10 MINUTES**

TOTAL TIME: **15 MINUTES**

INGREDIENTS

4 TABLESPOONS UNSALTED BUTTER

1 CUP BLUEBERRIES

1 CUP BLACKBERRIES

1 CUP RASPBERRIES

½ CUP STRAWBERRIES

⅓ CUP LIGHT BROWN SUGAR

1 TABLESPOON HONEY

½ TEASPOON SALT

3 TABLESPOONS FRESH LEMON JUICE

1 TEASPOON LEMON ZEST

DIRECTIONS

1. Place the butter in a saucepan and cook over medium heat until melted. Add the berries, brown sugar, honey, and salt and stir. Cook for 5 to 6 minutes while mashing the berries so that they release their juices.

2. Add the lemon juice and lemon zest and cook for another 2 minutes. Remove from heat and let stand for 5 minutes. Enjoy by itself or spoon over slices of Pound Cake (see page 41) or Shortbread (see page 293).

Mixed Berry Clafoutis

YIELD: **6 SERVINGS**

ACTIVE TIME: **20 MINUTES**

TOTAL TIME: **1 HOUR**

INGREDIENTS

1 STICK UNSALTED BUTTER, MELTED

1 CUP GRANULATED SUGAR, PLUS 2 TEASPOONS

⅔ CUP ALL-PURPOSE FLOUR

½ TEASPOON SALT

1 TEASPOON PURE VANILLA EXTRACT

3 EGGS, BEATEN

1 CUP WHOLE MILK

1 CUP FRESH BLUEBERRIES

1 CUP FRESH RASPBERRIES

1 CUP FRESH BLACKBERRIES OR STRAWBERRIES

CONFECTIONERS' SUGAR, FOR TOPPING

DIRECTIONS

1. Preheat the oven to 400°F.

2. Place 6 tablespoons of the butter, ½ cup of the granulated sugar, the flour, salt, vanilla, eggs, and milk in a mixing bowl and stir until blended and smooth. Set aside.

3. Use the remaining butter to grease a cast-iron skillet (a gratin dish or tart pan can also be used). Place the cast-iron skillet in the oven to warm up.

4. Remove the skillet from the oven, add ½ cup of the granulated sugar, and shake to evenly distribute over the bottom. Add the berries and then pour the batter over the berries. Sprinkle with the remaining sugar and return the skillet to the oven. Bake until the clafoutis is puffy, golden brown, and set in the center, about 35 minutes.

5. Remove from the oven, sprinkle with confectioners' sugar, and serve warm or at room temperature.

Triple Berry Galette

YIELD: **4 TO 6 SERVINGS**

ACTIVE TIME: **20 MINUTES**

TOTAL TIME: **1 HOUR**

INGREDIENTS

1 BALL OF LEAF LARD PIECRUST DOUGH (SEE PAGE 33)

ALL-PURPOSE FLOUR, FOR DUSTING

1 CUP FRESH BLUEBERRIES

1 CUP FRESH BLACKBERRIES

1 CUP FRESH RASPBERRIES

½ CUP GRANULATED SUGAR, PLUS 1 TABLESPOON

JUICE OF ½ LEMON

3 TABLESPOONS CORNSTARCH

PINCH OF SALT

1 EGG, BEATEN

DIRECTIONS

1. Preheat the oven to 400°F.

2. Roll out the ball of dough to 9" on a flour-dusted work surface and then place it on a parchment-lined baking sheet.

3. Place the berries, ½ cup of sugar, lemon juice, cornstarch, and salt in a mixing bowl and stir until the berries are evenly coated.

4. Spread the mixture over the crust, making sure to leave 1½" of crust at the edge. Fold the crust over the filling, brush the folded crust with the beaten egg, and sprinkle the remaining sugar over it.

5. Place the galette in the oven and bake until the filling is bubbly and has thickened, about 35 minutes. Remove from the oven and let cool before serving.

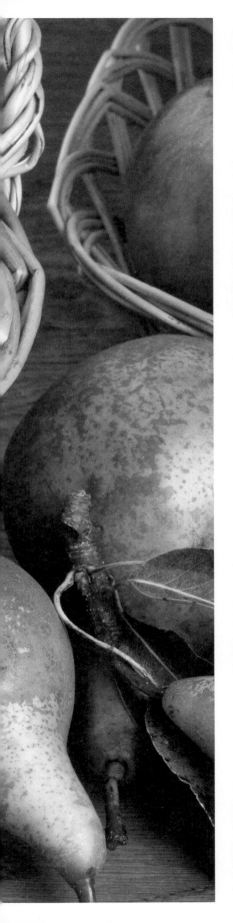

CHAPTER 8

APPLES & PEARS

Signs of humanity's deep affinity for the apple are everywhere. Synonymous with wholesomeness, intellect, and, thanks to Steve Wozniak and Steve Jobs, innovation, it is widely believed to be the first fruit that humans cultivated.

Its characterization as irresistible temptation is also deeply embedded in human consciousness. Cast as the initiator of both the fall in the Garden and the Trojan War, and the vessel that the wicked queen chose in her desperate attempt to take down Snow White, the idea that we are powerless against the apple's sweetness carries considerable weight. And, when that flavor is combined with sugar and spice and couched in an apple pie or a tarte Tatin, it's easy to see why.

The considerable attention the apple receives frequently crowds out the pear, but its sweet, creamy flesh and a flavor that carries strong notes of vanilla and citrus just may put you firmly on the side of this underdog.

APPLE OF YOUR EYE

While tradition recognizes the Granny Smith, with its tart taste and firm flesh, as the clear favorite, those who are fortunate to have access to the Northern Spy, which prefers cooler climates, swear that it is the best option when baking apple pies. Those who want straight sweetness in a pie trumpet the Honeycrisp, as it is not only sweet, but sturdy enough to not turn to mush in the oven.

All-American Apple Pie

YIELD: **8 TO 10 SERVINGS**

ACTIVE TIME: **35 MINUTES**

TOTAL TIME: **2 HOURS**

INGREDIENTS

8 CUPS PEELED, CORED, AND SLICED APPLES

2 TABLESPOONS FRESH LEMON JUICE

½ CUP GRANULATED SUGAR

2 TEASPOONS CINNAMON

PINCH OF SALT

¼ CUP ALL-PURPOSE FLOUR, PLUS MORE FOR DUSTING

2 BALLS OF LEAF LARD PIECRUST DOUGH (SEE PAGE 33)

1 EGG, BEATEN

DIRECTIONS

1. Place the apple slices, lemon juice, and sugar in a large saucepan and cook over medium heat until the apples are just beginning to soften.

2. Add the cinnamon and salt and cook for another minute. Strain the mixture through a fine sieve, reserve the liquid, and place the apples in a mixing bowl.

3. Return the reserved liquid to the saucepan, add the flour, and whisk to prevent lumps from forming. Cook until the liquid starts to thicken. Pour into the bowl containing the apples, stir to combine, and let cool completely. Preheat the oven to 450°F and grease a 9" pie plate.

4. When the apple mixture is cool, place the balls of dough on a flour-dusted work surface and roll them out so that they fit the pie plate. Place one of the crusts in the prepared pie plate and then evenly distribute the apple mixture inside of the crust. Place the remaining crust on top, crimp to seal, and cut 4 to 5 slits in the center. Brush the beaten egg over the top crust.

5. Place the pie in the oven and bake for 15 minutes. Reduce the temperature to 350°F and bake until the crust is golden brown and the filling is bubbling, about 30 minutes. Remove from the oven and let cool before serving.

Apple Upside Down Cake

YIELD: **8 TO 10 SERVINGS**

ACTIVE TIME: **15 MINUTES**

TOTAL TIME: **1 HOUR AND 45 MINUTES**

INGREDIENTS

10 TABLESPOONS UNSALTED BUTTER, MELTED

2 LBS. GOLDEN DELICIOUS APPLES, PEELED, CORED, AND SLICED

2 TEASPOONS FRESH LEMON JUICE

1 CUP PACKED LIGHT BROWN SUGAR

1 CUP ALL-PURPOSE FLOUR

1 TEASPOON BAKING POWDER

1 TABLESPOON CORNMEAL

½ TEASPOON SALT

¾ CUP GRANULATED SUGAR

2 LARGE EGGS

½ CUP SOUR CREAM

1 TEASPOON PURE VANILLA EXTRACT

DIRECTIONS

1. Preheat the oven to 350°F and grease a round 9″ cake pan with nonstick cooking spray.

2. Place 4 tablespoons of the butter in a cast-iron skillet and warm over medium-high heat. Add the apple slices and cook, while stirring occasionally, until they begin to caramelize, about 5 minutes. Add the lemon juice and a third of the brown sugar and cook, while stirring constantly, until the sugar has dissolved. Transfer the mixture to the cake pan, press into an even layer, and set aside.

3. Place the flour, baking powder, cornmeal, and salt in a mixing bowl and whisk until combined. Set aside.

4. Place the granulated sugar, remaining brown sugar, and eggs in a large bowl and beat until combined. Whisk in the remaining butter, the sour cream, and vanilla until they have been incorporated.

5. Add the wet mixture to the dry mixture and whisk until combined, taking care not to overmix. Pour the batter over the fruit in the pan, place the cake in the oven, and bake until golden brown and a toothpick inserted into the center comes out clean, about 35 minutes. Remove the pan from the oven and let cool for 20 minutes.

6. Invert the cake onto a large platter and place any fruit stuck to the bottom of the pan on top of the cake. Let cool for 30 minutes before serving.

Cider-Glazed Apple Bundt Cake

YIELD: **8 TO 10 SERVINGS**

ACTIVE TIME: **25 MINUTES**

TOTAL TIME: **2 HOURS AND 45 MINUTES**

INGREDIENTS

2 CUPS APPLE CIDER

3¾ CUPS ALL-PURPOSE FLOUR

1½ TEASPOONS BAKING POWDER

½ TEASPOON BAKING SODA

1½ TEASPOONS SALT

¾ TEASPOON CINNAMON

¼ TEASPOON ALLSPICE

¾ CUP CONFECTIONERS' SUGAR

2 STICKS UNSALTED BUTTER, MELTED

1½ CUPS PACKED DARK BROWN SUGAR

3 LARGE EGGS

2 TEASPOONS PURE VANILLA EXTRACT

1½ LBS. GRANNY SMITH APPLES, PEELED, CORED, AND GRATED

DIRECTIONS

1. Preheat the oven to 350°F and grease a Bundt pan with nonstick cooking spray.

2. Place the cider in a saucepan and cook over high heat until it has reduced by half, about 10 minutes. Set aside.

3. Place the flour, baking powder, baking soda, salt, cinnamon, and allspice in a large bowl and whisk until combined. Place confectioners' sugar in a separate bowl.

4. Add 2 tablespoons of the reduced cider to the confectioners' sugar and whisk until smooth. Cover with plastic wrap and set aside. Pour the remaining cider reduction into a large mixing bowl. Add the butter, brown sugar, eggs, and vanilla and whisk until smooth. Pour the cider-and-eggs mixture over the flour mixture and stir until almost all of the flour has been incorporated.

5. Add the apples and stir until combined. Transfer the mixture to the Bundt pan and smooth the top with a rubber spatula. Place in the oven and bake until a toothpick inserted into the center of the cake comes out clean, about 1 hour.

6. Remove the cake from the oven and set on a wire rack. Let cool for 10 minutes. Invert cake onto the wire rack and let cool for 20 minutes.

7. Stir the glaze and drizzle over the cake. Let the cake cool completely before serving.

Dutch Apple Baby

YIELD: **4 SERVINGS**

ACTIVE TIME: **20 MINUTES**

TOTAL TIME: **1 HOUR**

INGREDIENTS

4 TABLESPOONS UNSALTED BUTTER

2 FIRM AND TART APPLES, CORED, PEELED, AND SLICED

¼ CUP GRANULATED SUGAR, PLUS 3 TABLESPOONS

1 TABLESPOON CINNAMON

¾ CUP ALL-PURPOSE FLOUR

¼ TEASPOON SALT

¾ CUP WHOLE MILK

4 EGGS

1 TEASPOON PURE VANILLA EXTRACT

CONFECTIONERS' SUGAR, FOR DUSTING

DIRECTIONS

1. Preheat the oven to 425°F and place a rack in the middle position. Warm a cast-iron skillet over medium-high heat. Add the butter and apples and cook, while stirring, until the apples soften, about 3 to 4 minutes. Add the ¼ cup of sugar and the cinnamon and cook for another 3 or 4 minutes. Distribute the apples evenly over the bottom of the skillet and remove from heat.

2. In a large bowl, mix the remaining sugar, flour, and salt together. In a smaller bowl, whisk together the milk, eggs, and vanilla extract. Add the wet mixture to the dry mixture and stir to combine. Pour the resulting batter over the apples.

3. Put the skillet in the oven and bake until puffy and golden brown, about 20 minutes. Remove the skillet from the oven and let cool for a few minutes. Run a knife along the edge of the skillet to loosen the dessert and then, using oven mitts or pot holders, invert it onto a large plate. Dust with the confectioners' sugar and serve warm.

LES FLEURS DU MAL

The apple is the fruit most commonly cast as the temptation Eve could not resist. The origin of this association is believed to be the result of a clever pun made by Saint Jerome, a fourth-century scholar of scripture. Asked by Pope Damasus to translate the Hebrew Bible into the Latin spoken by the common man, Jerome stumbled upon a delicious coincidence when working on the Book of Genesis. In the Hebrew version, the generic term *peri*, which can pertain to any fruit, is used. But Jerome, perhaps in a desire to capture the gravity of the moment, selected *malus*, which is the Latin word for both "apple" and "evil." Apple had a wider meaning in Jerome's time than it does today, but as the fruit grew in popularity, the association became fixed in people's minds.

Apple Strudel

YIELD: **4 TO 6 SERVINGS**

ACTIVE TIME: **25 MINUTES**

TOTAL TIME: **1 HOUR AND 30 MINUTES**

INGREDIENTS

¾ LB. APPLES, PEELED, CORED, AND CUT INTO ½-INCH PIECES

¼ TEASPOON LEMON ZEST

1 TEASPOON FRESH LEMON JUICE

1½ TABLESPOONS GRANULATED SUGAR

DASH OF CINNAMON

¼ TEASPOON GROUND GINGER

2 PINCHES OF SALT

4 TABLESPOONS UNSALTED BUTTER, MELTED

7 SHEETS FROZEN PHYLLO DOUGH, THAWED

1 TABLESPOON CONFECTIONERS' SUGAR, PLUS MORE FOR DUSTING

DIRECTIONS

1. Preheat the oven to 350°F.

2. Place the apples, lemon zest, lemon juice, granulated sugar, cinnamon, ginger, and a pinch of salt in a large mixing bowl and toss until the apples are evenly coated. Place the mixture in a skillet and cook over medium heat until the apples begin to release their liquid. Remove from heat and let stand for 10 minutes before draining the mixture.

3. Place the melted butter in a bowl and stir in the remaining salt.

4. Brush a sheet of phyllo dough with some of the salted butter and lightly dust it with some of the confectioners' sugar. Repeat with the remaining sheets of phyllo dough, stacking them on top of one another after they have been dressed.

5. Place the apple mixture in the center of the phyllo sheets, leaving 2″ of dough open on the bottom and sides. Fold the bottom and sides over the filling so that they overlap and gently press down to seal. Place on a parchment-lined baking sheet and bake, while rotating the sheet halfway through, until the strudel is golden brown, 30 to 40 minutes. Remove from the oven, transfer to a cutting board, and let cool slightly. Slice into desired portions and dust with additional confectioners' sugar before serving.

Smoked Apple Crisp

YIELD: **8 TO 10 SERVINGS**

ACTIVE TIME: **35 MINUTES**

TOTAL TIME: **2 HOURS AND 30 MINUTES**

INGREDIENTS

1 CUP HICKORY OR APPLEWOOD CHIPS

4 LBS. APPLES, SLICED (BALDWIN OR GRANNY SMITH RECOMMENDED)

1 CUP GRANULATED SUGAR

1 CUP ALL-PURPOSE FLOUR

1 TABLESPOON CINNAMON

1 CUP OATS

1 CUP BROWN SUGAR

¼ TEASPOON BAKING SODA

¼ TEASPOON BAKING POWDER

1 STICK UNSALTED BUTTER, AT ROOM TEMPERATURE

1 TEASPOON NUTMEG

DIRECTIONS

1. Soak the wood chips in a bowl of water 1 hour before you are ready to cook the apples.

2. Bring your smoker to 250°F. Place the soaked wood chips in the smoking tray and place the apples in the smoker. Smoke for 8 to 10 minutes. Remove the apples and set aside.

3. Preheat the oven to 350°F. Place the sugar, flour, 2 teaspoons of the cinnamon, oats, brown sugar, baking soda, and baking powder in a mixing bowl and mix by hand until combined. Add the butter and mix until the butter has been incorporated and the mixture is a coarse, crumbly meal.

4. Place the apples in a bowl with the remaining cinnamon, the nutmeg, and half of the crumble. Toss until the apples are evenly coated. Transfer this mixture into a greased baking dish, top with the remaining crumble, and bake until golden brown, about 35 to 45 minutes.

YOU DO HAVE A SMOKER

If you don't have a smoker, that doesn't mean this preparation is out of reach—you can easily turn your gas or charcoal grill into an effective approximation of a smoker. To use a grill to smoke the apples, prepare one side of the grill for indirect heat. To do this, bank the coals to one side of a charcoal grill or leave one of the burners off on a gas grill. When the grill is 300°F, place the soaked wood chips on the coals or in a smoker box for a gas grill. Place the apples over indirect heat, cover the grill, and smoke for 8 to 10 minutes.

Apple Turnovers

YIELD: **4 SERVINGS**

ACTIVE TIME: **25 MINUTES**

TOTAL TIME: **1 HOUR AND 15 MINUTES**

INGREDIENTS

2 APPLES, PEELED, CORED, AND CHOPPED

¾ CUP GRANULATED SUGAR

1 TABLESPOON FRESH LEMON JUICE

PINCH OF SALT

¼ CUP APPLESAUCE

1 SHEET FROZEN PUFF PASTRY, THAWED

ALL-PURPOSE FLOUR, FOR DUSTING

1 TEASPOON CINNAMON

DIRECTIONS

1. Preheat the oven to 375°F.

2. Place the apples, 10 tablespoons of the sugar, lemon juice, and salt in a food processor and pulse until the apples are minced. Strain through a fine sieve, reserve the liquid, and place the solids in a small bowl. Stir in the applesauce and let sit for 5 minutes.

3. Place the sheet of puff pastry on a flour-dusted work surface and cut it into quarters. Place 2 tablespoons of the apple mixture in the middle of each quarter and brush the edges with some of the reserved liquid. Fold a bottom corner of each quarter to the opposing top corner and crimp to seal. Place the sealed pastries in the refrigerator for 10 minutes.

4. Place the remaining sugar and the cinnamon in a small bowl and stir to combine.

5. Place the turnovers on a parchment-lined baking sheet and brush the tops with some of the reserved liquid. Sprinkle with the cinnamon-and-sugar mixture, place the sheet in the oven, and bake, while rotating the baking sheet halfway through, until the turnovers are golden brown, about 25 minutes. Remove from the oven, transfer to wire racks, and let cool.

Tarte Tatin

YIELD: **6 TO 8 SERVINGS**

ACTIVE TIME: **30 MINUTES**

TOTAL TIME: **2 HOURS**

INGREDIENTS

1⅓ CUPS ALL-PURPOSE FLOUR, PLUS MORE FOR DUSTING

½ TEASPOON SALT

¾ CUP GRANULATED SUGAR, PLUS 1 TABLESPOON

2 STICKS UNSALTED BUTTER, CUT INTO SMALL PIECES

1 EGG, BEATEN

8 TO 10 APPLES, PEELED, CORED, AND SLICED

DIRECTIONS

1. To make the pastry, whisk together the flour, salt, and the tablespoon of sugar in a large bowl. Add half of the butter and use your fingers or a pastry blender to work the mixture until it is a collection of coarse clumps. Add the egg and work the mixture until the dough just holds together. Shape it into a ball, cover it with plastic wrap, and refrigerate for 1 hour. If preparing ahead of time, the dough will keep in the refrigerator overnight.

2. Place the remaining butter in a 10-inch cast-iron skillet and melt over medium heat. When the butter is melted, remove the skillet from heat and sprinkle the remaining sugar evenly over the butter. Place the apple slices in a circular pattern, starting at the edge of the pan and working in. The pieces should overlap and face the same direction. Place either 1 or 2 slices in the center when finished working in from the outside. As the tart bakes, the slices will slide down a bit.

3. Place the skillet over high heat and cook until the juices in the pan are a deep amber color, about 10 minutes. Remove from heat and turn the apples over. Place the skillet back over high heat and cook for 5 minutes. Remove the skillet from heat.

4. Preheat the oven to 375°F and place a rack in the middle position. Take the chilled dough out of the refrigerator and, working on a lightly floured surface, roll it out into a circle just big enough to cover the skillet. While being careful not to burn your fingers on the hot skillet, gently drape the dough over the apples and tuck it in around the sides. Put the skillet in the oven and bake until the pastry is golden brown, about 25 minutes.

5. Remove the skillet from the oven, allow to cool for about 5 minutes, and then run a knife around the edges to loosen the tart. Using oven mitts or pot holders, carefully invert the tart onto a large plate. Place any apples that are stuck to the skillet back in place on the tart. Let cool for 5 more minutes before serving.

Baked Stuffed Apples

YIELD: **6 SERVINGS**

ACTIVE TIME: **15 MINUTES**

TOTAL TIME: **1 HOUR**

INGREDIENTS

6 PINK LADY APPLES

3 TABLESPOONS UNSALTED BUTTER, MELTED

6 TABLESPOONS BLACKBERRY JAM

2 OZ. GOAT CHEESE, CUT INTO 6 ROUNDS

DIRECTIONS

1. Preheat the oven to 350°F. Slice the tops off of the apples and set aside. Use a paring knife to cut a circle around the apples' cores and then scoop out the centers. Make sure to leave a ½″ thick wall inside the apple.

2. Rub the inside and outside of the apples with some of the melted butter. Place the jam and goat cheese in a mixing bowl and stir to combine. Fill the apples' cavities with the mixture, place the tops back on the apples, and set them aside.

3. Warm a cast-iron skillet over medium-high heat. Add the remaining butter, place the apples in the skillet, and place the skillet in the oven. Bake until tender, 25 to 30 minutes. Remove from the oven and let cool briefly before serving.

Apple Cider Doughnuts

YIELD: 18 DOUGHNUTS

ACTIVE TIME: 30 MINUTES

TOTAL TIME: 1 HOUR AND 20 MINUTES

INGREDIENTS

1½ CUPS APPLE CIDER

2½ CUPS GRANULATED SUGAR

5 TABLESPOONS UNSALTED BUTTER, AT ROOM TEMPERATURE

2 LARGE EGGS, AT ROOM TEMPERATURE

3½ CUPS ALL-PURPOSE FLOUR, PLUS MORE FOR DUSTING

1¼ TEASPOONS SALT

2 TEASPOONS BAKING POWDER

1 TEASPOON BAKING SODA

3½ TABLESPOONS GROUND CINNAMON

½ TEASPOON GRATED NUTMEG

½ CUP BUTTERMILK

1 TABLESPOON PURE VANILLA EXTRACT

CANOLA OIL, FOR FRYING

DIRECTIONS

1. Place the apple cider in a saucepan and bring to a simmer over medium-high heat. Cook until the cider has reduced to approximately ⅓ cup. Remove from heat and let cool completely.

2. Place 1 cup of the sugar and the butter in the mixing bowl of a stand mixer and beat until the mixture is pale and fluffy. Add the eggs one at a time and beat until completely incorporated before adding the next one. Place the flour, salt, baking powder, baking soda, ½ tablespoon of the cinnamon, and nutmeg in another mixing bowl, whisk to combine, and set the mixture aside.

3. Add the buttermilk, cooled reduced cider, and vanilla into the bowl of the stand mixer. Add the flour mixture and beat on low speed until combined.

4. Generously dust a work surface with flour and place the dough on it. Pat it into a rectangle that is ¾" thick. Sprinkle the dough generously with flour, transfer to a parchment-lined baking sheet, cover with plastic wrap, and place in the freezer for 20 minutes.

5. Remove the dough from the freezer and use a floured biscuit cutter or mason jar to cut it into rounds. Place the doughnuts on another parchment-lined baking sheet and place them in the freezer for 5 minutes.

6. Place the remaining sugar and cinnamon in a bowl, stir to combine, and set the mixture aside.

7. Add canola oil to a Dutch oven until it is 3" deep and heat it to 350°F. Working in batches of three doughnuts, place the doughnuts in the hot oil and fry until golden brown, about 1 minute. Turn the doughnuts over and fry for another minute. Transfer the cooked doughnuts to a paper towel-lined plate to drain.

8. When the doughnuts are still warm but cool enough to handle, dredge them in the cinnamon-and-sugar mixture and serve immediately.

Granny Smith Sorbet

YIELD: **2 CUPS**

ACTIVE TIME: **15 MINUTES**

TOTAL TIME: **8 HOURS AND 15 MINUTES**

INGREDIENTS

3 GRANNY SMITH APPLES, CORED AND QUARTERED

1 TABLESPOON SLICED GINGER

1 CINNAMON STICK

1 TABLESPOON MAPLE SYRUP

1½ TEASPOONS BROWN SUGAR

1 TEASPOON NUTMEG

3 WHOLE CLOVES

1 ORANGE, HALVED

¾ CUP GRANULATED SUGAR, PLUS 1 TABLESPOON

2 TABLESPOONS FRESH LEMON JUICE

DIRECTIONS

1. Place the apples, ginger, cinnamon stick, maple syrup, brown sugar, nutmeg, whole cloves, and orange halves in a large stockpot and cover with cold water.

2. Bring to a boil over medium-high heat. Cover the stockpot and reduce the heat so that the mixture simmers. Cook for 1 hour.

3. After 1 hour, remove the pot from heat, strain, and either discard the solids or reserve them for another preparation.

4. Place the liquid, granulated sugar, and lemon juice in a large bowl and stir until the sugar has dissolved. Pour the mixture into a large container, cover, and place in the refrigerator until completely chilled.

5. Pour the mixture into an ice cream maker and churn until the desired consistency is achieved. Cover the churned sorbet and freeze for 6 hours before serving.

Pear Galette with Maple Caramel

YIELD: **6 TO 8 SERVINGS**

ACTIVE TIME: **30 MINUTES**

TOTAL TIME: **1 HOUR AND 45 MINUTES**

DIRECTIONS

1. To prepare the dough, place the flour, cinnamon, nutmeg, cloves, salt, and sugar in a bowl and whisk to combine. Divide the butter into tablespoons and place them in the freezer for 15 minutes.

2. Place the flour mixture and the frozen pieces of butter in a food processor and blitz until combined. Gradually add the water and blitz until the dough just holds together. Remove from the food processor, place on a lightly floured work surface, and knead until all of the ingredients are thoroughly incorporated. Place in the refrigerator for 20 minutes before rolling out.

3. Preheat the oven to 400°F and prepare the filling. Place the sugar and cinnamon in a bowl, stir to combine, and set aside. Place the pears, lemon zest, minced ginger, and butter in a bowl and gently toss, being careful not to break the slices of pear.

4. Place the dough on a lightly floured work surface and roll out into a 12" circle that is approximately ¼" thick. Place it on a parchment-lined baking sheet and then place the pear slices on the dough in layers, making sure to leave 1½" of dough uncovered around the edge. Sprinkle each layer with the sugar-and-cinnamon mixture before adding the next layer.

5. Fold the edge of the dough over the filling and crimp. Brush this crust with the egg yolk and sprinkle with the sugar-and-cinnamon mixture. Place the galette in the oven and bake until the crust is golden brown and the pears are tender, about 25 minutes.

6. While the galette is baking, prepare the maple caramel. Place the butter in a saucepan and melt over medium heat. Add the sugar and salt and cook, while stirring constantly, until the sugar is dissolved, about 5 minutes. Add the maple syrup and cook until the mixture is smooth and thick. Remove from heat.

7. Remove the galette from the oven, drizzle the maple caramel over the top, and let cool for 5 to 10 minutes before serving.

INGREDIENTS

FOR THE DOUGH

1½ CUPS ALL-PURPOSE FLOUR,
PLUS MORE FOR DUSTING

1 TEASPOON CINNAMON

¼ TEASPOON NUTMEG

¼ TEASPOON GROUND CLOVES

1½ TEASPOONS SALT

2 TEASPOONS BROWN SUGAR

2 STICKS UNSALTED BUTTER

½ CUP ICE-COLD WATER

YOLK OF 1 EGG, BEATEN

FOR THE FILLING

¼ CUP GRANULATED SUGAR

2 TEASPOONS CINNAMON

3 ANJOU PEARS, CORED AND CUT
INTO ¼-INCH SLICES

1½ TABLESPOONS LEMON ZEST

½ TABLESPOON MINCED GINGER

2 TABLESPOONS UNSALTED
BUTTER, CUT INTO SMALL PIECES

FOR THE MAPLE CARAMEL

1 STICK UNSALTED BUTTER

1 CUP DARK BROWN SUGAR

½ TEASPOON SALT

½ CUP MAPLE SYRUP

Pear Clafoutis

YIELD: **4 TO 6 SERVINGS**

ACTIVE TIME: **20 MINUTES**

TOTAL TIME: **1 HOUR**

INGREDIENTS

1½ STICKS UNSALTED BUTTER, MELTED

1 CUP GRANULATED SUGAR, PLUS 2 TEASPOONS

⅔ CUP ALL-PURPOSE FLOUR

½ TEASPOON SALT

1 TEASPOON PURE ALMOND EXTRACT

3 EGGS

1 CUP WHOLE MILK

4 PEARS, CORED AND SLICED

CONFECTIONERS' SUGAR, FOR TOPPING (OPTIONAL)

DIRECTIONS

1. Preheat oven to 400°F.

2. Place half of the butter and sugar, the flour, salt, almond extract, eggs, and milk in a mixing bowl and stir until combined. Set the batter aside.

3. Put 2 tablespoons of the butter in a cast-iron skillet and place it in the oven as it warms up.

4. Place another skillet over medium-high heat and add the remaining butter, the pears, and the ½ cup of the sugar. Cook, while stirring, until the pears are just soft and glazed, about 3 minutes.

5. Remove the skillet from the oven and pour in half of the batter. Spoon the cooked pears over the batter, cover with the remaining batter, and sprinkle the remaining sugar on top. Place in the oven and bake until it is puffy and golden brown, about 30 minutes. Remove from the oven and sprinkle confectioners' sugar on top, if desired.

Sour Cream & Pear Pie

YIELD: **6 TO 8 SERVINGS**

ACTIVE TIME: **25 MINUTES**

TOTAL TIME: **2 HOURS**

INGREDIENTS

1 LEAF LARD PIECRUST
(SEE PAGE 33)

1¼ CUPS SOUR CREAM

¾ CUP GRANULATED SUGAR

¾ CUP ALL-PURPOSE FLOUR

¼ TEASPOON SALT, PLUS A PINCH

2 TEASPOONS PURE VANILLA
EXTRACT

1 EGG

4 TO 5 CUPS PEELED AND SLICED
PEARS

3 TABLESPOONS GRADE B REAL
MAPLE SYRUP

¼ CUP PACKED LIGHT BROWN
SUGAR

½ TEASPOON GROUND CARDAMOM

3 TABLESPOONS UNSALTED
BUTTER, CHILLED AND CUT INTO
SLIVERS

DIRECTIONS

1. Place the crust in a greased 9″ pie plate and preheat the oven to 400°F.

2. Place the sour cream, sugar, ¼ cup of the flour, the ¼ teaspoon salt, vanilla, and egg in a mixing bowl and whisk until combined. Stir in the pear slices and evenly distribute the mixture in the crust.

3. Place the remaining flour and salt, the maple syrup, brown sugar, and cardamom in a bowl and stir to combine. Add the butter and work the mixture with a pastry blender until coarse crumbs start to form. Place the mixture in the refrigerator.

4. Place the pie in the oven and bake for 15 minutes. Reduce the temperature to 350°F and bake for another 30 minutes. Remove pie from oven, take the butter-and-brown sugar mixture out of the refrigerator, and sprinkle it over the pie. Bake for another 20 to 25 minutes until topping is golden brown. Remove from the oven and allow to cool before serving.

Pear & Ginger Crumble

INGREDIENTS

9 TABLESPOONS UNSALTED
BUTTER, CHILLED

4 PEARS

1 TEASPOON GROUND GINGER

1 CUP ALL-PURPOSE FLOUR

½ CUP PACKED DARK BROWN
SUGAR

½ CUP ROLLED OATS

VANILLA ICE CREAM (SEE PAGE 152
FOR HOMEMADE), FOR SERVING

DIRECTIONS

1. Preheat oven to 350°F.

2. Place 1 tablespoon of the butter in a cast-iron skillet and melt it over medium heat.

3. Trim the tops and bottoms from the pears, cut them into quarters, remove the cores, and cut each quarter in half. Lay the slices in the melted butter. Sprinkle the pear slices with the ginger, cook until they start to brown, and remove the skillet from heat.

4. Place the flour and brown sugar in a bowl and stir to combine. Cut the remaining butter into slices, add them to the bowl, and use your fingers to work the mixture until a coarse meal forms. Add the rolled oats, combine, and then spread the mixture on top of the pears.

5. Put the skillet in the oven and bake until the pears are bubbling and the crumble topping is brown, about 25 minutes. Remove the skillet from the oven and let cool for a few minutes. Top each serving with a scoop of ice cream.

Chai-Poached Pears

YIELD: **4 SERVINGS**

ACTIVE TIME: **10 MINUTES**

TOTAL TIME: **1 HOUR AND 30 MINUTES**

INGREDIENTS

3 BAGS OF CHAI TEA

2 CINNAMON STICKS

4 WHOLE CLOVES

2 TEASPOONS GRATED NUTMEG

½ CUP GRANULATED SUGAR

4 RIPE PEARS, LEFT WHOLE OR PEELED AND SLICED

DIRECTIONS

1. Bring a saucepan of water to a boil. Add the tea bags, cinnamon sticks, cloves, and nutmeg, reduce the heat, and simmer for 10 minutes. Turn off the heat and let mixture steep for 30 minutes.

2. Remove spices and tea bags from the water. Add the sugar and cook over low heat, while stirring, until the sugar is dissolved. Place the pears in the simmering tea and cook, while spooning the tea over the pears, until they are fork-tender, about 40 minutes. Turn the pears in the water as they cook to ensure that they are cooked evenly.

3. Remove the pears from liquid, transfer them to the serving dishes, and spoon some of the liquid over the top.

CHAPTER 9

T A R T

Sometimes the palate sounds the cry for a respite from straight sweetness.
Occasionally, the temperature rises so high that the thought of carrying
a heavy baked good around in your stomach is too much to bear.

Enter the tart dessert, which will rush to your aid in such circumstances.
Able to be both decadent and light, to be refreshing while also sweet,
the pleasantly sour treats in this chapter are able to satisfy in ways
that no other class of desserts can.

SHE'S A JOLLY GOODFELLOW

On its face, the lemon meringue pie seems like yet another confection the French are responsible for, but it is in fact as American as apple pie.

In the early days of the American experiment, Philadelphia was the bustling cultural center of the nation. Amidst that era's dynamism, Elizabeth Goodfellow opened a pastry shop and a cooking school, one of the country's first. While Elizabeth never published her own recipes, her students (Eliza Leslie, a popular cookbook author of the early 19th century, was counted among Goodfellow's flock) served as the Plato to Goodfellow's Socrates. While handing down her recipes and knowledge to the public, they couldn't help but convey her propensity for covering lemon custard pie with meringue. Unknown before the 19th century, in part because lemons were rare outside of the large cities, Goodfellow's pie took the burgeoning nation by storm and quickly became one of its classic desserts.

Lemon Meringue Pie

YIELD: **8 SERVINGS**

ACTIVE TIME: **30 MINUTES**

TOTAL TIME: **1 HOUR AND 30 MINUTES**

INGREDIENTS

FOR THE FILLING

¼ CUP CORNSTARCH

¼ CUP ALL-PURPOSE FLOUR

1¾ CUPS GRANULATED SUGAR

¼ TEASPOON SALT

2 CUPS WATER

YOLKS OF 4 EGGS, LIGHTLY BEATEN

½ CUP FRESH LEMON JUICE

1½ TABLESPOONS LEMON ZEST

2 TABLESPOONS UNSALTED BUTTER

1 LEAF LARD PIECRUST
(SEE PAGE 33), BLIND BAKED

FOR THE MERINGUE

WHITES OF 4 EGGS

¼ TEASPOON CREAM OF TARTAR

PINCH OF SALT

½ CUP GRANULATED SUGAR

1 TEASPOON FRESH LEMON JUICE

DIRECTIONS

1. To prepare the filling, place the cornstarch, flour, sugar, and salt in a saucepan and stir until well combined. Add the water in a slow stream and stir until incorporated. Cook the mixture over medium heat, while stirring occasionally, until it is thick, about 20 minutes. Remove from heat.

2. While whisking constantly, add ¼ cup of the mixture in the saucepan into the beaten egg yolks. Stir the tempered eggs into the saucepan and place it over medium-low heat.

3. Add the lemon juice, lemon zest, and butter and stir constantly until the mixture is thick enough to coat the back of a wooden spoon. Remove the mixture from heat and let it cool completely. Preheat the oven to 400°F.

4. Add the cooled filling to the baked piecrust and use a rubber spatula to smooth the top.

5. To prepare the meringue, place the egg whites, cream of tartar, and salt in a mixing bowl and beat with a handheld mixer until stiff peaks start to form. Gradually add the sugar and beat until the sugar is dissolved and the mixture is very stiff. Gently fold in the lemon juice.

6. Spread the meringue over the filling and use a large spoon or a spatula to create swirled peaks. Place in the oven and bake until peaks of meringue are light brown, about 6 minutes. Remove from the oven and let the pie cool completely before serving.

Lemon Brûlée

YIELD: **6 SERVINGS**

ACTIVE TIME: **30 MINUTES**

TOTAL TIME: **5 HOURS AND 30 MINUTES**

INGREDIENTS

2 CUPS HEAVY CREAM

¼ CUP GRANULATED SUGAR

ZEST OF 2 LEMONS

YOLKS OF 5 LARGE EGGS

PINCH OF SALT

3 TABLESPOONS FRESH LEMON JUICE

½ TEASPOON PURE VANILLA EXTRACT

BOILING WATER, AS NEEDED

3 TABLESPOONS CASTER SUGAR, FOR TOPPING

DIRECTIONS

1. Preheat the oven to 325°F and place six ramekins in a large baking dish.

2. Place the cream, granulated sugar, and lemon zest in a saucepan and bring to a simmer over medium heat.

3. Place the egg yolks and salt in a mixing bowl and beat until combined.

4. While whisking constantly, incrementally add the warm cream mixture to the beaten eggs until it has all been incorporated.

5. Add the lemon juice and vanilla extract and whisk to incorporate. Divide the mixture between the six ramekins.

6. Add boiling water to the dish until it reaches approximately halfway up the ramekins. Place the dish in the oven and bake for approximately 30 minutes, until the centers of the custards are just short of set. Remove and let cool in the dish for 15 minutes.

7. Transfer the ramekins to the refrigerator and chill for at least 4 hours.

8. Remove and distribute the caster sugar evenly over the tops of the custards. Use a kitchen torch or your oven's broiler to caramelize the sugar. Serve immediately.

Lemony Rice Pudding Pie

YIELD: **6 TO 8 SERVINGS**

ACTIVE TIME: **10 MINUTES**

TOTAL TIME: **2 HOURS AND 10 MINUTES**

INGREDIENTS

3 CUPS LEMON CURD
(SEE PAGE 387)

2 CUPS WHOLE MILK

1 TEASPOON PURE VANILLA
EXTRACT

1½ TO 2 CUPS COOKED RICE
(BROWN RICE PREFERRED)

1 GRAHAM CRACKER CRUST
(SEE PAGE 34)

1 CUP WHIPPED CREAM
(SEE PAGE 53)

CINNAMON, FOR GARNISH
(OPTIONAL)

DIRECTIONS

1. Place the Lemon Curd and milk in a large mixing bowl and whisk to combine. Add the vanilla and cooked rice and stir to combine.

2. Evenly distribute the filling in the piecrust, smoothing the top with a rubber spatula. Cover the pie with plastic wrap and place in the refrigerator for 2 hours.

3. Preheat the broiler on your oven. Remove the pie from the refrigerator and place it underneath the broiler. Broil until the top starts to brown, about 5 minutes. Remove and top each slice with Whipped Cream and cinnamon, if desired.

Lemon Layer Cake

YIELD: **10 TO 12 SERVINGS**

ACTIVE TIME: **30 MINUTES**

TOTAL TIME: **1 HOUR AND 30 MINUTES**

INGREDIENTS

FOR THE CAKE

1 CUP WHOLE MILK, AT ROOM TEMPERATURE

WHITES OF 6 LARGE EGGS, AT ROOM TEMPERATURE

2 TEASPOONS PURE VANILLA EXTRACT

2¼ CUPS CAKE FLOUR

1¾ CUPS GRANULATED SUGAR

4 TEASPOONS BAKING POWDER

1 TEASPOON SALT

1½ STICKS UNSALTED BUTTER, DIVIDED INTO TABLESPOONS AND AT ROOM TEMPERATURE

2 CUPS LEMON CURD (SEE PAGE 387)

FOR THE FROSTING

WHITES OF 2 LARGE EGGS

1 CUP GRANULATED SUGAR

¼ CUP WATER

1 TABLESPOON FRESH LEMON JUICE

1 TABLESPOON CORN SYRUP

DIRECTIONS

1. Preheat the oven to 350°F and grease two round 9" cake pans with nonstick cooking spray.

2. Place the milk, egg whites, and vanilla in a bowl and whisk until combined.

3. Place the flour, sugar, baking powder, and salt in a mixing bowl and whisk to combine. Add the butter one piece at a time and work it into the mixture with a pastry blender. When the mixture is crumbly and all of the butter has been incorporated, gradually add the milk mixture and beat until the batter is fluffy. Scrape the bowl as needed while mixing the cake batter.

4. Divide the batter between the cake pans, place in the oven, and bake until a toothpick inserted in the center of the cakes comes out clean, about 25 minutes. Remove from the oven, let cool in pans for 10 minutes, and then transfer the cakes to wire racks to cool completely.

5. When the cakes have cooled, spread half of the Lemon Curd over the top of one of the cakes. Place the other cake on top, flat-side up, spread the remaining curd on the top of this cake, and set the cake aside.

6. To prepare the frosting, bring 1" of water to a gentle simmer in a saucepan. Place the ingredients in a large heatproof bowl, place the bowl over the saucepan, and stir until the mixture starts to thicken. Remove from heat and beat until stiff peaks form and the mixture has cooled to room temperature. Spread the frosting over the outside of the cake and serve.

Lemon Tea Cake

YIELD: **6 TO 8 SERVINGS**

ACTIVE TIME: **30 MINUTES**

TOTAL TIME: **1 HOUR AND 30 MINUTES**

INGREDIENTS

¾ CUP GRANULATED SUGAR

ZEST OF 2 LEMONS

6 TABLESPOONS UNSALTED BUTTER, CUT INTO SMALL PIECES

2 EGGS

1 CUP ALL-PURPOSE FLOUR

1 TEASPOON BAKING POWDER

½ CUP WHOLE MILK

CONFECTIONERS' SUGAR, FOR DUSTING

DIRECTIONS

1. Preheat the oven to 350°F and grease a round 9" cake pan. In a large bowl, combine the sugar and lemon zest. Add the butter and beat until the mixture is light and fluffy. Add the eggs one at a time, stirring to incorporate thoroughly before adding the next one.

2. Place the flour and baking powder in a measuring cup and stir to combine. Alternate adding the flour mixture and the milk to the butter-and-sugar mixture, stirring after each addition until it has been incorporated.

3. Transfer the batter to the cake pan, place it in the oven, and bake for about 30 to 35 minutes, until the top is golden brown and a toothpick inserted in the middle comes out clean. Remove and let cool before dusting with confectioners' sugar and cutting into wedges.

Lemon Squares

YIELD: **12 TO 16 SQUARES**

ACTIVE TIME: **15 MINUTES**

TOTAL TIME: **1 HOUR**

INGREDIENTS

1 STICK UNSALTED BUTTER

⅓ CUP CONFECTIONERS' SUGAR

1 CUP ALL-PURPOSE FLOUR, PLUS 2 TABLESPOONS

PINCH OF SALT

2 LARGE EGGS, AT ROOM TEMPERATURE

1 CUP GRANULATED SUGAR

⅓ CUP FRESH LEMON JUICE

1 TABLESPOON LEMON ZEST

DIRECTIONS

1. Preheat the oven to 350°F and grease a square 8″ cake pan with nonstick cooking spray.

2. Place the butter, ¼ cup of the confectioners' sugar, the 1 cup of flour, and salt in a mixing bowl and stir until combined. Press mixture into the baking pan and bake for 20 minutes, or until it is set and lightly browned. Remove from the oven and set aside.

3. Place the eggs, granulated sugar, remaining flour, lemon juice, and lemon zest in a mixing bowl and beat with a handheld mixer on medium until well combined.

4. Pour the mixture over the crust and bake for 20 minutes, or until just browned. The custard should still be soft. Let the pan cool on a wire rack before dusting with the remaining confectioners' sugar and cutting into bars.

Miniature Lemon Tarts

INGREDIENTS

FOR THE DOUGH

1½ STICKS UNSALTED BUTTER, AT ROOM TEMPERATURE

⅔ CUP CREAM CHEESE, AT ROOM TEMPERATURE

1½ CUPS ALL-PURPOSE FLOUR

½ CUP CONFECTIONERS' SUGAR, PLUS MORE FOR DUSTING

FOR THE FILLING

2 CUPS GRANULATED SUGAR

5 TABLESPOONS ALL-PURPOSE FLOUR

4 EGGS

ZEST AND JUICE OF 2 LEMONS

DIRECTIONS

1. To prepare the dough, place the butter and cream cheese in the mixing bowl of a stand mixer and beat until just combined. Place flour and confectioners' sugar in a separate bowl and whisk to combine. Add the dry mixture to the butter-and-cream cheese mixture and beat until the dough just holds together. Work the mixture with your hands until it is smooth and homogenous.

2. Spoon approximately 1 tablespoon of dough into the wells of two greased muffin tins. Press down and spread the dough to fill the wells. Set the tins aside and preheat the oven to 350°F.

3. To prepare the filling, place the sugar and flour in a mixing bowl and stir to combine. Add the eggs, whisk to incorporate, and then add the lemon zest and juice. Whisk until incorporated.

4. Fill the tart shells with the filling, place the tarts in the oven and bake until the shells are golden brown, about 20 minutes. Remove and let cool in the pan for 15 minutes.

5. Run a knife around the edge of each tart, remove from the wells, dust with confectioners' sugar, and serve.

Lemon Curd Tart with Torched Meringue

YIELD: **6 TO 8 SERVINGS**

ACTIVE TIME: **30 MINUTES**

TOTAL TIME: **1 HOUR AND 30 MINUTES**

INGREDIENTS

FOR THE DOUGH

6 TABLESPOONS UNSALTED
BUTTER, AT ROOM TEMPERATURE

3 TABLESPOONS SIFTED
CONFECTIONERS' SUGAR

1 EGG

¼ TEASPOON PURE VANILLA
EXTRACT

6 TABLESPOONS ALL-PURPOSE
FLOUR, PLUS MORE FOR DUSTING

½ TEASPOON BAKING POWDER

½ TEASPOON SALT

FOR THE FILLING & MERINGUE

3 CUPS LEMON CURD
(SEE PAGE 387)

1 CUP GRANULATED SUGAR

½ CUP EGG WHITES

PINCH OF SALT

DIRECTIONS

1. To prepare the dough, place the butter in the mixing bowl of a stand mixer fitted with the paddle attachment and beat on low until it is smooth. Add the sugar and beat on medium until the mixture is light and fluffy. Add the egg and beat until fully incorporated. Add the vanilla and beat until incorporated. Scrape down the bowl as needed while mixing the dough.

2. Add the flour, baking powder, and salt and beat on low until incorporated and the dough just holds together. Cover in plastic wrap and place in the refrigerator for 1 hour.

3. Remove the dough from the refrigerator, place on a flour-dusted work surface, and roll out to fit a greased 9" tart pan. Place the dough in the pan and fill it with the Lemon Curd. Set the tart aside while you prepare the meringue.

4. Bring 2" of water to a boil in a saucepan and fit the stand mixer with the whisk attachment. As the water warms, place the sugar, egg whites, and salt in a metal mixing bowl and beat until combined.

5. Place the bowl over the boiling water and whisk until the mixture reaches 150°F. Immediately pour the mixture into the mixing bowl of the stand mixer and beat until stiff peaks form. Spread the meringue on top of the tart and use a kitchen torch to toast the top of the meringue. You can also toast the meringue in a 400°F oven for 6 minutes.

Lemon Curd

YIELD: **2 CUPS**

ACTIVE TIME: **15 MINUTES**

TOTAL TIME: **30 MINUTES**

INGREDIENTS

1 CUP FRESH LEMON JUICE

4 TEASPOONS LEMON ZEST

6 LARGE EGGS

1⅓ CUPS GRANULATED SUGAR

2 STICKS UNSALTED BUTTER

DIRECTIONS

1. Place all of the ingredients the mixing bowl of a stand mixer fitted with the paddle attachment. Beat on medium speed until well combined.

2. Pour the mixture into a saucepan and cook over low heat until it is thick enough to coat the back of a spoon, about 10 minutes.

3. Pour the lemon curd into a serving dish, place in the refrigerator, and chill until it thickens further.

Lemon Posset

YIELD: **6 SERVINGS**

ACTIVE TIME: **30 MINUTES**

TOTAL TIME: **4 HOURS**

INGREDIENTS

2 CUPS HEAVY CREAM

⅔ CUP GRANULATED SUGAR

1 TABLESPOON LEMON ZEST

6 TABLESPOONS FRESH LEMON JUICE

WHIPPED CREAM (SEE PAGE 53)

1½ CUPS BLUEBERRIES, FOR GARNISH

DIRECTIONS

1. Place the heavy cream, sugar, and lemon zest in a saucepan and bring to a boil, while stirring, over medium heat. Cook until the sugar has dissolved and the mixture has reduced slightly, about 10 minutes.

2. Remove the saucepan from heat and stir in the lemon juice. Let the mixture stand until a skin forms on the top, about 20 minutes. Strain through a fine sieve and transfer the mixture to the refrigerator. Chill until set, about 3 hours.

3. About 10 minutes before you are ready to serve the desserts, remove from the refrigerator and let the mixture come to room temperature. Place the Whipped Cream in the bottom of a serving dish and then alternate layers of the posset and Whipped Cream. Garnish each serving with the blueberries and serve.

Lemon Curd & Grape Clafoutis

YIELD: **6 TO 8 SERVINGS**

ACTIVE TIME: **15 MINUTES**

TOTAL TIME: **45 MINUTES**

INGREDIENTS

3 CUPS LEMON CURD
(SEE PAGE 387)

1 TABLESPOON FRESH LEMON
JUICE

1 TEASPOON LEMON ZEST

2 TABLESPOONS UNSALTED BUTTER

1 TABLESPOON LIGHT BROWN
SUGAR

2 TO 3 CUPS SEEDLESS GRAPES

2 TABLESPOONS GRANULATED
SUGAR

DIRECTIONS

1. Preheat the oven to 350°F.

2. Place the Lemon Curd, lemon juice, and lemon zest in a mixing bowl and stir to combine. Set the mixture aside.

3. Place a cast-iron skillet over medium heat and melt the butter in it. Add the brown sugar and cook, while stirring constantly, until the sugar is dissolved. Carefully remove pan from heat.

4. Spread the lemon curd mixture in the skillet. Distribute the grapes evenly in the custard. Sprinkle with the granulated sugar.

5. Put the skillet in the oven and bake until the custard is set, about 30 minutes.

6. Remove the skillet from the oven and allow to cool before serving.

Limoncello Fruit Salad

YIELD: **6 SERVINGS**

ACTIVE TIME: **5 MINUTES**

TOTAL TIME: **10 MINUTES**

INGREDIENTS

1 PINT OF STRAWBERRIES, HULLED AND QUARTERED

1 PINT OF BLUEBERRIES

1 PINT OF BLACKBERRIES

1 TEASPOON LEMON ZEST

2 CUPS PEELED AND DICED KIWI

2 CUPS PITTED, PEELED, AND DICED PEACHES

1 TABLESPOON FRESH LEMON JUICE

¼ CUP LIMONCELLO

2 TABLESPOONS GRANULATED SUGAR

¼ CUP CHOPPED MINT LEAVES

DIRECTIONS

1. Place all of the ingredients in a bowl, toss to combine, and refrigerate until ready to serve.

Lemon Granita

INGREDIENTS

1 TABLESPOON LEMON ZEST

¾ CUP FRESH LEMON JUICE

1 CUP WATER

½ CUP GRANULATED SUGAR

1 TABLESPOON GRATED GINGER

DIRECTIONS

1. Place all of ingredients in a food processor and blitz until well combined and no large pieces remain.

2. Run the mixture through a fine sieve and pour liquid into a square 8″ cake pan. Place in freezer and scrape with a fork once an hour to loosen tiny, icy flakes.

3. When enough flakes have accumulated, divide them between the serving dishes.

The Ice Storm

YIELD: **4 TO 6 SERVINGS**

ACTIVE TIME: **30 MINUTES**

TOTAL TIME: **2 HOURS**

INGREDIENTS

1 CUP WHOLE MILK

¾ CUP GRANULATED SUGAR

½ CUP FRESH LIME JUICE

1 PACKAGE OF GELATIN

YOLKS OF 2 LARGE EGGS, AT ROOM TEMPERATURE

¼ TEASPOON CORNSTARCH

2½ TEASPOONS LIME ZEST, PLUS MORE FOR GARNISH

WHITES OF 5 LARGE EGGS, AT ROOM TEMPERATURE

PINCH OF CREAM OF TARTAR

¾ CUP HEAVY CREAM

LIME WHEELS, FOR GARNISH

DIRECTIONS

1. Place the milk and ½ cup of the sugar in a saucepan and cook over medium-low heat, while stirring occasionally, until the sugar has dissolved, about 5 minutes.

2. Place the lime juice in a small bowl, add the gelatin, and stir to combine. Set the mixture aside and prepare an ice water bath in a large bowl.

3. Place the egg yolks, half of the remaining sugar, and the cornstarch in a bowl and beat until the mixture has thickened. While whisking constantly, gradually add the hot milk mixture to the egg yolk mixture until it has all been incorporated. Place the tempered eggs in the saucepan and cook, while stirring, over medium-low heat until it is consistency of heavy cream. Strain the mixture into a mixing bowl, stir in the lime juice-and-gelatin mixture and the lime zest, and place the bowl in the prepared ice water bath. Stir the mixture occasionally as it cools into a custard.

4. Place the egg whites and cream of tartar in a mixing bowl and beat until foamy. Add the remaining sugar and beat until soft peaks form. Remove the bowl containing the custard from the ice water bath and whisk in one-third of the egg white mixture. Add the remaining egg white mixture and fold to incorporate it.

5. Beat the heavy cream until soft peaks form. Fold into the custard and transfer that mixture into a bowl or soufflé dish. Place in the freezer for approximately 1½ hours, until set. Garnish with lime wheels and additional lime zest before serving.

Key Lime Pie

YIELD: **6 TO 8 SERVINGS**

ACTIVE TIME: **10 MINUTES**

TOTAL TIME: **1 HOUR**

INGREDIENTS

2 CUPS HEAVY CREAM

¼ CUP GRANULATED SUGAR

⅓ CUP FRESH KEY LIME JUICE

1 TABLESPOON GELATIN

½ CUP SWEETENED CONDENSED MILK

1 GRAHAM CRACKER CRUST (SEE PAGE 34)

WHIPPED CREAM (SEE PAGE 53), FOR GARNISH

KEY LIME ZEST AND/OR KEY LIME WHEELS, FOR GARNISH

DIRECTIONS

1. Place the cream in a mixing bowl and beat until soft peaks start to form. Add the sugar and beat until stiff peaks start to form.

2. Place the key lime juice and gelatin in a small saucepan and stir until the gelatin has dissolved. Cook over medium heat until the mixture starts to thicken, about 3 to 5 minutes. Remove the pan from heat and allow to cool slightly. Stir in the condensed milk and then fold this mixture into the whipped cream resulting from Step 1.

3. Pour the filling into the crust, cover with plastic wrap, and place in the refrigerator. Chill until set, about 45 minutes. Garnish with Whipped Cream and key lime zest and/or wheels.

THAT'S THE KEY

The key lime tree is native to Malaysia, but the name of this golf ball-sized citrus comes from the Florida Keys, where the trees brought by the Spanish came to flourish—at least until the majority of the groves were wiped out by a hurricane. Today, most key limes come from Mexico.

When selecting key limes, keep in mind that the green ones are actually unripe. They will have higher levels of acidity and tartness, which can be fine in some preparations, but for desserts you'll want to seek out yellow key limes, as they are sweeter.

Gingersnap & Key Lime Tart

YIELD: **6 TO 8 SERVINGS**

ACTIVE TIME: **20 MINUTES**

TOTAL TIME: **1 HOUR AND 30 MINUTES**

INGREDIENTS

FOR THE CRUST

8 TO 10 GINGERSNAP COOKIES

1 TEASPOON GRATED GINGER

1 STICK UNSALTED BUTTER, MELTED

FOR THE FILLING

1 (14 OZ.) CAN OF SWEETENED CONDENSED MILK

½ CUP FRESH KEY LIME JUICE

YOLKS OF 4 LARGE EGGS

1 TABLESPOON PURE VANILLA EXTRACT

WHIPPED CREAM (SEE PAGE 53), FOR GARNISH

1 TABLESPOON KEY LIME ZEST, FOR GARNISH

DIRECTIONS

1. Preheat the oven to 350°F and grease a 9" tart pan with nonstick cooking spray.

2. To prepare the crust, place the cookies in a food processor and blitz until they are crumbs. You can also put the cookies in a resealable plastic bag and use a rolling pin to grind them into crumbs.

3. Place the crumbs in a bowl and add the ginger. Add the melted butter and stir until the mixture is like wet sand. Press the mixture into the greased tart pan.

4. Place the crust in the oven and bake until it is firm, about 10 minutes. Remove from the oven and let cool. Reduce the temperature in the oven to 325°F.

5. To prepare the filling, place the condensed milk, key lime juice, egg yolks, and vanilla in a bowl and mix until combined. Pour the filling into the cooled crust.

6. Put the tart in the oven and bake for about 20 to 30 minutes, until the filling has set into a soft custard. Remove from the oven and let cool completely before serving. Top each slice with Whipped Cream and a sprinkle of the key lime zest.

Lemon-Lime Frozen Yogurt

YIELD: **4 TO 6 SERVINGS**

ACTIVE TIME: **20 MINUTES**

TOTAL TIME: **6 HOURS AND 20 MINUTES**

INGREDIENTS

2 CUPS PLAIN GREEK YOGURT

½ CUP WATER

1 CUP SIMPLE SYRUP

2 TABLESPOONS FRESH LIME JUICE

1 TABLESPOON FRESH LEMON JUICE

1 TEASPOON LEMON ZEST

1 TEASPOON LIME ZEST

½ TEASPOON PURE VANILLA EXTRACT

DIRECTIONS

1. Place all of the ingredients in a mixing bowl and whisk until well combined.

2. Pour the mixture into an ice cream maker and churn until it reaches the consistency of soft-serve ice cream.

3. Pour the churned mixture into an airtight container and freeze for 6 hours before serving.

Strawberry Rhubarb Pie

YIELD: **6 TO 8 SERVINGS**

ACTIVE TIME: **20 MINUTES**

TOTAL TIME: **1 HOUR AND 30 MINUTES**

INGREDIENTS

4 CUPS STRAWBERRIES, HULLED AND HALVED

4 CUPS CHOPPED RHUBARB

1 CUP GRANULATED SUGAR

¼ CUP CORNSTARCH

ZEST OF ½ ORANGE

PINCH OF SALT

2 BALLS OF LEAF LARD PIECRUST DOUGH (SEE PAGE 33), CHILLED

ALL-PURPOSE FLOUR, FOR DUSTING

2 TABLESPOONS UNSALTED BUTTER, CUT INTO SMALL PIECES

1 EGG, BEATEN

DIRECTIONS

1. Preheat the oven to 400°F and grease a 9" pie plate.

2. Place the strawberries, rhubarb, sugar, cornstarch, orange zest, and salt in a large mixing bowl and stir to combine. Set the mixture aside.

3. Place the balls of dough on a flour-dusted work surface and roll them out to fit the prepared pie plate. Transfer one of the crusts to the pie plate, fill it with the strawberry-and-rhubarb mixture, and dot the mixture with the butter.

4. Cut the other crust into 1" thick strips. Lay some of the strips over the pie and trim the strips so that they fit. To make a lattice crust, lift every other strip and fold them back so you can place another strip across those strips that remain flat. Lay the folded strips back down over the cross-strip. Fold back the strips that you laid the cross-strip on top of, and repeat until the lattice covers the surface of the pie.

5. Seal the edges and brush the crust with the egg, taking care not to get any egg on the filling. Place the pie on a baking sheet, place it in the oven, and bake for 20 minutes. Reduce the temperature to 350°F and bake until the filling is bubbling and the crust is golden brown, about 40 minutes. Remove and let cool before serving.

Strawberry Rhubarb Crisp

YIELD: **4 SERVINGS**

ACTIVE TIME: **15 MINUTES**

TOTAL TIME: **45 MINUTES**

INGREDIENTS

1½ CUPS CHOPPED RHUBARB

1½ CUPS HULLED AND SLICED STRAWBERRIES

2 TABLESPOONS GRANULATED SUGAR

⅓ CUP ALL-PURPOSE FLOUR, PLUS 2 TEASPOONS

4 TABLESPOONS UNSALTED BUTTER, CHILLED AND CUT INTO SMALL PIECES

¼ CUP BROWN SUGAR

¾ CUP OATS

WHIPPED CREAM (SEE PAGE 53), FOR SERVING

DIRECTIONS

1. Preheat the oven to 450°F. Place the rhubarb, strawberry slices, granulated sugar, and the 2 teaspoons of flour in a bowl and stir to combine. Toss to coat the fruit and then transfer to a 10-inch cast-iron skillet.

2. Place the butter and the brown sugar in a bowl and use a fork to combine. Add the oats and remaining flour and work the mixture until it is crumbly. Sprinkle over the fruit mixture in the skillet.

3. Put the skillet in the oven and bake until the topping is golden brown and the filling is bubbling, about 30 minutes. Serve warm and top each portion with Whipped Cream.

Strawberry Rhubarb Ricotta Cake with Lemon Meringue

YIELD: **4 SERVINGS**

ACTIVE TIME: **30 MINUTES**

TOTAL TIME: **1 HOUR AND 30 MINUTES**

INGREDIENTS

FOR THE CAKE

1 STICK UNSALTED BUTTER, AT ROOM TEMPERATURE

½ CUP GRANULATED SUGAR

2 EGGS

¼ TEASPOON PURE VANILLA EXTRACT

2 TEASPOONS LEMON ZEST

¾ CUP RICOTTA CHEESE

¾ CUP ALL-PURPOSE FLOUR

1 TEASPOON BAKING POWDER

½ TEASPOON SALT

½ CUP HULLED AND MINCED STRAWBERRIES, PLUS MORE FOR GARNISH

½ CUP RHUBARB JAM (SEE RECIPE)

FOR THE LEMON MERINGUE

1 CUP GRANULATED SUGAR

½ CUP WATER

4 EGG WHITES

1 TABLESPOON FRESH LEMON JUICE

DIRECTIONS

1. Preheat the oven to 350°F and grease a 9 x 5-inch loaf pan. To prepare the cakes, place the butter and sugar in the mixing bowl of a stand mixer fitted with the paddle attachment and beat on high until the mixture is smooth and a pale yellow. Reduce speed to medium, add the eggs one at a time, and beat until incorporated. Add the vanilla, lemon zest, and ricotta and beat until the mixture is smooth.

2. Place the flour, baking powder, and salt in a mixing bowl and whisk to combine. Reduce the speed of the mixer to low, add the dry mixture, and beat until incorporated. Scrape the mixing bowl as needed while mixing the batter.

3. Add the strawberries and fold to incorporate. Place the batter in the loaf pan, place it in the oven, and bake until a toothpick inserted into the center comes out clean, about 35 minutes. Remove from the oven and let cool to room temperature in the pan.

4. To prepare the meringue, place the sugar and water in a saucepan and cook on high until the mixture is 240°F. While the simple syrup is heating up, place the egg whites and lemon juice in the mixing bowl of the stand mixer fitted with the whisk attachment. Beat at medium speed until soft peaks form, about 2 to 3 minutes.

5.   When the simple syrup reaches 240°F, slowly add it to the beaten egg whites with the mixer running. Raise the speed to high and beat until stiff peaks form. To test whether the meringue is ready, remove the whisk attachment and turn it so that the whisk is facing up. The meringue should hold its shape. If desired, transfer the meringue to a pastry bag fitted with a piping tip.

6.   Remove the cooled cake from the pan and cut it into 8 equal pieces. Spread some of the Rhubarb Jam over four of the pieces. Cover the jam with some of the meringue and then place the unadorned pieces of cake on top. Spread more meringue on top and toast with a pastry torch until golden brown. Garnish with additional strawberries and serve.

RHUBARB JAM

4 CUPS CHOPPED RHUBARB

1 CUP WATER

¾ CUP GRANULATED SUGAR

½ TEASPOON SALT

1 TEASPOON PECTIN

1.   Place all of the ingredients, except for the pectin, in a saucepan and cook over high heat, stirring occasionally to prevent sticking. Cook until nearly all of the liquid has evaporated.

2.   Add the pectin and stir the mixture for 1 minute. Transfer to a sterilized mason jar and allow to cool completely before applying the lid and placing it in the refrigerator, where the jam will keep for up to 1 week.

Rhubarb & Champagne Soup with Lemon & Poppy Seed Mascarpone

YIELD: **4 SERVINGS**

ACTIVE TIME: **45 MINUTES**

TOTAL TIME: **50 MINUTES**

INGREDIENTS

4 CUPS CHOPPED RHUBARB

1 CUP RASPBERRIES

1 CUP ORANGE JUICE

1 CUP WATER

2 CUPS CHAMPAGNE

LEMON & POPPY SEED
MASCARPONE (SEE RECIPE)

DIRECTIONS

1. Place the rhubarb, raspberries, orange juice, and water in a large saucepan and bring to a boil over medium heat. Reduce the heat and simmer for 20 minutes.

2. Transfer the mixture to a food processor and puree, while slowly adding the Champagne, until the puree has a creamy texture. Strain through a fine sieve and place in the refrigerator until chilled.

3. To serve, ladle the soup into bowls and top each with a dollop of the Lemon & Poppy Seed Mascarpone.

LEMON & POPPY SEED MASCARPONE

½ CUP MASCARPONE CHEESE

1 TABLESPOON FRESH LEMON JUICE

1 TABLESPOON POPPY SEEDS

1 TABLESPOON GRANULATED SUGAR

1. Place all of the ingredients in a mixing bowl and whisk until thoroughly combined. Place in the refrigerator until the soup is ready.

Cranberry Sorbet

YIELD: **3 CUPS**

ACTIVE TIME: **20 MINUTES**

TOTAL TIME: **5 HOURS**

INGREDIENTS

½ LB. FRESH CRANBERRIES

2¾ CUPS WATER

13 TABLESPOONS GRANULATED SUGAR

1 CUP ORANGE JUICE

½ TEASPOON CORNSTARCH

DIRECTIONS

1. Place the cranberries, 9 oz. of the water, and 5 tablespoons of the sugar in a medium saucepan and cook over medium heat until all of the cranberries pop open. Transfer the mixture to the blender and puree until smooth, starting at a low speed and increasing to high. Strain through a fine sieve and place in the refrigerator until chilled.

2. Place the remaining water and sugar in a saucepan and bring to a boil, while stirring, until the sugar is dissolved. Remove from heat and let cool completely.

3. Place the cranberry puree, simple syrup, orange juice, and cornstarch in a bowl and mix until combined.

4. Pour the mixture into an ice cream maker and churn until the desired texture has been reached.

5. Transfer to the freezer and freeze for at least 4 hours, until it is set.

Cranberry & Apple Crisp

YIELD: **4 SERVINGS**

ACTIVE TIME: **20 MINUTES**

TOTAL TIME: **1 HOUR**

INGREDIENTS

¾ CUP GRANULATED SUGAR

¼ CUP ALL-PURPOSE FLOUR, PLUS 2½ TABLESPOONS

1 TEASPOON SALT

⅓ TEASPOON CINNAMON

½ TEASPOON NUTMEG

⅛ TEASPOON GROUND CLOVES

2½ CUPS DICED NORTHERN SPY APPLES

1 CUP FRESH CRANBERRIES

¾ CUP OATS

¼ CUP BROWN SUGAR

2 TEASPOONS ORANGE ZEST

6 TABLESPOONS UNSALTED BUTTER, MELTED

DIRECTIONS

1. Preheat the oven to 375°F. Place the sugar, 2½ tablespoons of flour, half the salt, the cinnamon, nutmeg, and cloves in a mixing bowl and stir to combine. Add the apples and cranberries and toss until the apples are evenly coated.

2. Place the oats, the remaining flour, brown sugar, remaining salt, orange zest, and half of the melted butter in a mixing bowl and stir to combine. Add the remaining butter and stir until incorporated.

3. Divide the apple-and-cranberry mixture between four ramekins, leaving ½" at the top of each. Top with the crumble, place the ramekins on a baking sheet, and bake until the crumble is golden brown and the filling is bubbly, 35 to 40 minutes. Remove and let cool slightly before serving.

Sour Cherry Pie

YIELD: **6 TO 8 SERVINGS**

ACTIVE TIME: **30 MINUTES**

TOTAL TIME: **2 HOURS**

INGREDIENTS

3¾ CUPS MONTMORENCY CHERRIES, PITTED

2¾ CUPS GRANULATED SUGAR

2½ TABLESPOONS WATER

¼ CUP CORNSTARCH

1 LEAF LARD PIECRUST (SEE PAGE 33)

½ CUP ALL-PURPOSE FLOUR, PLUS MORE FOR DUSTING

½ CUP DARK BROWN SUGAR

⅔ CUP OATS

6 TABLESPOONS UNSALTED BUTTER, CHILLED AND CUT INTO SMALL PIECES

DIRECTIONS

1. Grease a 9" pie plate.

2. Place cherries and the granulated sugar in a saucepan and cook, while stirring, until the sugar has dissolved.

3. Place the water and cornstarch in a bowl and stir to combine. Add this mixture to the saucepan, stir to combine, and cook until the mixture is syrupy. Remove from heat and let cool completely. Preheat the oven to 350°F.

4. Place the crust in the pie plate, add the sour cherry filling, and crimp the edge of the piecrust.

5. Place the flour, brown sugar, oats, and butter in a mixing bowl and work the mixture until it is combined and crumbly. Spread the mixture over the filling, place the pie in the oven, and bake until the crust is golden brown and the filling is bubbly, about 50 minutes. Remove and briefly let cool before serving.

CHAPTER 10

TROPICAL

When we have ground ourselves down and recognize that we desperately need to take a step back and set things right, our imaginations inevitably offer up the crystal blue water, warm sand, and lush vegetation of the tropics as a potential balm.

It is no surprise, then, that when we need something sweet to lift ourselves at the end of a long day, the mind will occasionally set its sights on a tropical taste. From the perfectly sweet flavor and creamy texture that coconuts and bananas supply, to the beguiling mixture of tart and sweet in each slice of kiwi, the confections in this chapter will have you back on track in no time.

Coconut Macaroons

YIELD: **15 TO 20 MACAROONS**

ACTIVE TIME: **15 MINUTES**

TOTAL TIME: **1 HOUR**

INGREDIENTS

1 CUP UNSWEETENED SHREDDED COCONUT

2 TABLESPOONS HONEY

2 TABLESPOONS COCONUT OIL

½ CUP ALL-PURPOSE FLOUR

1 TEASPOON PURE VANILLA EXTRACT

¼ TEASPOON SALT

4 OZ. MILK CHOCOLATE, CHOPPED

DIRECTIONS

1. Place all of the ingredients, except for the chocolate, in a food processor and blitz until well combined.

2. Roll tablespoons of the mixture into balls and place them on a parchment-lined baking sheet. Place in the refrigerator for 30 minutes.

3. Place the chocolate in a microwave-safe bowl. Microwave on medium until melted, removing to stir every 20 seconds.

4. Remove the baking sheet from the refrigerator and dip the balls halfway into the melted chocolate. Place them back on the baking sheet, drizzle any remaining chocolate over the top, and place them in the refrigerator until the chocolate is hardened.

Coconut & Lemon Sandwich Cookies

YIELD: **24 COOKIES**

ACTIVE TIME: **20 MINUTES**

TOTAL TIME: **3 HOURS AND 30 MINUTES**

INGREDIENTS

FOR THE COOKIES

1 CUP UNSWEETENED SHREDDED COCONUT

2 STICKS UNSALTED BUTTER, AT ROOM TEMPERATURE

⅓ CUP GRANULATED SUGAR

1 TABLESPOON LEMON ZEST

1 TEASPOON LEMON OIL

2 CUPS ALL-PURPOSE FLOUR

½ TEASPOON SALT

FOR THE FILLING

1 CUP CONFECTIONERS' SUGAR

4 TABLESPOONS UNSALTED BUTTER

1 TABLESPOON LEMON ZEST

1 TABLESPOON FRESH LEMON JUICE

2 TABLESPOONS LIGHT CORN SYRUP

DIRECTIONS

1. Preheat the oven to 325°F.

2. To prepare the cookies, place the coconut on a baking sheet, place it in the oven, and toast, while removing to stir occasionally, until lightly browned, about 10 to 12 minutes.

3. Place the butter, sugar, lemon zest, and lemon oil in the mixing bowl of a stand mixer and beat at low speed until combined. Increase the speed to high and beat for 3 to 4 minutes, until the mixture is light and fluffy. Slowly add the flour and salt and beat until a soft dough forms. Add the toasted coconut and beat until incorporated.

4. Place the dough on a sheet of waxed paper and form it into a 2½" thick log. Cover in plastic wrap and refrigerate for at least 2 hours.

5. Preheat the oven to 350°F. Cut the dough into ¼" thick slices and place them on parchment-lined baking sheets. Place the cookies in the oven and bake until the edges are brown, about 10 minutes. Remove from the oven and let the cookies cool on the baking sheets for 2 minutes before transferring them to wire racks to cool completely.

6. To prepare the filling, place all of the ingredients in a mixing bowl and beat until the mixture is light and fluffy.

7. Spread approximately 1 teaspoon of the filling on a cookie and top with another cookie. Repeat until all of the cookies and filling have been used. Refrigerate for 15 minutes before serving.

INGREDIENTS

FOR THE COCONUT CREAM

WHITES OF 4 LARGE EGGS

1 CUP GRANULATED SUGAR

PINCH OF SALT

4 STICKS UNSALTED BUTTER, CUT INTO SMALL PIECES AND AT ROOM TEMPERATURE

¼ CUP CREAM OF COCONUT

1 TEASPOON PURE VANILLA EXTRACT

FOR THE CAKE

2¼ CUPS SIFTED CAKE FLOUR, PLUS MORE FOR DUSTING

1 CUP GRANULATED SUGAR

1 TABLESPOON BAKING POWDER

¾ TEASPOON SALT

1½ STICKS UNSALTED BUTTER, DIVIDED INTO TABLESPOONS AND AT ROOM TEMPERATURE

WHITES OF 5 LARGE EGGS

1 LARGE EGG

1 TEASPOON PURE VANILLA EXTRACT

¾ CUP CREAM OF COCONUT

¼ CUP WATER

2 CUPS SWEETENED SHREDDED COCONUT

Coconut Layer Cake

YIELD: **8 TO 10 SERVINGS**

ACTIVE TIME: **35 MINUTES**

TOTAL TIME: **1 HOUR AND 30 MINUTES**

DIRECTIONS

1. Preheat the oven to 350°F and grease two round 9" cake pans with nonstick cooking spray.

2. To prepare the coconut cream, place 2" of water in a saucepan and bring to a gentle simmer. Place the egg whites, sugar, and salt in a metal mixing bowl and place the bowl over the saucepan. Cook, while whisking constantly, for about 2 minutes. Remove the bowl from heat and beat the mixture until it is shiny. Add the butter one piece at a time and beat until incorporated. Add the cream of coconut and vanilla extract and beat until well combined. Scrape down the bowl as needed while mixing. Set aside.

3. To prepare the cake, place the flour, sugar, baking powder, and salt in a mixing bowl and whisk to combine. Add the butter one piece at a time and work the mixture with a pastry blender until the mixture resembles a coarse meal.

4. Place the egg whites and the egg in a separate bowl and beat until combined. Add the vanilla, cream of coconut, and water and beat until well combined.

5. Add half of the wet mixture to the dry mixture and beat until light and fluffy. Slowly add the remaining half of the wet mixture and beat until incorporated. Scrape down the bowl as needed.

6. Divide the batter between the prepared pans, place in the oven, and bake until they are golden brown and a toothpick inserted into the center of each comes out clean, about 25 minutes. Remove from the oven and let the cakes cool in the pan for 10 minutes.

7. Place the cakes on wire racks and let cool to room temperature.

8. When the cakes are cool, spread some of the coconut cream over the top of one of the cakes. Place the other cake on top, flat-side up, and spread the remaining coconut cream over the entire cake. Sprinkle with the shredded coconut and serve.

Coconut & Brown Sugar Cake

YIELD: **8 SERVINGS**

ACTIVE TIME: **20 MINUTES**

TOTAL TIME: **1 HOUR AND 20 MINUTES**

INGREDIENTS

2 STICKS UNSALTED BUTTER

¼ CUP PACKED DARK BROWN SUGAR

2 CUPS SIFTED CAKE FLOUR, PLUS MORE FOR DUSTING

¾ CUP GRANULATED SUGAR

2 TEASPOONS BAKING POWDER

½ TEASPOON SALT

WHITES OF 4 EGGS

1 EGG

1 TEASPOON PURE VANILLA EXTRACT

¾ CUP CREAM OF COCONUT

¼ CUP WATER

1 CUP SWEETENED SHREDDED COCONUT

SUGAR GLAZE (SEE PAGE 42)

DIRECTIONS

1. Preheat the oven to 350°F. Place half of the butter in a large cast-iron skillet and warm over medium heat. When the butter is melted, sprinkle the brown sugar over the butter, reduce the heat to medium-low and let the sugar melt, taking care to not let the butter get too hot.

2. Place the flour, sugar, baking powder, and salt in a mixing bowl and whisk to combine. Add the remaining butter 1 tablespoon at a time and work the mixture with a pastry blender until the mixture resembles a coarse meal.

3. Place the egg whites and the egg in a separate bowl and beat until combined. Add the vanilla, cream of coconut, water, and coconut and beat until well combined.

4. Add half of the wet mixture to the dry mixture and beat until light and fluffy. Slowly add the remaining half of the wet mixture and beat until incorporated. Scrape down the bowl as needed.

5. Pour the batter into the skillet, place it in the oven, and bake until the cake is golden brown and a toothpick inserted in the center comes out clean, about 25 minutes.

6. Remove from the oven, let cool for 10 minutes, and invert the cake onto a large platter. Let the cake cool for another 15 minutes before applying the glaze and serving.

Coconut Dream Pie

YIELD: **8 SERVINGS**

ACTIVE TIME: **15 MINUTES**

TOTAL TIME: **1 HOUR**

INGREDIENTS

1 (14 OZ.) CAN OF UNSWEETENED COCONUT MILK

1 CUP WHOLE MILK

¾ CUP UNSWEETENED SHREDDED COCONUT, LIGHTLY TOASTED, PLUS MORE FOR TOPPING

10 TABLESPOONS GRANULATED SUGAR

3 EGGS

4½ TABLESPOONS CORNSTARCH

3 TABLESPOONS UNSALTED BUTTER

2 TEASPOONS PURE VANILLA EXTRACT

2 TEASPOONS PURE COCONUT EXTRACT

1 LEAF LARD PIECRUST (SEE PAGE 33), BLIND BAKED

WHIPPED CREAM (SEE PAGE 53)

DIRECTIONS

1. Place the coconut milk, milk, shredded coconut, and ½ cup of the sugar in a large saucepan and stir to combine. Bring to a simmer over medium heat.

2. While the mixture in the saucepan is warming, place the eggs, the remaining sugar, and the cornstarch in a mixing bowl and whisk until the mixture is smooth.

3. While whisking constantly, incorporate the mixture in the saucepan into the egg mixture in ½-cup increments. When you have incorporated 2 cups of the warmed mixture, whisk the tempered eggs into the saucepan and cook, while stirring constantly, until the mixture is thick enough to coat the back of a wooden spoon. Remove from heat, add the butter, vanilla, and coconut extract, and stir to incorporate.

4. Fill the piecrust with the mixture, cover it with plastic wrap, and refrigerate until cool.

5. When the filling is cool, top with the Whipped Cream and the additional coconut and serve.

Coconut Cream Float

YIELD: **4 SERVINGS**

ACTIVE TIME: **2 MINUTES**

TOTAL TIME: **2 MINUTES**

INGREDIENTS

1 PINT OF COCONUT ICE CREAM

2 TEASPOONS GRATED NUTMEG

3 (12 OZ.) BOTTLES OF QUALITY CREAM SODA

2 TABLESPOONS CHOCOLATE SYRUP

1 TABLESPOON SPICED RUM (OPTIONAL)

DIRECTIONS

1. Place ice cream in the bottom of four tall glasses. Grate nutmeg over ice cream.

2. Top each glass with the cream soda, chocolate syrup, and rum, if desired.

TAKING IT TO THE STREETS

This is a take on a very popular street food in Thailand that is known as *khanom krok*, or "candy bowl" because of the traditional shape, and the sweetness. To make the perfectly spherical cakes found on the streets of Bangkok, you will need to purchase an indented khanom krok pan, which is similar to the Dutch aebleskiver pan.

Coconut Pudding Pancakes

YIELD: **30 PANCAKES**

ACTIVE TIME: **20 MINUTES**

TOTAL TIME: **20 MINUTES**

INGREDIENTS

1½ CUPS COCONUT MILK

1½ CUPS RICE FLOUR

½ CUP SWEETENED COCONUT FLAKES

5 TABLESPOONS GRANULATED SUGAR

½ TEASPOON KOSHER SALT

1 CUP CREAM OF COCONUT

½ TABLESPOON TAPIOCA STARCH OR CORNSTARCH

2 TABLESPOONS VEGETABLE OIL

¼ CUP CORN KERNELS (OPTIONAL)

DIRECTIONS

1. Place the coconut milk, 1 cup of the rice flour, the coconut flakes, 1 tablespoon of the sugar, and the salt in a bowl and whisk vigorously until the sugar has dissolved. Set the mixture aside.

2. Place the cream of coconut, remaining rice flour, remaining sugar, and tapioca starch or cornstarch in another bowl and whisk until the starch dissolves. Add this mixture to the coconut milk mixture and stir until combined.

3. Place a cast-iron skillet over medium heat and coat it with some of the vegetable oil. For each cake, ladle about 2 tablespoons of the batter into the skillet and cook for approximately 1 minute. Top with the corn, if using.

4. Cover the pan and let the cakes steam until they are solid and nearly cooked through, about 5 minutes. Transfer the cooked cakes to a platter and tent it with foil to keep them warm. Repeat until all of the mixture has been used and replenish the vegetable oil if the skillet starts to look dry.

Coconut & Tapioca Soup

INGREDIENTS

5 CUPS WHOLE MILK

½ CUP GRANULATED SUGAR

SEEDS AND POD OF 1 VANILLA BEAN

1 CUP SMALL TAPIOCA PEARLS

1 (14 OZ.) CAN OF COCONUT MILK

COCONUT TUILE (SEE RECIPE)

MINT LEAVES, FOR GARNISH

DIRECTIONS

1. Place the milk, sugar, and vanilla seeds and pod in a large saucepan and bring to a boil.

2. Reduce heat so that the soup simmers and add the tapioca pearls. Cook until the tapioca pearls are soft, about 10 minutes.

3. Remove the pan from heat, stir in the coconut milk, and let stand until cool. Serve with the Coconut Tuile and garnish with the mint leaves.

COCONUT TUILE

⅓ CUP UNSWEETENED SHREDDED COCONUT

¼ CUP CONFECTIONERS' SUGAR

1 TABLESPOON ALL-PURPOSE FLOUR

1 TABLESPOON UNSALTED BUTTER, MELTED

WHITE OF 1 EGG

1. Place the coconut, confectioners' sugar, and flour in a mixing bowl and whisk to combine. Place the butter and the egg white in a separate bowl and whisk until combined.

2. Combine the mixtures and place in the refrigerator for 2 hours.

3. Preheat the oven to 350°F. Spread the chilled mixture on a greased baking sheet. Place in the oven and cook for 8 minutes, or until golden brown. Cut into desired portions and serve with the soup.

Piña Colada Pudding

YIELD: **4 TO 6 SERVINGS**

ACTIVE TIME: **10 MINUTES**

TOTAL TIME: **10 MINUTES**

INGREDIENTS

1 (8 OZ.) PACKAGE OF CREAM CHEESE, AT ROOM TEMPERATURE

2 CUPS WHIPPED CREAM (SEE PAGE 53), PLUS MORE FOR TOPPING

½ TEASPOON PURE VANILLA EXTRACT

1 (20 OZ.) CAN OF CRUSHED PINEAPPLE

½ CUP SWEETENED SHREDDED COCONUT

DIRECTIONS

1. Place the cream cheese and Whipped Cream in a bowl and beat until light and fluffy. Mix in the vanilla.

2. Drain the pineapple in a colander and then press down to squeeze out as much liquid as possible.

3. Fold the coconut into the cream cheese mixture. Scoop into serving dishes and top with the pineapple and additional Whipped Cream.

Pineapple Upside Down Cake

YIELD: **8 TO 10 SERVINGS**

ACTIVE TIME: **1 HOUR**

TOTAL TIME: **2 HOURS**

INGREDIENTS

FOR THE TOPPING

4 TABLESPOONS UNSALTED BUTTER

1 (20 OZ.) CAN OF PINEAPPLE RINGS AND THE JUICE

½ CUP PACKED DARK BROWN SUGAR

FOR THE CAKE

4 TABLESPOONS UNSALTED BUTTER, CHILLED

1 CUP PACKED LIGHT BROWN SUGAR

2 EGGS

1 CUP BUTTERMILK

1 TEASPOON PURE VANILLA EXTRACT

1½ CUPS ALL-PURPOSE FLOUR

1½ TEASPOONS BAKING POWDER

½ TEASPOON SALT

DIRECTIONS

1. Preheat the oven to 350°F.

2. To prepare the topping, place a cast-iron skillet over medium-high heat. Add the butter, the juice from the can of pineapples, and the brown sugar and stir until the liquid comes to a boil and starts to thicken. Continue cooking until the sauce darkens and gains the consistency of caramel. Remove from heat and place the pineapple rings in the liquid, working from the outside in. Put the skillet in the oven while preparing the batter.

3. To prepare the cake, place the butter and light brown sugar in a mixing bowl and beat until light and creamy. Add the eggs one at a time and incorporate thoroughly before adding the next. Add the buttermilk and vanilla extract, stir to incorporate, and set the mixture aside.

4. Place the flour, baking powder, and salt in a separate bowl and whisk to combine. Add the dry mixture to the wet mixture and stir to combine.

5. Remove the skillet from the oven and pour the batter over the topping. Return to the oven and bake until the cake is golden and a knife inserted in the middle comes out clean, 35 to 40 minutes. Remove from the oven and let the cake rest for 10 minutes.

6. While using pot holders to hold the skillet, invert the cake onto a plate. If some of the topping is stuck to the skillet, gently remove it and place it back on the cake. Let cool for a few more minutes before slicing.

Pineapple Popsicles

YIELD: **12 POPSICLES**

ACTIVE TIME: **15 MINUTES**

TOTAL TIME: **6 HOURS**

INGREDIENTS

1½ CUPS WATER

¾ CUP GRANULATED SUGAR

JUICE OF ½ LEMON

½ CUP PINEAPPLE JUICE

POPSICLE STICKS

DIRECTIONS

1. Place the water and sugar in a saucepan and heat over medium-high heat until the sugar has dissolved.

2. Add lemon juice and the pineapple juice and stir to combine.

3. Turn off the heat and let the mixture cool. Pour the mixture into popsicle molds and transfer to the freezer. After 30 minutes, insert the popsicle sticks and place the popsicles back in the freezer until frozen solid, about 5 hours.

Pineapple Cream Tart

YIELD: **6 TO 8 SERVINGS**

ACTIVE TIME: **30 MINUTES**

TOTAL TIME: **2 HOURS AND 30 MINUTES**

INGREDIENTS

½ CUP GRANULATED SUGAR

3 TABLESPOONS CORNSTARCH

¼ TEASPOON SALT

1¾ CUPS WHOLE MILK

¾ CUP PINEAPPLE JUICE

YOLKS OF 3 EGGS, BEATEN

1 TABLESPOON UNSALTED BUTTER

1 TART PASTRY SHELL (SEE PAGE 38)

1 (20 OZ.) CAN OF PINEAPPLE RINGS OR CHUNKS

¾ CUP SHREDDED COCONUT

DIRECTIONS

1. Place the sugar, cornstarch, salt, and milk in a saucepan and whisk until smooth. Cook, while stirring constantly, over medium-low heat until the mixture starts to thicken and is about to boil. Remove from heat, add the pineapple juice, and stir to combine.

2. While whisking constantly, add a large spoonful of the hot mixture to the egg yolks. When it is incorporated, whisk another large spoonful of the mixture into the eggs. Place the tempered eggs in the saucepan and whisk vigorously to combine. Place the saucepan over low heat, add the butter, and cook, while stirring continuously, until the mixture is thick enough to coat the back of a wooden spoon.

3. Pour the custard into the pastry shell and distribute evenly. Cover the tart with plastic wrap and place in the refrigerator for 2 hours.

4. Remove the tart from the refrigerator and arrange the pineapple on top. Sprinkle the coconut over the tart and serve.

YIELD: **6 SERVINGS**

ACTIVE TIME: **10 MINUTES**

TOTAL TIME: **10 MINUTES**

Bananas Foster

INGREDIENTS

2 STICKS UNSALTED BUTTER

1 CUP PACKED LIGHT BROWN SUGAR

6 BANANAS, CUT LENGTHWISE AND HALVED

½ CUP DARK RUM

½ CUP HEAVY CREAM

VANILLA ICE CREAM (SEE PAGE 152 FOR HOMEMADE), FOR SERVING

CINNAMON, FOR SERVING

DIRECTIONS

1. Place a cast-iron skillet over medium-high heat and add the butter and brown sugar. Once the butter and sugar are melted, add the bananas to the pan and cook until they start to caramelize, about 3 minutes. Shake the pan and spoon some of the sauce over the bananas.

2. Remove the pan from heat and add the rum. Using a long match or wand lighter, carefully light the rum on fire. Place the pan back on the heat and shake the pan until the flames are gone. Add the cream and stir to incorporate.

3. Divide the bananas and sauce between the serving dishes. Top each serving with ice cream and sprinkle cinnamon over the top.

FOSTER PARENTS

Boozy, simple, and in possession of unique charm: it should come as no surprise that Bananas Foster originated in New Orleans. That beginning came about in the 1950s, when the Crescent City served as a major port for the bananas being shipped from Central and South America. Observing the glut of quality produce being laid at their doorstep, Owen Brennan—owner of Brennan's, a restaurant that remains a leading light on the New Orleans culinary scene—challenged his sister, Ella, and his chef, Paul Blangé, to come up with a dessert that incorporated the tropical fruit. Blangé easily handled that task, and his showstopping treat—named for Owen's friend, the New Orleans businessman Richard Foster—remains a fixture on menus today. It remains particularly popular at its place of origin, as Brennan's sets 35,000 pounds of bananas alight a year, according to neworleans.com.

Graceland Pie

YIELD: **6 TO 8 SERVINGS**

ACTIVE TIME: **30 MINUTES**

TOTAL TIME: **1 HOUR**

INGREDIENTS

¾ CUP GRANULATED SUGAR

⅓ CUP ALL-PURPOSE FLOUR

¼ TEASPOON SALT

2 CUPS WHOLE MILK

YOLKS OF 3 EGGS, BEATEN

2 TABLESPOONS UNSALTED BUTTER

1¼ TEASPOONS PURE VANILLA
EXTRACT

4 BANANAS, SLICED

CREAMY NATURAL PEANUT
BUTTER, WARMED, FOR DRIZZLING

1 GRAHAM CRACKER CRUST (SEE
PAGE 34), MADE WITH CHOCOLATE
GRAHAM CRACKERS

WHIPPED CREAM (SEE PAGE 53)

DEHYDRATED BANANA CHIPS, FOR
GARNISH

¼ CUP CRISPY, CHOPPED BACON,
FOR GARNISH (OPTIONAL)

DIRECTIONS

1. Place the sugar, flour, and salt in a saucepan and whisk to combine. Whisk the milk into the mixture and bring to a simmer, while stirring constantly, over medium heat. Simmer, while stirring, for 2 minutes and then remove the pan from heat.

2. While whisking constantly, stir a small amount of the warmed mixture into the beaten egg yolks. Add the tempered egg yolks to the saucepan, place the pan back over medium heat, and cook until the mixture thickens and starts bubbling, while whisking constantly. Remove from heat, add the butter and vanilla, and stir until combined. Add half of the sliced bananas, stir to coat, and let the mixture cool.

3. While the mixture is cooling, place the peanut butter in a saucepan and warm over medium heat until it starts to melt.

4. Place the remaining bananas in the piecrust and then pour the cooled banana cream over the bananas. Cover with Whipped Cream, drizzle the peanut butter over it, and arrange the dehydrated banana chips and bacon pieces, if using, on top.

FIT FOR A KING

The size of Elvis Presley's legend means that we are far better acquainted with The King's daily routine and peccadillos than one might expect. While Elvis had a number of outsized appetites—including for something he tabbed the Fool's Gold Loaf, a loaf of Italian bread filled with a pound of bacon, peanut butter, and jelly—it can be argued that none is better known than his love of fried peanut butter, banana, and bacon sandwiches. Elvis scribes are divided on whether his mother, or his longtime cook, Pauline Nicholson, is responsible for cultivating this hunger in Elvis, and whether the bananas should be caramelized in a frying pan in the canonical version. But, as anyone brave enough to try the bizarre trio knows, there is no denying that The King was on to something.

Banana Cream Tart

YIELD: **6 TO 8 SERVINGS**

ACTIVE TIME: **15 MINUTES**

TOTAL TIME: **15 MINUTES**

INGREDIENTS

2 CUPS PASTRY CREAM
(SEE PAGE 50)

2 LARGE BANANAS, SLICED

1 TART PASTRY SHELL
(SEE PAGE 38)

WHIPPED CREAM (SEE PAGE 53)

CHOCOLATE SHAVINGS, FOR
TOPPING

DIRECTIONS

1. Place the Pastry Cream in the bowl of a stand mixer fitted with the paddle attachment. Beat on low until it is smooth and creamy.

2. Stir the banana slices into the Pastry Cream. Pour this mixture into the tart shell and smooth the top with a rubber spatula.

3. Spread the Whipped Cream on top of the banana filling and sprinkle the chocolate shavings over the tart. Store in the refrigerator until ready to serve.

Banana Pudding

YIELD: **10 TO 12 SERVINGS**

ACTIVE TIME: **20 MINUTES**

TOTAL TIME: **5 HOURS AND 20 MINUTES**

INGREDIENTS

6 CUPS VANILLA PUDDING
(SEE PAGE 175)

3 CUPS WHOLE MILK

1 (14 OZ.) CAN OF SWEETENED
CONDENSED MILK

1 TEASPOON PURE VANILLA
EXTRACT

2 CUPS WHIPPED CREAM
(SEE PAGE 53)

1 (11 OZ.) BOX OF NILLA WAFERS

3 BANANAS, SLICED

DIRECTIONS

1. Place the pudding, milk, and sweetened condensed milk in a bowl and whisk until thoroughly combined.

2. Add the vanilla extract and half of the Whipped Cream and whisk to incorporate.

3. Line the bottom of a serving dish with some of the Nilla Wafers. Top with some of the banana slices and then cover with some of the pudding mixture. Repeat this layering process until all of the pudding mixture, Nilla Wafers, and bananas have been used.

4. Spread the remaining Whipped Cream on top and place in the refrigerator for 5 hours.

Candied Plantains

YIELD: **4 SERVINGS**

ACTIVE TIME: **5 MINUTES**

TOTAL TIME: **10 MINUTES**

INGREDIENTS

1 TABLESPOON UNSALTED BUTTER

½ TEASPOON SALT

1 TABLESPOON GRANULATED SUGAR

2 SWEET PLANTAINS

⅓ CUP APPLE JUICE

1 TEASPOON CINNAMON

1 TEASPOON GRATED NUTMEG

DIRECTIONS

1. Place the butter in a saucepan and melt over medium heat. Add the salt and sugar to the melted butter and cook until the sugar has dissolved and the mixture turns golden brown.

2. Peel and cut the plantains into slices that are ⅓" thick. Place them in the saucepan and cook until tender, approximately 4 minutes.

3. Add the apple juice and let the mixture come to a boil. Cook until the sauce has thickened, about 1 minute. Remove pan from the heat and stir in the cinnamon and nutmeg.

4. Scoop into serving dishes and drizzle some of the sauce over the top of each portion.

Chilled Cantaloupe & Ginger Soup

YIELD: **4 SERVINGS**

ACTIVE TIME: **25 MINUTES**

TOTAL TIME: **2 HOURS AND 25 MINUTES**

INGREDIENTS

2 CANTALOUPES, FLESH CHOPPED AND SHELLS RESERVED

2 TEASPOONS GRATED GINGER

2 TABLESPOONS FRESH LEMON JUICE

4 CUPS CHAMPAGNE, CHILLED

¼ CUP GRANULATED SUGAR

WHIPPED CREAM (SEE PAGE 53), FOR SERVING

DIRECTIONS

1. Place the cantaloupe, ginger, and lemon juice in a food processor and puree until smooth. Strain through a fine sieve and then chill in the refrigerator for 2 hours.

2. Just before serving, add the Champagne and whisk to combine. Add the sugar slowly, tasting as you go, making sure you have just enough to emphasize the melon's flavor. Pour into bowls or the reserved cantaloupe shells and top each with a dollop of Whipped Cream.

Strawberry & Kiwi Tart

YIELD: **6 TO 8 SERVINGS**

ACTIVE TIME: **30 MINUTES**

TOTAL TIME: **3 HOURS AND 30 MINUTES**

INGREDIENTS

½ CUP CREAM CHEESE, AT ROOM TEMPERATURE

½ CUP GRANULATED SUGAR

1 TEASPOON PURE VANILLA EXTRACT

1 CUP HEAVY CREAM

1 TART PASTRY SHELL (SEE PAGE 38)

3 KIWIS, PEELED AND SLICED

1½ CUPS STRAWBERRIES, HULLED AND HALVED

3 TABLESPOONS SEEDLESS STRAWBERRY JAM

1 TABLESPOON WATER

DIRECTIONS

1. Place the cream cheese and sugar in the mixing bowl of a stand mixer fitted with the paddle attachment. Beat on low speed until the mixture is very smooth. Add the vanilla and beat to incorporate.

2. Place the cream in a separate bowl and beat with a handheld mixer on high speed until stiff peaks form. Add the whipped cream to the cream cheese mixture and fold to combine. Place the mixture in the pastry shell and evenly distribute.

3. Working from the outside to the center, alternate slices of the kiwi and strawberries on top of the filling. Place the tart in the refrigerator for 1 hour.

4. Place the jam and the water in a saucepan, stir to combine, and warm over low heat. When the jam starts to liquefy, remove the saucepan from heat and brush the mixture over the tart. Place in the refrigerator for 2 hours before serving.

459

Mango Creamsicles

YIELD: **10 TO 12 POPSICLES**

ACTIVE TIME: **5 MINUTES**

TOTAL TIME: **5 HOURS AND 30 MINUTES**

INGREDIENTS

FLESH OF 3 RIPE MANGOS, CHOPPED

2½ CUPS COCONUT MILK

1 TABLESPOON FRESH LEMON JUICE

POPSICLE STICKS

DIRECTIONS

1. Place the mango, coconut milk, and lemon juice in a blender and puree until smooth.

2. Pour into popsicle molds and freeze. After 30 minutes, insert a popsicle stick into each mold.

3. Freeze until the popsicles are frozen solid, about 5 hours.

Mango with Lime-Pepper Syrup

YIELD: **4 SERVINGS**

ACTIVE TIME: **15 MINUTES**

TOTAL TIME: **15 MINUTES**

INGREDIENTS

FLESH OF 2 LARGE MANGOS, DICED

¾ CUP HONEY, PLUS MORE AS NEEDED

ZEST AND JUICE OF 2 LIMES

2 TABLESPOONS FRESH YUZU OR LEMON JUICE

8 WHOLE BLACK PEPPERCORNS

1 CUP GREEK YOGURT, STIRRED

DIRECTIONS

1. Place a dry cast-iron skillet over high heat. Add the mangos and cook, while turning once, until they are slightly charred, about 3 minutes.

2. Reduce the heat to low and add the honey, lime zest, lime juice, yuzu or lemon juice, and the peppercorns. Cook until the honey is melted, while stirring to coat the mangos.

3. Remove from heat and let cool slightly. Remove the mangos with a slotted spoon and leave the peppercorns in the skillet. Divide the mangos between 4 small dishes.

4. Top with a dollop of the yogurt, drizzle with additional honey, and serve immediately.

Tropical Fruit Salad

YIELD: **10 TO 12 SERVINGS**

ACTIVE TIME: **10 MINUTES**

TOTAL TIME: **10 MINUTES**

INGREDIENTS

ZEST AND JUICE OF 1 LIME

¼ CUP CHOPPED FRESH MINT LEAVES

1 TABLESPOON HONEY

4 KIWIS, PEELED AND SLICED

FLESH OF 1 PINEAPPLE, DICED

FLESH OF 1 MANGO, DICED

1 CUP HULLED AND SLICED STRAWBERRIES

2 CUPS RED SEEDLESS GRAPES, HALVED

1 CUP BLUEBERRIES

DIRECTIONS

1. Place the lime zest, lime juice, mint, and honey in a small bowl, stir to combine, and set aside.

2. Place the remaining ingredients in a large bowl and toss until evenly distributed. Add the dressing, toss to coat, and serve.

Strawberry Daiquiri

YIELD: **2 SERVINGS**

ACTIVE TIME: **1 MINUTE**

TOTAL TIME: **1 MINUTE**

INGREDIENTS

1 LB. FROZEN STRAWBERRIES

½ CUP FRESH LIME JUICE

2 TABLESPOONS GRANULATED SUGAR

1 TABLESPOON HONEY

½ CUP WHITE RUM (OPTIONAL)

DIRECTIONS

1. Place all of the ingredients in a blender, puree until smooth, and pour into tall glasses.

Piña Colada

INGREDIENTS

1 CUP FROZEN PINEAPPLE CHUNKS

1 CUP ICE

½ CUP PINEAPPLE JUICE

½ CUP CREAM OF COCONUT

½ CUP WHITE RUM (OPTIONAL)

½ CUP DARK RUM (OPTIONAL)

1 TEASPOON GRATED NUTMEG

DIRECTIONS

1. Place all of the ingredients in a blender, puree until smooth, pour into tall glasses, and serve with a straw.

CHAPTER 11

THE DECADENT DUO:

CARAMEL

& CHEESE

In a book crammed with luscious desserts, it is not easy to get singled out as decadent. But treats built around caramel and cheese are deserving of such distinction, as the enjoyment of them feels particularly devilish.

By pushing the science of sweet to its limit, each bite of a caramel cake or ice cream forces our eyes to roll back in pleasure. The response cheesy desserts produce is equally ecstatic, as their unequalled richness forces us to realize that the point of a dessert is not actually the burst of sugar we receive, but the enjoyment of experiencing something that seems too good to be true.

Caramel Cake

YIELD: **6 SERVINGS**

ACTIVE TIME: **30 MINUTES**

TOTAL TIME: **3 HOURS**

INGREDIENTS

FOR THE ICING

4 TABLESPOONS UNSALTED BUTTER

1 CUP EVAPORATED MILK

⅔ CUP GRANULATED SUGAR

⅔ TEASPOON PURE VANILLA EXTRACT

FOR THE CAKE

5 TABLESPOONS UNSALTED BUTTER

2 TABLESPOONS VEGETABLE OIL

7 TABLESPOONS GRANULATED SUGAR

2 LARGE EGGS, AT ROOM TEMPERATURE

2 TEASPOONS EGG YOLK, AT ROOM TEMPERATURE

2 TEASPOONS PURE VANILLA EXTRACT

1 CUP SIFTED CAKE FLOUR

⅓ TEASPOON BAKING POWDER

PINCH OF SALT

⅓ CUP SOUR CREAM

DIRECTIONS

1. To prepare the icing, place the butter, evaporated milk, and sugar in a saucepan and cook over medium heat, while stirring occasionally, until the butter and sugar have melted. Reduce the heat to low and cook, while stirring occasionally, until the mixture is deep golden brown and thick, about 1½ hours. Remove from heat, stir in the vanilla, and let cool.

2. To prepare the cakes, preheat the oven to 350°F and grease three round 9″ cake pans with nonstick cooking spray.

3. Place the butter, oil, and sugar in the mixing bowl of a stand mixer and beat on high until the mixture is light and fluffy, about 5 to 6 minutes. Reduce the speed to medium and incorporate the eggs one at a time. Add the egg yolk and vanilla and beat until incorporated.

4. Sift the flour, baking powder, and salt into a separate mixing bowl. Reduce the mixer's speed to low and alternate adding the flour mixture and the sour cream to the wet mixture. Beat until thoroughly incorporated.

5. Divide the batter between the three cake pans, place them in the oven, and bake until a toothpick inserted into the center of each comes out clean, about 25 minutes. Remove the cakes from the oven, let cool in the pans for 10 minutes, and then transfer to wire racks to cool completely.

6. When the cakes and the icing are cool, spread some of the icing on top of one of the cakes. Place another cake on top, flat-side up, and spread more of the icing on top. Place the last cake on top, again flat-side up, and cover the entire cake with the remaining icing.

Tres Leches Cake

YIELD: **8 SERVINGS**

ACTIVE TIME: **1 HOUR**

TOTAL TIME: **24 HOURS**

INGREDIENTS

1 CUP ALL-PURPOSE FLOUR

1 TABLESPOON BAKING POWDER

6 LARGE EGGS, SEPARATED

1 CUP GRANULATED SUGAR

1 (14 OZ.) CAN OF SWEETENED CONDENSED MILK

1 (12 OZ.) CAN OF EVAPORATED MILK

1½ CUPS HEAVY CREAM

½ CUP WHITE RUM

DULCE DE LECHE (SEE SIDEBAR)

DIRECTIONS

1. Preheat the oven to 325°F and grease a square 8″ cake pan with nonstick cooking spray.

2. Place the flour and baking powder in a mixing bowl and whisk to combine. Place the egg whites in a large mixing bowl and beat with a handheld mixer at medium-high speed until stiff peaks form. Place the egg yolks and the sugar in another mixing bowl and beat at medium speed until the mixture is pale and thick, about 3 minutes. Add the beaten egg whites and the dry mixture to the egg yolk mixture and beat until the mixture is smooth.

3. Pour the batter into the pan, place in the oven, and bake until golden brown and a toothpick inserted in the center comes out clean, about 25 minutes. Remove from the oven, let cool in the pan for 10 minutes, and then place on a wire rack to cool completely.

4. Place the condensed milk, evaporated milk, heavy cream, and rum in a 9 x 13-inch baking dish and whisk to combine. Cut the cooled cake into 3″ squares and place them in the baking dish, while turning once or twice in the liquid. Tilt the dish and spoon the liquid over the squares until they are saturated. Pour all but a thin layer of the liquid out of the dish, cover, and refrigerate overnight.

5. To serve, place the cake on the serving plates and drizzle the Dulce de Leche over the top.

DULCE DE LECHE

You can purchase Dulce de Leche at the store (Nestle produces a popular version). Or, if you have some time, you can make it at home. If making at home, place 4 cups whole milk, 1½ cups sugar, and the seeds of a vanilla bean in a saucepan and bring to a simmer, stirring occasionally, over medium heat. When the sugar has dissolved, add ½ teaspoon baking soda, stir to incorporate, and reduce the heat to low. Gently simmer, stirring occasionally, until the mixture is caramel-colored and has reduced by three-quarters, about 3 hours. Strain and store in the refrigerator for up to 1 month.

Salted Caramel
Ice Cream

YIELD: **3 CUPS**

ACTIVE TIME: **30 MINUTES**

TOTAL TIME: **24 HOURS**

INGREDIENTS

1¼ CUPS GRANULATED SUGAR

2¼ CUPS HEAVY CREAM

½ TEASPOON SALT

SEEDS OF ½ VANILLA BEAN

1 CUP WHOLE MILK

3 LARGE EGGS, BEATEN

CARAMEL (SEE PAGE 57), WARMED,
FOR SERVING

WALNUTS, FOR SERVING
(OPTIONAL)

DIRECTIONS

1. Place 1 cup of the sugar in a cast-iron skillet and warm over medium heat, while stirring, until it starts to melt. Stop stirring and swirl the skillet until it is a dark amber color. Add 1¼ cups of the cream, being careful as the mixture will spatter, and cook, while stirring, until the caramel has dissolved. Transfer to a bowl, stir in the salt and vanilla, and let cool to room temperature.

2. Place the milk, remaining cream, and remaining sugar in a saucepan and bring to a boil, while stirring occasionally, over medium heat. Remove the pan from heat.

3. While whisking constantly, slowly add half of the milk mixture to the eggs. Pour the tempered eggs into the saucepan and cook, while stirring constantly, over medium heat until the custard is thick enough to coat the back of a wooden spoon. Strain through a fine sieve and then stir in cooled caramel. Place the custard in the refrigerator and chill overnight.

4. Place the custard in an ice cream maker and churn until the desired texture is achieved. Cover and store in the freezer until firm, about 6 hours. To serve, scoop the ice cream into serving bowls and top with the Caramel and walnuts, if desired.

Salted Caramel Macaroons

YIELD: **16 MACAROONS**

ACTIVE TIME: **20 MINUTES**

TOTAL TIME: **2 HOURS**

INGREDIENTS

6 TABLESPOONS UNSALTED BUTTER, MELTED

3 TABLESPOONS WHOLE MILK

¾ LB. SOFT CARAMELS

1 TEASPOON SALT

4 CUPS SWEETENED SHREDDED COCONUT

4 OZ. DARK CHOCOLATE CHIPS

DIRECTIONS

1. Place the butter, milk, caramels, and salt in a small saucepan and cook over medium heat. Once the caramels and butter have melted, add the coconut and stir until the coconut is coated.

2. Line a baking sheet with parchment paper and scoop tablespoons of the caramel-and-coconut mixture onto the sheet. Let stand for 1 hour.

3. Place the chocolate chips in a microwave-safe bowl and microwave on medium until melted, removing to stir every 20 seconds.

4. Dip half of the cooled macaroons into the melted chocolate and place them back on the baking sheet. Once all the macaroons have been dipped, drizzle the remaining chocolate over the top. Place in the refrigerator and chill until the chocolate has hardened, about 30 minutes.

Salted Caramel & Pecan Pie

YIELD: **8 SERVINGS**

ACTIVE TIME: **45 MINUTES**

TOTAL TIME: **1 HOUR AND 30 MINUTES**

INGREDIENTS

1 LEAF LARD PIECRUST
(SEE PAGE 33)

½ CUP CHOPPED PECANS

1½ CUPS MIXED SALTED NUTS

1¾ CUPS GRANULATED SUGAR

⅓ CUP DARK CORN SYRUP

¼ CUP WATER

¾ CUP HEAVY CREAM

2 TABLESPOONS DARK RUM

1 TEASPOON SALT

3 LARGE EGGS, BEATEN

DIRECTIONS

1. Preheat the oven to 350°F and place the rolled-out piecrust in a greased 9″ pie plate.

2. Place the pecans and the mixed nuts in a bowl and stir to combine. Set the mixture aside.

3. Place the sugar, corn syrup, and water in a saucepan and cook, while stirring constantly, until the sugar has dissolved. Raise heat to medium-high and continue to stir until the mixture comes to a boil and begins to turn dark brown, about 10 minutes. Remove from heat.

4. Stir in the cream, being careful as the mixture will spatter. Place the saucepan over medium-low heat, add the rum and salt, and cook, while stirring, until the mixture is smooth. Ladle into a large bowl and let cool.

5. When the mixture is cool, whisk in the eggs and pour the mixture into the piecrust. Sprinkle the nut mixture over the top, place in the oven, and bake until a knife inserted in the center comes out clean, about 45 minutes. Remove and let cool completely before serving.

Caramel Popcorn

YIELD: **4 TO 6 SERVINGS**

ACTIVE TIME: **10 MINUTES**

TOTAL TIME: **40 MINUTES**

INGREDIENTS

13 CUPS FRESHLY POPPED POPCORN

CARAMEL (SEE PAGE 57), WARMED

DIRECTIONS

1. Place the popcorn in a large bowl and drizzle the caramel over the top. Toss until the popcorn is evenly coated.

2. Pour the popcorn onto a parchment-lined baking sheet in an even layer. Let stand for 30 minutes before serving.

Caramel Apples

INGREDIENTS

4 GRANNY SMITH APPLES

POPSICLE STICKS

CARAMEL (SEE PAGE 57), WARMED

CHOPPED NUTS, SPRINKLES, OR
PREFERRED TOPPING

DIRECTIONS

1. Place the apples in the refrigerator and chill for 2 hours. This will ensure that the apples remain crisp after they are coated.

2. Remove the apples from the refrigerator and insert a popsicle stick in each one.

3. Dip the apples in the warmed Caramel, turning to ensure that they are coated evenly. Roll the caramel-covered apples in chopped nuts, sprinkles, or your preferred topping.

4. Place apples on a parchment-lined baking sheet and chill in the refrigerator for 2 hours before serving.

Caramel & Pecan Bars

INGREDIENTS

½ LB. PECAN HALVES

1 CUP ALL-PURPOSE FLOUR

⅓ CUP CONFECTIONERS' SUGAR

¼ TEASPOON SALT

2 STICKS UNSALTED BUTTER

1 LARGE EGG, AT ROOM TEMPERATURE

½ TEASPOON PURE VANILLA EXTRACT

¼ TEASPOON PURE ALMOND EXTRACT

WHOLE MILK, AS NEEDED

¾ CUP PACKED LIGHT BROWN SUGAR

¼ CUP LIGHT CORN SYRUP

¼ CUP HEAVY CREAM

DIRECTIONS

1. Preheat the oven to 375°F. Line a square 8″ cake pan with aluminum foil and grease the foil with nonstick cooking spray.

2. Place the pecans on a baking sheet, place them in the oven, and toast until lightly browned, about 5 minutes. Remove and set aside.

3. Place the flour, confectioners' sugar, and salt in a food processor and blitz for 5 seconds. Add half of the butter and pulse until mixture resembles a coarse meal.

4. Place the egg, vanilla extract, and almond extract in a small cup and whisk until well combined. Drizzle the liquid into the food processor and pulse until a stiff dough forms. If dough is too dry, add milk in 1-teaspoon increments until it holds together.

5. Transfer the dough to the prepared baking pan and press down on it until it is firmly packed and approximately ¾″ high. Place the dough in the freezer for 15 minutes. Remove, prick with a fork, place in the oven, and bake until lightly browned, about 10 minutes. Remove and let cool.

6. While the crust is baking, place the remaining butter, brown sugar, and corn syrup in a saucepan and bring to a boil over high heat, while whisking constantly. Boil for 2 minutes, remove pan from heat, and stir in the heavy cream and toasted pecans, being careful as the mixture will splatter.

7. Spoon the butter-and-pecan topping over the baked crust and smooth the top with a rubber spatula. Place in the oven and bake until the topping is bubbling and dark brown, about 20 minutes. Remove from the oven and let cool completely in the pan before cutting into bars.

YIELD: **8 SERVINGS**

ACTIVE TIME: **45 MINUTES**

TOTAL TIME: **1 HOUR AND 30 MINUTES**

INGREDIENTS

¾ CUP WARM WATER (110°F),
PLUS 1 TABLESPOON

½ TEASPOON BAKING SODA

½ LB. PITTED DATES, CHOPPED

1¼ CUPS ALL-PURPOSE FLOUR

½ TEASPOON BAKING POWDER

¾ TEASPOON SALT

1¾ CUPS PACKED DARK BROWN
SUGAR

2 LARGE EGGS

1 STICK UNSALTED BUTTER,
HALF MELTED, HALF AT ROOM
TEMPERATURE

1½ TABLESPOONS PURE
VANILLA EXTRACT

1 CUP HEAVY CREAM

DASH OF FRESH LEMON JUICE

Date & Toffee Pudding Cakes

DIRECTIONS

1. Place the ¾ cup of warm water, baking soda, and half of the dates in a large mason jar and soak for 5 minutes. The liquid should cover the dates.

2. Preheat the oven to 350°F and grease 8 ramekins with nonstick cooking spray. Bring water to boil in a small saucepan.

3. Place the flour, baking powder, and ½ teaspoon of the salt in a large bowl and whisk to combine.

4. Place ¾ cup of the brown sugar and the remaining dates in a blender or food processor and blitz until the mixture is fine. Drain the soaked dates, reserve the liquid, and set them aside. Add the reserved liquid to the blender with the eggs, melted butter, and vanilla and puree until smooth. Add the puree and soaked dates to the flour mixture and fold to combine.

5. Fill each ramekin two-thirds of the way with the batter, place the filled ramekins in a large roasting pan, and pour the boiling water in the roasting pan so that it goes halfway up each ramekin.

6. Cover tightly with aluminum foil and place the pan in the oven. Bake until each cake is puffy and the surfaces are spongy but firm, about 40 minutes. Remove the ramekins from the roasting pan and let cool on a wire rack for 10 minutes.

7. Place the remaining butter in a saucepan and warm over medium-high heat. When the butter is melted, add the remaining brown sugar and salt and whisk until smooth. Cook, while stirring occasionally, until the brown sugar has dissolved. Slowly add the cream, while stirring constantly, until it has all been incorporated and the mixture is smooth. Reduce heat to low and simmer until the mixture starts to bubble. Remove from heat and stir in the lemon juice.

8. To serve, invert each cake into a bowl or onto a dish, spoon a generous amount of the sauce over each, and serve.

New York Cheesecake

INGREDIENTS

2½ LBS. CREAM CHEESE, AT ROOM TEMPERATURE

1½ CUPS GRANULATED SUGAR

PINCH OF SALT

⅓ CUP SOUR CREAM

2 TEASPOONS FRESH LEMON JUICE

1 TABLESPOON PURE VANILLA EXTRACT

YOLKS FROM 2 LARGE EGGS

6 LARGE EGGS

1 GRAHAM CRACKER CRUST (SEE PAGE 34), IN A SPRINGFORM PAN

DIRECTIONS

1. Preheat the oven to 200°F.

2. Place the cream cheese, half of the sugar, and the salt in the mixing bowl of a stand mixer fitted with the paddle attachment. Beat at medium-low speed until combined. Add the remaining sugar, beat until combined, and then add the sour cream, lemon juice, and vanilla. Beat at low speed until combined, add the egg yolks, and beat at medium-low speed until well-combined. Scrape down the bowl as needed.

3. Incorporate the eggs two at a time. When all of the eggs have been incorporated, pour the mixture through a fine sieve, pressing down with a rubber spatula to help the mixture through.

4. Pour the mixture into the crust and let it rest for 10 minutes. Use a fork to pop any air bubbles that surface. Place the cheesecake in the oven and bake for 45 minutes. Remove from the oven and pop any bubbles that have risen to the surface. Return to the oven and bake until the center of the cake is 165°F, about 2 hours. Remove the cake from the oven and raise the oven temperature to 500°F.

5. Place the cheesecake in the oven and bake until the top is golden brown, 5 to 10 minutes. Remove from the oven and let cool until barely warm, about 2½ hours. Cover in plastic wrap and place in the refrigerator until set, about 6 hours.

6. To serve, remove the sides of the pan and allow the cake to sit at room temperature for 30 minutes before slicing.

NEW YORK, I LOVE YOU

Without a doubt, people love the New York cheesecake above all other versions. But many who would not tolerate another form of this rich, cheesy treat would be nonplussed if asked to identify what it is exactly that produces the famed dense and satiny texture.

That beloved thickness is the result of cream cheese, heavy cream and/or sour cream, eggs, and, occasionally, egg yolks being baked at a low temperature for a long period of time, and very briefly at a high temperature. The rich result, which was made iconic at New York's now-closed Lindy's deli, is unadulterated by any other flavoring, allowing the sweet and tangy flavor to linger on the thickly coated tongues of its fans.

No-Bake Cheesecake

YIELD: **8 TO 10 SERVINGS**

ACTIVE TIME: **20 MINUTES**

TOTAL TIME: **4 TO 5 HOURS**

INGREDIENTS

1 (14 OZ.) CAN OF SWEETENED CONDENSED MILK

1 TEASPOON PURE VANILLA EXTRACT

½ TEASPOON GRATED NUTMEG

2 (8 OZ.) PACKAGES OF CREAM CHEESE, AT ROOM TEMPERATURE

¼ CUP FRESH LEMON JUICE

1 GRAHAM CRACKER CRUST (SEE PAGE 34), IN A SPRINGFORM PAN

FRESH FRUIT, FOR TOPPING (OPTIONAL)

CONFECTIONERS' SUGAR, FOR TOPPING (OPTIONAL)

DIRECTIONS

1. Place the sweetened condensed milk, vanilla, nutmeg, and cream cheese in the bowl of an electric mixer and beat until well combined. Add the lemon juice and beat until incorporated.

2. Pour cream cheese mixture into the Graham Cracker Crust and cover with plastic wrap. Place in the refrigerator for 3 to 4 hours.

3. To serve, remove the cheesecake from the refrigerator and let sit at room temperature for 30 minutes. Top with fresh fruit or confectioners' sugar, if desired.

Bloody Good Chocolate Cheesecake

YIELD: **6 TO 8 SERVINGS**

ACTIVE TIME: **1 HOUR**

TOTAL TIME: **24 HOURS**

INGREDIENTS

FOR THE CRUST

1 STICK UNSALTED BUTTER, MELTED

1 CUP GRANULATED SUGAR

1½ TABLESPOONS WATER

⅓ CUP UNSWEETENED COCOA POWDER

1½ CUPS ALL-PURPOSE FLOUR

FOR THE FILLING

4½ CUPS CREAM CHEESE, AT ROOM TEMPERATURE

1⅓ CUPS GRANULATED SUGAR

4 EGGS

2 TABLESPOONS BLOOD ORANGE CURD (SEE SIDEBAR)

2 CUPS SOUR CREAM

FOR THE GANACHE

1⅓ CUPS BITTERSWEET CHOCOLATE CHIPS

3 TABLESPOONS BUTTER

1⅓ CUPS HEAVY CREAM

3 TABLESPOONS SUGAR

DIRECTIONS

1. Preheat the oven to 350°F. To prepare the crust, place the butter and sugar in the mixing bowl of a stand mixer fitted with the paddle attachment. Beat at medium speed until the mixture is light and fluffy. Add the remaining ingredients and beat until fluffy.

2. Press the mixture into a 9" springform pan. Place the pan in the oven and bake for 30 minutes. Remove and let cool. Lower the oven temperature to 300°F.

3. Wipe out the mixing bowl of the stand mixer. Add the cream cheese and 1 cup of the sugar and beat on medium speed until combined. Incorporate the eggs one at a time, scraping down the mixing bowl after each has been incorporated. Add the Blood Orange Curd, beat until incorporated, and pour the mixture into the crust. Place in the oven and bake until the center jiggles slightly, about 1 hour. Turn off the oven and leave the pan in the oven for 1 hour.

4. Remove the cheesecake from the oven and preheat the oven to 300°F. Place the sour cream and the remaining sugar in a mixing bowl and stir to combine. Spread this mixture over the top of the cheesecake. Place in the oven and bake for 20 minutes. Remove from the oven and let cool until just warm. Cover with plastic wrap and place in the refrigerator overnight.

5. Remove the cheesecake from the refrigerator and let come to room temperature as you prepare the ganache. To prepare the ganache, place the chocolate chips and butter in a mixing bowl and set aside. Place the cream and sugar in a saucepan and bring to a boil over medium heat, while stirring. When the sugar has dissolved, pour the mixture over the chocolate and butter and let stand for 5 minutes.

6. Stir the ganache until it is smooth and then spread it over the top of the cheesecake. Let the cheesecake stand for 10 minutes before serving.

BLOOD ORANGE CURD

YOLKS OF 6 EGGS

½ CUP GRANULATED SUGAR

ZEST AND JUICE OF 2 BLOOD ORANGES

ZEST AND JUICE OF 1 LEMON

1 STICK UNSALTED BUTTER, CUT INTO SMALL PIECES AND AT ROOM TEMPERATURE

1. Place the egg yolks and sugar in a small saucepan and whisk to combine. Add the citrus zests and juices and cook, while stirring constantly, over medium-low heat, until the mixture is thick enough to coat the back of a spoon, about 10 minutes. Make sure that the mixture does not come to a boil as it cooks.

2. Strain through a fine sieve while gently pressing down with a rubber spatula. Add the butter, stir until melted, and refrigerate until chilled.

Pumpkin Cheesecake

YIELD: **6 TO 8 SERVINGS**

ACTIVE TIME: **20 MINUTES**

TOTAL TIME: **24 HOURS**

INGREDIENTS

2 CUPS FINELY GROUND
GINGERSNAPS

3 TABLESPOONS DARK BROWN
SUGAR

6 TABLESPOONS UNSALTED
BUTTER, MELTED

1 CUP CANNED PUMPKIN PUREE

1 (8 OZ.) PACKAGE OF CREAM
CHEESE, AT ROOM TEMPERATURE

½ TEASPOON ALLSPICE

½ TEASPOON GRATED NUTMEG

1 TEASPOON CINNAMON

½ TEASPOON SALT

1 (14 OZ.) CAN OF SWEETENED
CONDENSED MILK

1 CUP WHIPPED CREAM
(SEE PAGE 53)

DIRECTIONS

1. Place the ground gingersnaps, brown sugar, and melted butter in a mixing bowl and stir to combine. Press the mixture into the bottom of a 9″ springform pan.

2. Place the pumpkin and cream cheese in the mixing bowl of a stand mixer fitted with the paddle attachment. Beat on medium until light and fluffy. Add the allspice, nutmeg, cinnamon, and salt and beat until thoroughly combined.

3. With the mixer running, slowly add the condensed milk. When it has been incorporated, add the Whipped Cream, and fold to incorporate it.

4. Pour the mixture into the crust. Place the cheesecake in the refrigerator overnight. Let sit at room temperature for 30 minutes before serving.

Chocolate Cheesecake Tart

YIELD: **6 TO 8 SERVINGS**

ACTIVE TIME: **40 MINUTES**

TOTAL TIME: **7 HOURS AND 30 MINUTES**

INGREDIENTS

8 TO 10 OREO COOKIES, FILLING SCRAPED OFF

2 TABLESPOONS UNSWEETENED COCOA POWDER

2 TABLESPOONS KAHLUA

1 STICK UNSALTED BUTTER, MELTED

2 (8 OZ.) PACKAGES OF CREAM CHEESE, AT ROOM TEMPERATURE

1 CUP GRANULATED SUGAR

½ TEASPOON PURE VANILLA EXTRACT

2 EGGS

DIRECTIONS

1. Preheat the oven to 350°F. Place the cookies in a food processor or blender and pulse until they are crumbs. You can also put the cookies in a large resealable plastic bag and use a rolling pin to crush them.

2. Put the crumbs in a large bowl and add 1 tablespoon of the unsweetened cocoa powder, the Kahlua, and butter. Stir until combined and then press the mixture into a greased 9″ springform pan. Place the pan in the oven and bake until the crust is firm, about 10 minutes. Remove the pan from the oven and let it cool. Reduce oven temperature to 325°F.

3. Place the cream cheese and sugar in the mixing bowl of a stand mixer fitted with the paddle attachment. Beat on medium speed until low. Add the remaining cocoa powder, vanilla, and eggs and beat until they have been incorporated.

4. Scrape the mixture into the cooled crust, put tart in the oven, and bake until the filling is set, about 40 minutes. Remove from the oven, briefly allow to cool, and refrigerate for 6 hours before serving.

Cheesecake-Filled Strawberries

YIELD: **4 TO 6 SERVINGS**

ACTIVE TIME: **25 MINUTES**

TOTAL TIME: **1 HOUR AND 30 MINUTES**

INGREDIENTS

⅓ CUP HEAVY CREAM

1 (8 OZ.) PACKAGE OF CREAM CHEESE, AT ROOM TEMPERATURE

½ CUP CONFECTIONERS' SUGAR

1 TEASPOON PURE VANILLA EXTRACT

¼ TEASPOON SALT

2 PINTS OF FRESH STRAWBERRIES, HULLED AND CORED

4 GRAHAM CRACKERS, GROUND, FOR TOPPING (OPTIONAL)

SLIVERED ALMONDS, FOR TOPPING (OPTIONAL)

DIRECTIONS

1. Place the heavy cream in a mixing bowl and beat it until soft peaks form. Add the cream cheese, confectioners' sugar, vanilla, and salt and beat until the mixture is light and fluffy. Transfer the mixture into a piping bag or a large resealable plastic bag.

2. Pipe the mixture into the cavities in the strawberries until it is mounded on top. If using a plastic bag to pipe the mixture into the strawberries, cut a small opening in one of the bottom corners and squeeze the mixture into the cavity you made in the strawberries. You want the filling to form a mound on top of the strawberries without overflowing.

3. Sprinkle graham cracker crumbs or slivered almonds on top and then place the stuffed strawberries in the refrigerator for 1 hour before serving.

Blue Cheese & Walnut Tart with Pears and Honey

YIELD: **4 TO 6 SERVINGS**

ACTIVE TIME: **15 MINUTES**

TOTAL TIME: **45 MINUTES**

INGREDIENTS

1 BALL OF TART PASTRY SHELL DOUGH (SEE PAGE 38)

2 TABLESPOONS CHOPPED THYME LEAVES

1 CUP CRUMBLED BLUE CHEESE

1 HANDFUL OF WALNUTS

1 PEAR, CORED AND SLICED

HONEY, TO TASTE

DIRECTIONS

1. Preheat the oven to 550°F.

2. Roll the dough out to approximately ¼" thick and form it into the desired shape. Place it on a parchment-lined baking sheet and place it in the oven until it starts to turn golden brown, 10 to 15 minutes. Remove from the oven and let cool.

3. Sprinkle the thyme, blue cheese, and walnuts evenly over the dough.

4. Distribute the pear slices, place in the oven, and cook until the crust is crispy and the cheese is melted, about 10 to 15 minutes.

5. Remove from the oven, let cool for 5 minutes, and drizzle the honey over the tart. Slice and serve immediately.

Quark Panna Cotta with Rosé Raspberry Sauce

YIELD: **6 SERVINGS**

ACTIVE TIME: **40 MINUTES**

TOTAL TIME: **24 HOURS**

INGREDIENTS

FOR THE PANNA COTTA

2½ CUPS HEAVY CREAM

⅔ CUP WHOLE MILK

⅔ CUP GRANULATED SUGAR

½ TEASPOON SALT

1 TEASPOON PURE VANILLA
EXTRACT

2 CUPS QUARK CHEESE

½ OZ. GELATIN (2 ENVELOPES)

6 TABLESPOONS HONEY

RASPBERRIES, FOR GARNISH

TOASTED ALMONDS, FOR GARNISH

MINT LEAVES, FOR GARNISH

FOR THE SAUCE

2 CUPS ROSÉ

⅓ CUP GRANULATED SUGAR

¼ TEASPOON SALT

2 CUPS RASPBERRIES

DIRECTIONS

1. To prepare the panna cotta, place the cream, milk, sugar, salt, and vanilla in a saucepan and bring to a boil over medium heat, taking care that the mixture does not boil over. Remove from heat.

2. Place the quark in a small mixing bowl and ladle about 1 cup of the mixture in the saucepan into the bowl. Whisk to combine and then pour the tempered quark into the saucepan.

3. Bring the mix back to a boil and then remove the saucepan from heat. Place the gelatin in a large mixing bowl and pour the warmed mixture into it, while whisking constantly to prevent lumps from forming. Pour into the serving dishes and place in the refrigerator to set overnight.

4. Approximately 2 hours before you will serve the panna cotta, prepare the sauce. Place the Rosé in a small saucepan and cook over medium-high heat until it has reduced by half. Add the remaining ingredients, bring the mixture to a boil, and then reduce heat so that the mixture simmers. Simmer for 20 minutes. Transfer the mixture to a blender and puree until smooth. Strain through a fine sieve and place the sauce in the refrigerator to cool completely.

5. When the panna cottas are set, pour 1 tablespoon of honey over each serving. Pour the sauce on top of the honey and garnish with raspberries, toasted almonds, and mint.

Rustico with Honey Glaze

YIELD: **8 SERVINGS**

ACTIVE TIME: **15 MINUTES**

TOTAL TIME: **30 MINUTES**

INGREDIENTS

VEGETABLE OIL, FOR FRYING

4 SHEETS FROZEN PUFF PASTRY, THAWED

WHITE OF 1 EGG, BEATEN

½ LB. MOZZARELLA CHEESE, SLICED

1 CUP HONEY

DIRECTIONS

1. Add vegetable oil to a Dutch oven until it is 2″ deep and bring to 350°F over medium-high heat.

2. Cut eight 5″ circles and eight 4″ circles from the sheets of puff pastry.

3. Place a slice of cheese in the center of each 5″ circle. Place a 4″ circle over the cheese, fold the bottom circle over the edge, and pinch to seal.

4. Place one or two rustico in the oil and fry until the dough is a light golden brown and crispy, about 2 to 3 minutes. Remove from oil and transfer to a paper towel-lined cooling rack. Repeat until all eight wraps have been fried.

5. To serve, drizzle the honey over the top of each rustico.

CHAPTER 12

HOLIDAY FAVORITES

& OTHER UNIQUE CONFECTIONS

We like to pretend that the holidays are all about family. But, if we're being honest, we know that the food plays just as important a role. Once we have the time and a number of occasions to lift our spirits, we can unwind and enjoy ourselves to the fullest.

That combination has caused a number of confections to become signposts that the good times are here at last. From the pumpkin pie that has become an essential part of a Thanksgiving spread to the king cakes that rule Mardi Gras in New Orleans, this chapter focuses on those seasonal desserts that are bound together by how beloved they are.

Sugar Cookies

YIELD: **24 COOKIES**

ACTIVE TIME: **20 MINUTES**

TOTAL TIME: **2 HOURS**

INGREDIENTS

1½ STICKS UNSALTED BUTTER

¾ CUP GRANULATED SUGAR

1 LARGE EGG, AT ROOM TEMPERATURE

1 TEASPOON PURE VANILLA EXTRACT

½ TEASPOON SALT

2½ CUPS ALL-PURPOSE FLOUR, PLUS MORE FOR DUSTING

CONFECTIONERS' SUGAR (OPTIONAL)

SUGAR GLAZE (SEE PAGE 42) (OPTIONAL)

PREFERRED SPRINKLES (OPTIONAL)

DIRECTIONS

1. Place the butter and sugar in a mixing bowl and beat at low speed with a handheld mixer until combined. Increase the speed to high and beat until the mixture is light and fluffy. Add the egg, vanilla, and salt and beat for 1 minute. Slowly add flour to the mixture and beat until it is a stiff dough.

2. Divide the dough in half and wrap each half in plastic wrap. Press each piece of dough into a pancake. Refrigerate dough for 1 hour. The dough will keep in the refrigerator for up to 2 days.

3. Preheat the oven to 350°F. Place the pieces of dough on a flour-dusted work surface and roll each to a thickness of ¼". Cut cookies into desired shapes with flour-dusted cookie cutters and place them on parchment-lined baking sheets. Place in the oven and bake until the edges start to brown, about 10 minutes.

4. Remove from the oven, let the cookies rest on baking sheets for 2 minutes, and then transfer to wire racks to cool completely. Decorate with the confectioners' sugar, glaze, and/or sprinkles, if desired.

Stained Glass Cookies

YIELD: **24 COOKIES**

ACTIVE TIME: **20 MINUTES**

TOTAL TIME: **2 HOURS**

INGREDIENTS

2 STICKS UNSALTED BUTTER

¾ CUP GRANULATED SUGAR

½ CUP PACKED LIGHT BROWN SUGAR

1 LARGE EGG, AT ROOM TEMPERATURE

½ TEASPOON PURE RUM EXTRACT

½ TEASPOON SALT

3¼ CUPS ALL-PURPOSE FLOUR, PLUS MORE FOR DUSTING

½ LB. PREFERRED HARD CANDY

DIRECTIONS

1. Place the butter and sugars in a mixing bowl and beat at low speed with a handheld mixer until combined. Increase the speed to high and beat until the mixture is light and fluffy. Add the egg, rum extract, and salt and beat for 1 minute. Slowly add the flour to the mixture and beat until it is a stiff dough.

2. Divide the dough in half and wrap each half in plastic wrap. Press the pieces of dough into a pancake and refrigerate for 1 hour. The dough will keep in the refrigerator for up to 2 days.

3. Place the hard candy in a resealable freezer bag and pound with a small saucepan until crushed. Preheat the oven to 350°F and line two baking sheets with parchment paper.

4. Place the dough on a flour-dusted work surface and roll each piece out to ¼". Cut into the desired shapes with flour-dusted cookie cutters. Use smaller cutters to create designs inside of the cookies, fill holes with crushed candy, and transfer cookies to the baking sheets. Bake cookies until the edges start to brown, about 10 minutes. Remove the cookies from the oven, let rest on baking sheets for 2 minutes, and then set on wire racks to cool completely.

Christmas in the Caribbean

YIELD: **36 COOKIES**

ACTIVE TIME: **20 MINUTES**

TOTAL TIME: **1 HOUR**

INGREDIENTS

3 TABLESPOONS CREAM CHEESE, AT ROOM TEMPERATURE

2 TABLESPOONS FRESH LIME JUICE, PLUS MORE AS NEEDED

1½ CUPS CONFECTIONERS' SUGAR

2½ CUPS ALL-PURPOSE FLOUR

¾ CUP CASTER SUGAR

¼ TEASPOON SALT

1 TEASPOON LIME ZEST

2 STICKS UNSALTED BUTTER, DIVIDED INTO TABLESPOONS AND AT ROOM TEMPERATURE

2 TEASPOONS PURE VANILLA EXTRACT

1½ CUPS SWEETENED SHREDDED COCONUT, MINCED

DIRECTIONS

1. Preheat the oven to 350°F. Place 1 tablespoon of the cream cheese and the lime juice in a mixing bowl and stir until the mixture is smooth. Add the confectioners' sugar and whisk until the mixture is smooth and thin, adding lime juice as needed until the glaze reaches the desired consistency. Set the glaze aside.

2. Place the flour, caster sugar, salt, and lime zest in another mixing bowl and beat until combined. Add the butter one piece at a time and use a pastry blender to work the mixture until it is a coarse meal. Add the vanilla and remaining cream cheese and work until incorporated.

3. Form the mixture into balls and place them on parchment-lined baking sheets. Place in the oven and bake until the cookies are a light brown, about 15 minutes. Remove from the oven and let cool to room temperature.

4. Brush the glaze over the cookies and sprinkle with the coconut. Allow the glaze to dry before serving.

Chrusciki

YIELD: **20 COOKIES**

ACTIVE TIME: **25 MINUTES**

TOTAL TIME: **1 HOUR AND 30 MINUTES**

INGREDIENTS

3 LARGE EGGS, AT ROOM
TEMPERATURE

¼ CUP WHOLE MILK

¾ CUP GRANULATED SUGAR

1 STICK UNSALTED BUTTER

1 TEASPOON BAKING SODA

1 TEASPOON PURE VANILLA
EXTRACT

½ TEASPOON SALT

½ TEASPOON GRATED NUTMEG

3½ CUPS ALL-PURPOSE FLOUR,
PLUS MORE FOR DUSTING

VEGETABLE OIL, FOR FRYING

1 CUP CONFECTIONERS' SUGAR,
FOR DUSTING

DIRECTIONS

1. Place the eggs, milk, granulated sugar, and butter in a mixing bowl and whisk until well combined. Whisk in the baking soda, vanilla, salt, and nutmeg, and then add the flour. Mix until a soft dough forms, cover the bowl tightly, and chill in the refrigerator for 1 hour. The dough will keep in the refrigerator for up to 3 days.

2. Dust a work surface with flour and roll out the dough to ¼" thick. Cut into 1" strips and then cut the strips on a diagonal every 3" to form diamond-shaped cookies.

3. Add vegetable oil to a Dutch oven until it is 1½" deep. Heat to 375°F and add the cookies a few at a time, using a slotted spoon to turn them as they brown. When cookies are browned all over, remove, set to drain on paper towels, and sprinkle with confectioners' sugar. Serve immediately.

Polvorones

INGREDIENTS

2 STICKS UNSALTED BUTTER, AT ROOM TEMPERATURE

1¾ CUPS CONFECTIONERS' SUGAR

1 CUP CAKE FLOUR, PLUS MORE FOR DUSTING

1 CUP SELF-RISING FLOUR

1 CUP ALMONDS, BLANCHED AND MINCED

½ TEASPOON PURE VANILLA EXTRACT

WARM WATER (110°F), AS NEEDED

DIRECTIONS

1. Preheat the oven to 350°F and line two baking sheets with parchment paper. Place the butter in a mixing bowl with 1¼ cups of the confectioners' sugar and beat at medium speed with a handheld mixer until light and fluffy. Add the flours, almonds, and vanilla and beat until the dough is just combined and very stiff. Add a few drops of water, if necessary, to make it pliable.

2. Remove tablespoons of the dough and roll them into balls. Place the balls on the baking sheets and flatten them slightly with the bottom of a glass that has been dipped in flour. Place in oven and bake until lightly browned, about 10 minutes. Remove from oven.

3. Sift the remaining sugar into a shallow bowl and use a spatula to transfer the cookies to the bowl. Roll the cookies in the sugar until they are evenly coated and then transfer them to wire racks to cool completely.

AROUND THE WORLD

Taking its name from the Spanish word *polvo*, meaning "powder," these confections are also popularly known as Mexican wedding cookies. But they originated in medieval Arabia, and were brought to Spain by the Moors when they took over Andalusia during the eighth century.

Gingerbread Cookies

YIELD: **24 COOKIES**

ACTIVE TIME: **20 MINUTES**

ACTIVE TIME: **2 HOURS**

INGREDIENTS

1½ STICKS UNSALTED BUTTER, AT ROOM TEMPERATURE

½ CUP PACKED LIGHT BROWN SUGAR

⅔ CUP MOLASSES

1 LARGE EGG, AT ROOM TEMPERATURE

1 TEASPOON BAKING SODA

1 TEASPOON GROUND GINGER

1 TEASPOON APPLE PIE SPICE

½ TEASPOON SALT

½ TEASPOON PURE VANILLA EXTRACT

¼ TEASPOON FRESHLY GROUND BLACK PEPPER

3 CUPS ALL-PURPOSE FLOUR, PLUS MORE FOR DUSTING

SUGAR GLAZE (SEE PAGE 42)

CANDIES, FOR DECORATION (OPTIONAL)

DIRECTIONS

1. Place the butter and brown sugar in a mixing bowl and beat at low speed with a handheld mixer until combined. Increase the speed to high and beat until the mixture is light and fluffy. Add the molasses, egg, baking soda, ginger, apple pie spice, salt, vanilla, and pepper and beat for 1 minute. Slowly add the flour to the mixture and beat until it is a stiff dough.

2. Divide the dough in half and wrap each half in plastic wrap. Flatten each piece into a pancake and refrigerate for 1 hour. The dough will keep in the refrigerator for up to 2 days.

3. Preheat the oven to 350°F and line two baking sheets with parchment paper. Place the dough on a flour-dusted work surface and roll to a thickness of ¼". Dip cookie cutters in flour and cut the dough into desired shapes. Transfer the cookies to the baking sheets and bake until firm, about 10 minutes.

4. Remove cookies from oven, let rest for 2 minutes, and then set on wire racks to cool completely. Decorate with the Sugar Glaze and candies, if desired.

Gingerbread Madeleines

INGREDIENTS

5 TABLESPOONS UNSALTED BUTTER, PLUS MORE FOR THE PAN

½ CUP BROWN SUGAR

2 EGGS

1 TABLESPOON MINCED GINGER

1¼ TEASPOONS PURE VANILLA EXTRACT

1½ TABLESPOONS MOLASSES

⅓ CUP WHOLE MILK

½ CUP ALL-PURPOSE FLOUR

½ CUP CAKE FLOUR

¼ TEASPOON BAKING POWDER

1½ TEASPOONS SALT

¼ TEASPOON GROUND CLOVES

¼ TEASPOON GRATED NUTMEG

1 TEASPOON CINNAMON

DIRECTIONS

1. Place the butter in a small saucepan and cook over medium heat until lightly brown. Remove from heat and let cool to room temperature.

2. Place the butter and the brown sugar in the bowl of a stand mixer fitted with the whisk attachment. Beat on high until light and frothy. Lower the speed, add the eggs one at a time, and beat until incorporated. Add the ginger, vanilla, molasses, and milk and beat until incorporated.

3. Sift the flours and baking powder into a bowl. Add the salt, cloves, nutmeg, and cinnamon and stir to combine.

4. Gradually add the dry mixture to the wet mixture and beat until the dry mixture has been thoroughly incorporated. Transfer the dough to the refrigerator and chill for 2 hours.

5. Preheat the oven to 375°F and brush each shell-shaped depression in the madeleine pan with butter. Place the pan in the freezer for at least 10 minutes.

6. Remove the pan from the freezer and the batter from the refrigerator. Fill each "shell" two-thirds of the way with batter, place the pan in the oven, and bake until a toothpick inserted into the center of a cookie comes out clean, about 12 minutes. Remove from the oven and place the cookies on a wire rack to cool slightly. Serve warm or at room temperature.

Gingerbread Ice Cream

INGREDIENTS

1½ CUPS HEAVY CREAM

1½ CUPS WHOLE MILK

2 TEASPOONS GROUND GINGER

2 TEASPOONS CINNAMON

1 TEASPOON NUTMEG

¼ TEASPOON GROUND CLOVES

2 TABLESPOONS MOLASSES

PINCH OF SALT

⅔ CUP GRANULATED SUGAR

YOLKS OF 5 EGGS

DIRECTIONS

1. Place all of the ingredients, except for the sugar and egg yolks, in a medium saucepan and cook over medium heat until the mixture starts to bubble.

2. Remove from heat and let the mixture steep for 30 minutes to 1 hour.

3. Strain, discard the solids, wipe out the saucepan, and return the liquid to it. Bring to a simmer over medium heat.

4. Place the sugar and egg yolks in a bowl and whisk until combined. Add a little bit of the mixture in the saucepan to the eggs, while stirring constantly to keep from cooking the eggs.

5. Add the tempered eggs to the saucepan and cook until the mixture is thick enough to coat the back of a wooden spoon. Remove from heat and let cool. Cover the pan and transfer to the refrigerator. Chill overnight.

6. When you are ready to make the ice cream, place the mixture in your ice cream maker and churn until the desired texture is achieved. Freeze for at least 6 hours before serving.

Pumpkin Pie

INGREDIENTS

1 (14 OZ.) CAN OF PUMPKIN PUREE
(NOT PUMPKIN PIE FILLING)

1 (12 OZ.) CAN OF EVAPORATED
MILK

2 EGGS, LIGHTLY BEATEN

½ CUP GRANULATED SUGAR

½ TEASPOON SALT

1 TEASPOON CINNAMON

¼ TEASPOON GROUND GINGER

¼ TEASPOON GROUND NUTMEG

1 LEAF LARD PIECRUST
(SEE PAGE 33), BLIND BAKED

DIRECTIONS

1. Preheat the oven to 400°F. In a large bowl, combine the pumpkin puree, evaporated milk, eggs, sugar, salt, cinnamon, ginger, and nutmeg. Stir to combine thoroughly.

2. Working with the crust in the pie plate, fill it with the pumpkin mixture. Smooth the surface with a rubber spatula.

3. Put the pie in the oven and bake for 15 minutes. Reduce the heat to 325°F and bake for an additional 30 to 45 minutes, until the filling is firm and a toothpick inserted in the middle comes out clean. Remove the pie from the oven and allow to cool before serving.

Spicy Pumpkin Pie

YIELD: **6 TO 8 SERVINGS**

ACTIVE TIME: **15 MINUTES**

TOTAL TIME: **1 HOUR AND 30 MINUTES**

INGREDIENTS

⅔ CUP PACKED DARK BROWN SUGAR

4 EGGS

1 (14 OZ.) CAN OF PUMPKIN PUREE (NOT PUMPKIN PIE FILLING)

1 TEASPOON CINNAMON

1 TEASPOON GROUND GINGER

½ TEASPOON GRATED NUTMEG

¼ TEASPOON GROUND CLOVES

CAYENNE PEPPER, TO TASTE

2 TABLESPOONS SPICED RUM

¼ TEASPOON SALT

1½ CUPS HEAVY CREAM

1 LEAF LARD PIECRUST (SEE PAGE 33), BLIND BAKED

12 TO 14 GINGERSNAPS

DIRECTIONS

1. Preheat the oven to 375°F.

2. Place the sugar, eggs, and pumpkin in a mixing bowl and beat until the sugar begins to dissolve. Add the spices, rum, salt, and the cream and beat until incorporated.

3. Cover the bottom of the blind-baked crust with the ginger snaps.

4. Pour the pumpkin mixture over the ginger snaps and smooth the surface with a rubber spatula. Place in the oven and bake until the filling is set and a toothpick inserted into the center comes out clean, about 45 minutes. Remove and let cool completely before serving.

Sweet Potato Pie

YIELD: **6 TO 8 SERVINGS**

ACTIVE TIME: **25 MINUTES**

TOTAL TIME: **2 HOURS**

INGREDIENTS

2 CUPS COOKED AND MASHED SWEET POTATOES

1½ CUPS EVAPORATED MILK

2 EGGS, LIGHTLY BEATEN

½ CUP GRANULATED SUGAR

½ TEASPOON SALT

1 TEASPOON CINNAMON

¼ TEASPOON GROUND GINGER

¼ TEASPOON GROUND NUTMEG

1 STICK UNSALTED BUTTER

1 CUP LIGHT BROWN SUGAR

1 BALL OF LEAF LARD PIECRUST DOUGH (SEE PAGE 33)

ALL-PURPOSE FLOUR, FOR DUSTING

DIRECTIONS

1. Preheat the oven to 400°F. Place the mashed sweet potatoes, evaporated milk, eggs, granulated sugar, salt, cinnamon, ginger, and nutmeg in a bowl and stir until combined.

2. Place a cast-iron skillet over medium heat and melt the butter in it. Add the brown sugar and cook, while stirring constantly, until the sugar is dissolved. Remove the pan from heat.

3. Place the piecrust dough on a flour-dusted work surface and roll it out to fit the skillet. Gently place it over the butter-and-brown sugar mixture. Place the skillet in the oven and bake for 15 minutes.

4. Remove the skillet from the oven and briefly let the crust cool. Fill the crust with the sweet potato mixture and use a rubber spatula to evenly distribute. Place the pie in the oven and bake for 15 minutes.

5. Reduce the heat to 325°F and bake until the filling is set and a toothpick inserted in the center comes out clean, about 30 minutes. Remove the skillet from the oven and let cool before serving.

Squash Whoopie Pies with Ginger Cream

YIELD: **12 SERVINGS**

ACTIVE TIME: **20 MINUTES**

TOTAL TIME: **1 HOUR**

INGREDIENTS

1⅓ CUPS ALL-PURPOSE FLOUR

1 TEASPOON CINNAMON

1 TEASPOON GROUND GINGER

¼ TEASPOON GROUND CLOVES

½ TEASPOON GRATED NUTMEG

½ TEASPOON BAKING SODA

½ TEASPOON BAKING POWDER

1 TEASPOON SALT

1 CUP PACKED LIGHT BROWN SUGAR

2 TABLESPOONS MAPLE SYRUP

1 CUP PUREED BUTTERNUT OR ACORN SQUASH

1 EGG

1 CUP VEGETABLE OIL

1⅓ CUPS CONFECTIONERS' SUGAR

4 TABLESPOONS UNSALTED BUTTER

1 (8 OZ.) PACKAGE OF CREAM CHEESE, AT ROOM TEMPERATURE

2 TEASPOONS GRATED GINGER

½ TEASPOON PURE VANILLA EXTRACT

DIRECTIONS

1. Preheat the oven to 350°F. Sift the flour, cinnamon, ground ginger, cloves, nutmeg, baking soda, baking powder, and salt into a mixing bowl.

2. Place the brown sugar, maple syrup, pureed squash, egg, and vegetable oil in a separate mixing bowl and stir until combined. Sift the dry mixture into the squash mixture and stir until it has been incorporated.

3. Use an ice cream scoop to place dollops of the batter onto a greased baking sheet. Make sure to leave plenty of space between the scoops. Place the sheet in the oven and bake until golden brown, about 10 to 15 minutes. Remove and let cool.

4. While the squash cakes are cooling, place the remaining ingredients in a bowl and beat with a handheld mixer until combined and fluffy.

5. When the cakes have cooled completely, spread the powdered sugar-and-butter filling on one of the cakes. Top with another cake and repeat until all of the cakes and filling have been used.

Rajndling

INGREDIENTS

2¼ CUPS ALL-PURPOSE FLOUR, PLUS MORE FOR DUSTING

1 CUP WHOLE MILK

5 TEASPOONS INSTANT YEAST

2 EGGS

½ CUP GRANULATED SUGAR

PINCH OF SALT

1 STICK UNSALTED BUTTER, CHOPPED INTO SMALL PIECES

¾ CUP PACKED LIGHT BROWN SUGAR

1 TEASPOON CINNAMON

½ CUP CHOPPED WALNUTS

½ CUP CHOPPED CRANBERRIES

CONFECTIONERS' SUGAR, FOR TOPPING

DIRECTIONS

1. Preheat the oven to 375°F. Combine the flour, 1 tablespoon of milk, yeast, eggs, and 1 teaspoon of the granulated sugar in a large mixing bowl and stir gently. Cover with a cloth and let stand in a naturally warm area for 30 minutes.

2. Add the remaining milk and granulated sugar, the salt, and the butter to the mixture and work it until it is a smooth dough. Let stand for 10 minutes and then roll out the dough until it is roughly as thick as your thumb.

3. Sprinkle the brown sugar and cinnamon over the dough and then add the walnuts and cranberries. Roll the dough up so that it maintains its length.

4. Grease a Bundt pan with nonstick cooking spray and place the dough in the pan. Bake until it is golden brown and a knife inserted into the center comes out clean, about 35 minutes. Remove from the oven and let cool before topping with the confectioners' sugar.

King Cake

YIELD: **8 TO 10 SERVINGS**

ACTIVE TIME: **40 MINUTES**

TOTAL TIME: **3 HOURS AND 30 MINUTES**

INGREDIENTS

⅓ CUP WHOLE MILK

1¾ TEASPOONS ACTIVE DRY YEAST

3 CUPS ALL-PURPOSE FLOUR, PLUS MORE FOR DUSTING

⅓ CUP CONFECTIONERS' SUGAR

¼ TEASPOON GRATED NUTMEG

1 TEASPOON LEMON ZEST

2 EGGS

YOLK OF 1 EGG

1 TEASPOON ORANGE BLOSSOM WATER

6 TABLESPOONS UNSALTED BUTTER, CUT INTO SMALL PIECES

1 TEASPOON SALT

5 TABLESPOONS WARM WATER (110°F)

3 TABLESPOONS GRANULATED SUGAR

YELLOW, PURPLE, AND GREEN FOOD COLORING (OPTIONAL)

CANDIED FRUIT, ROUGHLY CHOPPED

DIRECTIONS

1. Place the milk in a saucepan and heat to 100°F. Add the yeast, gently stir, and let the mixture rest for 5 minutes.

2. Place the mixture in a large mixing bowl. Add the flour, the confectioners' sugar, nutmeg, lemon zest, one of the eggs, the egg yolk, and the orange blossom water and beat until combined.

3. Transfer the dough to the mixing bowl of a stand mixer fitted with the dough hook attachment. Work the dough and gradually incorporate the butter. When all of the butter has been incorporated, add the salt and work the mixture until it is very smooth. This should take about 20 minutes. Place the dough in a naturally warm spot and let it rise until it has doubled in size, about 1 to 1½ hours.

4. Transfer the dough to flour-dusted work surface and shape it into a ball. Place the ball in a 9 x 13-inch baking dish lined with parchment and flatten it slightly. Make a small hole in the center of the dough and use your hands to gradually enlarge the hole and create a crown. Cover and let stand for 1 hour.

5. Preheat the oven to 320°F. Place the remaining egg and 1 tablespoon of the warm water in a measuring cup and beat to combine. Brush the crown with the egg wash. Place in the oven and bake until the crown is golden brown and a toothpick inserted into the center comes out clean, about 30 minutes.

6. Place the sugar and the remaining warm water in a mixing bowl and stir until the sugar has dissolved. Add the food coloring, if desired, and stir to combine. Brush the hot crown with the glaze and decorate with the chopped candied fruit.

HEAVY LIES THE CROWN

The end of the holiday season is a return to normalcy for everyone other than those who inhabit New Orleans. In the Crescent City, this time is the beginning of the true celebration, Mardi Gras, a ramping up that is traditionally marked by the consumption of king cake. Resting somewhere in the space between a coffee cake and cinnamon roll, the traditionally colorful cake typically has a small plastic baby hidden within. Whoever finds it must either bring the next cake or throw a party, sparking an unending cycle of enjoyment.

Orange Cake

INGREDIENTS

¾ CUP GRANULATED SUGAR

ZEST OF 2 ORANGES

1 STICK UNSALTED BUTTER, CUT INTO SMALL PIECES

3 EGGS

1½ CUPS ALL-PURPOSE FLOUR

1 TEASPOON BAKING POWDER

½ CUP ORANGE JUICE (FRESH SQUEEZED PREFERRED)

DIRECTIONS

1. Preheat the oven to 350°F and put a cast-iron skillet in the oven. In a large bowl, combine the sugar and orange zest. Add the butter and beat with a handheld mixer until the mixture is light and fluffy. Incorporate the eggs one at a time.

2. Place the flour and baking powder in a separate mixing bowl and whisk to combine. Alternate adding the flour mixture and the orange juice to the butter-and-sugar mixture, beating after each addition until it has been thoroughly incorporated.

3. Using pot holders or oven mitts, remove the skillet from the oven and pour the batter into it. Put the skillet in the oven and bake for about 30 to 35 minutes, until the top is golden, the cake springs to the touch, and a toothpick inserted in the middle comes out clean. Remove the cake from the oven and let it cool completely before cutting into wedges.

Honey Roasted Figs

YIELD: **4 SERVINGS**

ACTIVE TIME: **5 MINUTES**

TOTAL TIME: **10 MINUTES**

INGREDIENTS

6 TABLESPOONS HONEY

16 BLACK MISSION FIGS, HALVED

½ TEASPOON CINNAMON

GOAT CHEESE, CRUMBLED,
TO TASTE

DIRECTIONS

1. Place the honey in a nonstick skillet and warm over medium heat.

2. When the honey starts to liquefy, place the cut figs face down and cook until golden brown, about 5 minutes.

3. Sprinkle the cinnamon over the figs and gently stir to coat. Remove figs from the pan, top with the goat cheese, and serve.

Portuguese Vermicelli Pudding

YIELD: **4 SERVINGS**

ACTIVE TIME: **25 MINUTES**

TOTAL TIME: **45 MINUTES**

INGREDIENTS

ZEST OF 1 LEMON, CUT INTO STRIPS

2 CUPS WHOLE MILK, PLUS MORE AS NEEDED

2 TEASPOONS PURE VANILLA EXTRACT

1 TEASPOON DARK RUM

3 TABLESPOONS UNSALTED BUTTER

1 CINNAMON STICK

½ CUP GRANULATED SUGAR

4½ OZ. VERMICELLI, BROKEN INTO 2" PIECES

YOLKS OF 3 LARGE EGGS, BEATEN

GROUND CINNAMON, FOR GARNISH

DIRECTIONS

1. Place the strips of lemon zest, milk, vanilla, rum, butter, cinnamon stick, and sugar in a saucepan and cook, while stirring, over medium heat until the sugar dissolves. Slowly bring to a gentle boil, reduce the heat to low, cover, and simmer for 5 minutes.

2. Remove and discard the lemon zest and cinnamon stick, raise the heat to medium-high, and bring to a boil.

3. Add the vermicelli and cook, while stirring occasionally, for 10 minutes (you want to slightly overcook the pasta in this recipe). When the pasta is very soft and most of the liquid has been absorbed, remove the pan from heat and let cool for 10 minutes.

4. Slowly add one spoonful of the warm pasta mixture to the beaten eggs and stir until well combined. Add another spoonful and mix until well combined. Add the tempered eggs to the saucepan and stir until well combined. If the mixture seems too thick, add more milk, 1 tablespoon at a time, until the thickness is similar to that of rice pudding. Transfer the pudding to four ramekins, garnish with cinnamon, and serve.

Peppermint Bark

YIELD: **24 PIECES**

ACTIVE TIME: **15 MINUTES**

TOTAL TIME: **1 HOUR**

INGREDIENTS

¾ CUP CRUSHED PEPPERMINT CANDIES

¾ LB. SEMISWEET CHOCOLATE CHIPS

2 TEASPOONS VEGETABLE OIL

¾ LB. WHITE CHOCOLATE CHIPS

DIRECTIONS

1. Line a rimmed baking sheet with parchment paper and place the crushed peppermint candies in a mixing bowl.

2. Place the semisweet chocolate chips in a microwave-safe bowl. Microwave on medium until melted, removing to stir every 20 seconds.

3. Stir 1 teaspoon of the vegetable oil into the melted chocolate and then pour the chocolate onto the baking sheet, using a rubber spatula to distribute evenly. Place in the refrigerator until set, about 15 minutes.

4. Place the white chocolate chips in a microwave-safe bowl. Microwave on medium until melted, removing to stir every 20 seconds. Add the remaining oil, stir to combine, and pour the melted white chocolate on top of the hardened semisweet chocolate, using a rubber spatula to distribute evenly.

5. Sprinkle the peppermint pieces liberally over the white chocolate and lightly press down on them. Refrigerate until set, about 30 minutes. Break the bark into pieces and refrigerate until ready to serve.

YIELD: **16 BROWNIES**

ACTIVE TIME: **25 MINUTES**

TOTAL TIME: **1 HOUR AND 15 MINUTES**

Peppermint Brownies

INGREDIENTS

3 OZ. BITTERSWEET CHOCOLATE, CHOPPED

¼ CUP HEAVY CREAM, PLUS MORE AS NEEDED

1 CUP ALL-PURPOSE FLOUR

3 TABLESPOONS UNSWEETENED COCOA POWDER

½ TEASPOON SALT

1½ STICKS UNSALTED BUTTER, AT ROOM TEMPERATURE

2½ CUPS CONFECTIONERS' SUGAR

2 LARGE EGGS

½ TEASPOON PURE VANILLA EXTRACT

2 TO 4 DROPS OF RED FOOD COLORING (OPTIONAL)

¾ CUP CRUSHED PEPPERMINT CANDIES

DIRECTIONS

1. Preheat the oven to 350°F and grease a square 8″ cake pan. Combine the chocolate and 2 tablespoons of the cream in a microwave-safe bowl. Microwave on medium until the chocolate has melted and the mixture is smooth, removing to stir every 20 seconds.

2. Place the flour, cocoa powder, and salt in a mixing bowl and whisk until combined. Place 1 stick of the butter and ½ cup of the sugar in a separate mixing bowl and beat with a handheld mixer at low speed to combine. Increase the speed to high and beat until light and fluffy. Incorporate the eggs one at a time and then add chocolate-and-cream mixture and the vanilla. When incorporated, gradually add the flour-and-cocoa mixture and beat until smooth.

3. Scrape the batter into the prepared pan and distribute evenly with a rubber spatula. Place in the oven and bake until the brownies are firm and a toothpick inserted in the center comes out clean, about 15 minutes. Remove and allow to cool in the pan.

4. While the brownies are cooling, prepare the frosting. Place the remaining butter, sugar, and cream in a mixing bowl and beat at medium speed with a handheld mixer until light and fluffy. If using, add the red food coloring and beat until well combined. Add cream in 1-teaspoon increments if frosting is too thick. Spread frosting over cooled brownies, sprinkle the crushed peppermint candies on top, and cut into small bars.

Grasshopper Cookies

YIELD: **24 COOKIES**

ACTIVE TIME: **1 HOUR AND 30 MINUTES**

TOTAL TIME: **4 HOURS**

INGREDIENTS

FOR THE COOKIES

2 STICKS UNSALTED BUTTER

¼ CUP GRANULATED SUGAR

YOLK OF 1 LARGE EGG, AT ROOM TEMPERATURE

½ TEASPOON PURE VANILLA EXTRACT

½ TEASPOON BAKING POWDER

½ TEASPOON SALT

½ CUP UNSWEETENED COCOA POWDER

2 CUPS ALL-PURPOSE FLOUR

½ CUP SEMISWEET CHOCOLATE CHIPS, MELTED

FOR THE FILLING

½ CUP HEAVY CREAM

1½ TABLESPOONS LIGHT CORN SYRUP

¾ LB. QUALITY WHITE CHOCOLATE, MINCED

2 TABLESPOONS UNSALTED BUTTER

1 TEASPOON PURE MINT EXTRACT

¼ TEASPOON RED OR GREEN FOOD COLORING (OPTIONAL)

DIRECTIONS

1. To make the cookies, place the butter and sugar in a mixing bowl and beat at low speed with a handheld mixer to combine. Increase the speed to high and beat until light and fluffy. Beat in the egg yolk, vanilla, baking powder, and salt and then slowly add the cocoa powder and flour. Beat until a stiff dough forms.

2. Place the dough on a sheet of waxed paper and roll it into a log that is 2½" in diameter. Cover in plastic wrap and refrigerate for 2 hours. The dough will keep in the refrigerator for up to 2 days.

3. To prepare the filling, place the cream and corn syrup in a small saucepan and bring to a simmer. Stir in the white chocolate, butter, and mint extract, cover the pan, and remove from heat. Allow mixture to sit for 5 minutes. Stir well and, if using, stir in food coloring. Heat over very low heat if chocolate still has lumps. Press a sheet of waxed paper onto the surface and refrigerate.

4. Preheat the oven to 350°F. Line two baking sheets with parchment paper and cut the chilled dough into ½" thick slices. Place the cookies on the baking sheets, place them in the oven, and bake until the edges start to brown, about 10 minutes. Remove from the oven, let cool on the baking sheets for 2 minutes, and then place on a wire rack to cool completely.

5. When the cookies are cool, dip them in the melted chocolate until completely coated. Place the cookies back on the baking sheet and place it in the refrigerator until the chocolate has hardened, about 20 minutes.

6. Beat the filling with a handheld mixer on medium speed until it is light and fluffy. Place a dollop on the flat side of 1 cookie and top with the flat side of another cookie. Repeat until all of the cookies have been used.

Mint Chocolate Chip Milkshakes

YIELD: **4 SERVINGS**

ACTIVE TIME: **2 MINUTES**

TOTAL TIME: **2 MINUTES**

INGREDIENTS

2 PINTS OF MINT CHOCOLATE CHIP ICE CREAM

2 CUPS WHOLE MILK

¼ CUP CHOCOLATE SYRUP

¼ CUP CRÈME DE MENTHE (OPTIONAL)

WHIPPED CREAM (SEE PAGE 53), FOR SERVING

DIRECTIONS

1. Place all of the ingredients, except for the Whipped Cream, in a blender and blend until smooth.

2. Pour into tall glasses and top each with a dollop of Whipped Cream.

Lavender Ice Cream

YIELD: **3 CUPS**

ACTIVE TIME: **20 MINUTES**

TOTAL TIME: **24 HOURS**

INGREDIENTS

2 CUPS HEAVY CREAM

1 CUP HALF-AND-HALF

⅔ CUP HONEY

2 TABLESPOONS DRIED LAVENDER

YOLKS FROM 2 LARGE EGGS

PINCH OF SALT

DIRECTIONS

1. Place the cream, half-and-half, honey, and lavender in a medium saucepan and cook until it is about to boil. Remove from heat and let stand for at least 30 minutes. When cool, strain the mixture through a fine sieve to remove the lavender.

2. Place the mixture in a clean saucepan and cook over medium-low heat. Beat the egg yolks in a bowl and then add ¼ cup of the saucepan's contents to the yolks while whisking constantly. Incorporate another ¼ cup of the mixture, place the tempered eggs in the saucepan, stir in the salt, and cook over medium-low heat, stirring constantly to ensure that the mixture does not come to a boil.

3. When the mixture is thick enough to coat the back of a wooden spoon, remove the pan from heat and pour through a fine mesh sieve. Let cool completely, while stirring occasionally. Cover with plastic and place in the refrigerator overnight.

4. Pour the custard into an ice cream maker and churn until the desired consistency is achieved. Transfer to an airtight container and freeze for 6 hours before serving.

Orange & Rosemary Shortbread

YIELD: **24 COOKIES**

ACTIVE TIME: **20 MINUTES**

TOTAL TIME: **2 HOURS**

INGREDIENTS

4 STICKS UNSALTED BUTTER, AT ROOM TEMPERATURE

¼ CUP GRANULATED SUGAR

¼ CUP FRESH ORANGE JUICE

1 TABLESPOON ORANGE ZEST

2 TEASPOONS FRESH ROSEMARY LEAVES, MINCED

4½ CUPS ALL-PURPOSE FLOUR

CONFECTIONERS' SUGAR, TO TASTE

DIRECTIONS

1. Preheat the oven to 350°F and line two baking sheets with parchment paper.

2. Place all of the ingredients, except the flour and confectioners' sugar, in a mixing bowl and beat at low speed with a handheld mixer until the mixture is smooth and creamy.

3. Slowly add the flour and beat until a crumbly dough forms. Press the dough into a rectangle that is approximately ½" thick. Cover with plastic wrap and place the dough in the refrigerator for 1 hour.

4. Cut rounds out of the dough and place them on the baking sheets. Sprinkle with confectioners' sugar, place in the oven, and bake until the edges start to brown, about 15 minutes. Remove and let cool before serving.

Oatmeal Raisin Cookies

YIELD: **16 COOKIES**

ACTIVE TIME: **20 MINUTES**

TOTAL TIME: **1 HOUR**

INGREDIENTS

4 TABLESPOONS UNSALTED BUTTER

¼ TEASPOON CINNAMON

¾ CUP PACKED DARK BROWN SUGAR

½ CUP GRANULATED SUGAR

½ CUP VEGETABLE OIL

1 LARGE EGG

YOLK OF 1 LARGE EGG

1 TEASPOON PURE VANILLA EXTRACT

1 CUP ALL-PURPOSE FLOUR

½ TEASPOON BAKING SODA

¾ TEASPOON SALT

3 CUPS ROLLED OATS

½ CUP RAISINS

DIRECTIONS

1. Preheat the oven to 350°F.

2. Place the butter in a skillet and warm over medium-high heat until it is a dark golden brown and has a nutty aroma. Transfer to a mixing bowl and whisk in the cinnamon, brown sugar, granulated sugar, and vegetable oil. When the mixture is combined, add the egg, egg yolk, and vanilla and whisk until incorporated.

3. Place the flour, baking soda, and salt in a separate mixing bowl and whisk to combine. Add this mixture to the wet mixture and stir until well combined. Add the oats and raisins and stir until they are evenly distributed throughout the mixture.

4. Form the dough into 16 balls and divide them between two parchment-lined baking sheets. Press down on the balls of dough to flatten them slightly. Place the sheets in the oven and bake the cookies until the edges start to brown, about 10 minutes. Remove from the oven and let cool on the sheets for 5 minutes. Transfer to a wire rack and let cool completely.

Carrot Cake

YIELD: **6 TO 8 SERVING**

ACTIVE TIME: **30 MINUTES**

TOTAL TIME: **2 HOURS AND 30 MINUTES**

INGREDIENTS

2 CUPS GRATED CARROTS, PLUS MORE FOR TOPPING

2 CUPS GRANULATED SUGAR

1½ CUPS ALL-PURPOSE FLOUR

1½ TABLESPOONS BAKING SODA

1 TEASPOON SALT

1 TABLESPOON CINNAMON

3 EGGS

1¾ CUPS VEGETABLE OIL

2 TEASPOONS PURE VANILLA EXTRACT

½ CUP WALNUTS, CHOPPED (OPTIONAL)

CREAM CHEESE FROSTING (SEE PAGE 46)

DIRECTIONS

1. Preheat the oven to 350°F.

2. Place the carrots and sugar in a mixing bowl, stir to combine, and let the mixture sit for 10 minutes.

3. Place the flour, baking soda, salt, and cinnamon in a mixing bowl and stir to combine. Place the eggs, vegetable oil, and vanilla extract in a separate mixing bowl and stir to combine. Add the wet mixture to the dry mixture and stir until the mixture is a smooth batter. Stir in the carrots and, if desired, the walnuts.

4. Transfer the batter to a greased round 9″ cake pan and place the cake in the oven. Bake until the top is browned and a knife inserted into the center comes out clean, about 40 to 50 minutes.

5. Remove the cake from the oven, transfer to a wire rack, and let cool for 1 hour before applying the frosting. Top each slice with additional grated carrot before serving.

Grape-Nut Custard Pudding

YIELD: **12 SERVINGS**

ACTIVE TIME: **15 MINUTES**

TOTAL TIME: **1 HOUR AND 15 MINUTES**

INGREDIENTS

4 CUPS WHOLE MILK, WARMED

½ CUP GRAPE-NUTS

5 EGGS

1 TEASPOON PURE VANILLA EXTRACT

½ CUP GRANULATED SUGAR

1 TEASPOON CINNAMON

1 WHOLE NUTMEG

MAPLE SYRUP, FOR GARNISH

WHIPPED CREAM (SEE PAGE 53), FOR GARNISH

DIRECTIONS

1. Preheat the oven to 350°F.

2. Place the milk, Grape-Nuts, eggs, vanilla, and sugar in a bowl and stir until well combined.

3. Transfer the mixture to a baking dish and then place the dish in a roasting pan containing hot water. Place in the oven and cook for 15 minutes.

4. Remove the baking dish from the oven and stir the pudding. Return to the oven and cook until golden brown and a knife inserted into the center comes out clean, about 15 minutes.

5. Remove from the oven, sprinkle with cinnamon, and grate the nutmeg over the top. Let cool completely.

6. When the pudding is cool, top each serving with a drizzle of maple syrup and a dollop of Whipped Cream.

A TASTE OF THE OLD WORLD

This recipe dates back to 18th-century America, when New Englanders who had a hankering for the hasty pudding they left behind in England had to make the most of what was available, resulting in this dessert that leans heavily upon molasses and cornmeal. This latter ingredient, which the colonists referred to as "Indian flour," is what lends the dish its name.

Indian Pudding

YIELD: **8 SERVINGS**

ACTIVE TIME: **30 MINUTES**

TOTAL TIME: **8 HOURS AND 30 MINUTES**

INGREDIENTS

3 CUPS WHOLE MILK

1 CUP HEAVY CREAM

½ CUP CORNMEAL

½ CUP BLACKSTRAP MOLASSES

½ CUP LIGHT BROWN SUGAR

½ TEASPOON GINGER

½ TEASPOON NUTMEG

½ TEASPOON ALLSPICE

2 TEASPOONS CINNAMON

2 TEASPOONS SALT

5 EGGS

5 TABLESPOONS UNSALTED BUTTER

WHIPPED CREAM (SEE PAGE 53), FOR SERVING

DIRECTIONS

1. Preheat the oven to 275°F and grease a baking dish.

2. Place the milk in a large saucepan and cook over medium-high heat until it comes to a boil. Remove the saucepan from heat and set aside.

3. Place all of the remaining ingredients, except for the eggs, butter, and Whipped Cream, in a mixing bowl and stir to combine. Whisk this mixture into the heated milk.

4. Place the saucepan over medium-low heat and cook, while stirring, until the mixture begins to thicken. Remove the saucepan from heat.

5. Crack the eggs into a bowl and beat with a whisk. Add ½ cup of the hot molasses-and-cornmeal mixture and whisk to combine. Continue whisking in ½-cup increments of the mixture until all of it has been incorporated. Add the butter and whisk until it has been incorporated.

6. Pour the mixture into the prepared baking dish. Place the dish in a pan of water, place in the oven, and bake until it is set, about 2 hours.

7. Remove from the oven and let cool. When cool, transfer to the fridge for at least 6 hours. Serve with the Whipped Cream.

Cornmeal Cookies

YIELD: **24 COOKIES**

ACTIVE TIME: **20 MINUTES**

TOTAL TIME: **3 HOURS**

INGREDIENTS

1 STICK UNSALTED BUTTER

¾ CUP CONFECTIONERS' SUGAR

1 LARGE EGG, AT ROOM TEMPERATURE

½ TEASPOON PURE VANILLA EXTRACT

⅔ CUP ALL-PURPOSE FLOUR

¼ CUP FINELY GROUND CORNMEAL

2 TABLESPOONS CORNSTARCH

¼ TEASPOON SALT

DIRECTIONS

1. Place the butter and confectioners' sugar in a mixing bowl and beat at low speed with a handheld mixer to combine. Increase the speed to high and beat until light and fluffy. Add the egg and vanilla, beat for 1 minute, and then slowly add the flour, cornmeal, cornstarch, and salt. Beat until the mixture is a stiff dough.

2. Place the dough on a sheet of waxed paper and roll it into a log that is 2½" in diameter. Cover in plastic wrap and refrigerate for 2 hours. The dough will keep in the refrigerator for up to 2 days.

3. Preheat the oven to 350°F and line two baking sheets with parchment paper. Cut the chilled dough into ⅓" thick slices and arrange the cookies on the baking sheets. Place the cookies in the oven and bake until the edges start to brown, about 10 minutes. Remove from the oven, let cool on the sheets for 2 minutes, and then transfer the cookies to wire racks to cool completely.

Dirt Pudding

YIELD: **6 TO 8 SERVINGS**

ACTIVE TIME: **30 MINUTES**

TOTAL TIME: **1 HOUR AND 30 MINUTES**

INGREDIENTS

1 PACKAGE OF OREO COOKIES

1 (8 OZ.) PACKAGE OF CREAM CHEESE, AT ROOM TEMPERATURE

4 TABLESPOONS UNSALTED BUTTER, AT ROOM TEMPERATURE

1 CUP CONFECTIONERS' SUGAR

½ CUP WHOLE MILK

6 CUPS VANILLA PUDDING (SEE PAGE 175)

¾ CUP WHIPPED CREAM (SEE PAGE 53), PLUS MORE FOR TOPPING

CHOCOLATE SHAVINGS, FOR GARNISH

DIRECTIONS

1. Place the Oreos in a blender or food processor and blitz until they are finely ground.

2. Place the cream cheese, butter, and confectioners' sugar in a mixing bowl and beat until the mixture is light and fluffy.

3. Place the milk and pudding in a separate mixing bowl and stir to combine. Add the Whipped Cream and fold to incorporate.

4. Add the pudding mixture to the cream cheese mixture and stir until thoroughly combined.

5. In a serving bowl, alternate layers of the pudding-and-cream cheese mixture and the Oreo crumbs until all ingredients have been used.

6. Place in the refrigerator and chill for 1 hour. Top with additional Whipped Cream and chocolate shavings before serving.

Sopaipillas

YIELD: **24 SOPAIPILLAS**

ACTIVE TIME: **35 MINUTES**

TOTAL TIME: **1 HOUR**

INGREDIENTS

3 CUPS SELF-RISING FLOUR

1½ TEASPOONS BAKING POWDER

1 TEASPOON SALT

1 TEASPOON GRANULATED SUGAR

1 CUP WARM WATER (110°F)

VEGETABLE OIL, FOR FRYING

CONFECTIONERS' SUGAR, FOR SERVING

CINNAMON, FOR SERVING

HONEY, FOR SERVING

DIRECTIONS

1. Place the flour, baking powder, salt, and sugar in the bowl of a stand mixer fitted with the whisk attachment. Whisk until combined.

2. Turn the mixer on low speed and slowly drizzle in the warm water. Beat until a soft, smooth dough forms, about 8 minutes. Cover the bowl and let the dough rest for 20 minutes.

3. Place a Dutch oven over medium-high heat for 2 minutes. Add the oil until it is 2" deep. Reduce the heat to medium-low.

4. Divide the dough in half and pat each piece into a rectangle. Cut each rectangle into 12 squares and roll each square to ⅛" thick.

5. Raise the heat under the Dutch oven to medium and heat for 4 minutes. Working in batches of three, place the squares in the oil and use a pair of tongs to gently submerge each sopaipilla until puffy and golden, about 1 minute. Transfer to a paper towel-lined tray and continue until all of the squares have been fried. Serve immediately with confectioners' sugar, cinnamon, and honey.

Cinnamon Twists

YIELD: **24 TWISTS**

ACTIVE TIME: **15 MINUTES**

TOTAL TIME: **30 MINUTES**

INGREDIENTS

2 SHEETS FROZEN PUFF PASTRY, THAWED

1 CUP GRANULATED SUGAR

3½ TABLESPOONS CINNAMON

1 TEASPOON GRATED NUTMEG

1 EGG

1 CUP CARAMEL (SEE PAGE 57), WARMED, FOR SERVING

DIRECTIONS

1. Preheat oven to 375°F and roll out the sheets of puff pastry.

2. Combine the sugar, cinnamon, and nutmeg in a bowl. Beat the egg in a separate bowl.

3. Lightly brush the top of each pastry sheet with the egg and then sprinkle the sugar-and-spice mixture evenly across the tops of both sheets.

4. Cut the pastries into long strips and twist. Place strips on a parchment-lined baking sheet and bake until golden brown. Remove from the oven, flip each pastry over, and bake for an additional 2 to 3 minutes.

5. Remove twists from oven and allow to cool until just slightly warm. Serve with the Caramel on the side.

Bourbon Balls

YIELD: **24 COOKIES**

ACTIVE TIME: **15 MINUTES**

TOTAL TIME: **3 HOURS**

INGREDIENTS

2 STICKS UNSALTED BUTTER, AT ROOM TEMPERATURE

2 LBS. CONFECTIONERS' SUGAR

½ CUP BOURBON

½ TEASPOON SALT

MELTED CHOCOLATE, COCOA POWDER, CONFECTIONERS' SUGAR, OR SHREDDED COCONUT, FOR TOPPING

DIRECTIONS

1. Combine the butter and 1 pound of the confectioners' sugar in a mixing bowl and beat at low speed with a handheld mixer to combine. Increase the speed to high and beat until light and fluffy. Add the remaining sugar, bourbon, and salt and beat for 2 minutes. Transfer the mixture to the refrigerator and chill until firm, about 2 hours.

2. Line baking sheets with parchment paper and form tablespoons of the butter-and-bourbon mixture into balls. Coat the balls in melted chocolate, cocoa powder, confectioners' sugar, and/or shredded coconut and then transfer the sheets to the refrigerator. Chill for 45 minutes before serving.

Rosé Sorbet

YIELD: **6 SERVINGS**

ACTIVE TIME: **15 MINUTES**

TOTAL TIME: **24 HOURS**

INGREDIENTS

1⅓ CUPS GRANULATED SUGAR

1 (750 ML) BOTTLE OF ROSÉ

1 CUP WATER

DIRECTIONS

1. Place all of the ingredients in a saucepan and cook, while stirring, over medium-low heat until the sugar is completely dissolved. Raise the heat and bring to a boil.

2. Remove from heat and let cool completely. Cover and place the mixture in the refrigerator overnight.

3. Pour the mixture into an ice cream maker and churn until the desired consistency has been achieved. Transfer to the freezer and freeze for at least 6 hours before serving.

Roasted Parsnip Ice Cream

YIELD: **6 SERVINGS**

ACTIVE TIME: **20 MINUTES**

TOTAL TIME: **24 HOURS**

INGREDIENTS

1½ CUPS HEAVY CREAM

1½ CUPS WHOLE MILK

3 TO 4 CUPS ROASTED PARSNIP TRIMMINGS (THE STUFF YOU TYPICALLY THROW AWAY)

PINCH OF SALT

⅔ CUP GRANULATED SUGAR

YOLKS OF 5 EGGS

DIRECTIONS

1. Place the cream, milk, roasted parsnip pieces, and salt in a saucepan and cook over medium heat until the mixture starts to bubble. Remove it from heat and allow the mixture to steep for 30 minutes to 1 hour.

2. Strain the mixture through a fine sieve, pressing down on the pieces of parsnip to remove as much liquid as possible. Place the liquid in a saucepan and bring to a simmer. Discard the parsnip pieces.

3. Place the sugar and egg yolks in a bowl and whisk until combined.

4. Once the milk is simmering, add a little bit of the milk-and-cream mixture to the egg-and-sugar mixture and whisk constantly. Add the milk-and-cream mixture in small increments until all of it has been incorporated, while taking care not to cook the eggs.

5. Return the mixture to the saucepan and cook over low heat, while stirring, until it is thick enough to coat the back of a wooden spoon. Remove from heat and let cool. When cool, cover and transfer to the refrigerator. Chill overnight.

6. When you are ready to make ice cream, add the mixture to your ice cream maker and churn until the desired consistency has been achieved. Place the churned cream in the freezer for at least 6 hours before serving.

METRIC CONVERSIONS

U.S. Measurement	Approximate Metric Liquid Measurement	Approximate Metric Dry Measurement
1 teaspoon	5 ml	5 g
1 tablespoon or ½ ounce	15 ml	14 g
1 ounce or ⅛ cup	30 ml	29 g
¼ cup or 2 ounces	60 ml	57 g
⅓ cup	80 ml	76 g
½ cup or 4 ounces	120 ml	113 g
⅔ cup	160 ml	151 g
¾ cup or 6 ounces	180 ml	170 g
1 cup or 8 ounces or ½ pint	240 ml	227 g
1½ cups or 12 ounces	350 ml	340 g
2 cups or 1 pint or 16 ounces	475 ml	454 g
3 cups or 1½ pints	700 ml	680 g
4 cups or 2 pints or 1 quart	950 ml	908 g

INDEX

IMAGE CREDITS

ABOUT CIDER MILL PRESS
BOOK PUBLISHERS

❄ ❄ ❄

Good ideas ripen with time. From seed to harvest,
Cider Mill Press brings fine reading, information,
and entertainment together between the covers of its
creatively crafted books. Our Cider Mill bears fruit twice
a year, publishing a new crop of titles each spring and fall.

"Where Good Books Are Ready for Press"

Visit us online at
www.cidermillpress.com
or write to us at
PO Box 454
12 Spring St.
Kennebunkport, Maine 04046